Disability and Youth Spo

How can, or does, youth sport reconcile what seems to be a fundamental contradiction between understandings of sport and disability?

Has youth sport been challenged in any way?

Have alternative views of sport for disabled people been presented?

Examining some of the latest research, this book considers the relationship between sport and disability by exploring a range of questions such as these.

Disability and Youth Sport challenges current thinking and serves to stimulate progressive debate in this area. Drawing on a breadth of literature from sports pedagogy, sociology of sport, disability studies, inclusive education and adapted physical activity, a socially critical dialogue is developed where the voices of young disabled people are central. Topics covered include:

- the historical context of disability sport
- inclusion policy towards physical education and youth sport
- constructions of disability through youth sport
- the voices of young disabled people
- researching disability and youth sport.

With its comprehensive coverage and expert contributors from around the globe, this book is an ideal text for students at all levels with an interest in youth sport, disability studies, or sport policy.

Hayley Fitzgerald is a Senior Lecturer in Sport, Leisure and Culture at Leeds Metropolitan University, England. Prior to this, Hayley worked as a researcher at Loughborough University. She has also worked for a number of disability sport organizations in England, and has extensive experience of developing accessible research strategies.

International Studies in Physical Education and Youth Sport
Edited by Richard Bailey
Roehampton University, London, UK

Routledge's *International Studies in Physical Education and Youth Sport* series aims to stimulate discussion on the theory and practice of school physical education, youth sport, childhood physical activity and well-being. By drawing on international perspectives, both in terms of the background of the contributors and the selection of the subject matter, the series seeks to make a distinctive contribution to our understanding of issues that continue to attract attention from policy makers, academics and practitioners.

Also available in this series:

Children, Obesity and Exercise: A practical approach to prevention, treatment and management of childhood and adolescent obesity
Edited by Andrew P. Hills, Neil A. King and Nuala M. Byrne

Rethinking Gender and Youth Sport
Edited by Ian Wellard

The Pedagogy of Human Movement
Richard Tinning

Positive Youth Development Through Sport
Edited by Nicholas Holt

Young People's Voices in PE and Youth Sport
Edited by Mary O'Sullivan and Ann Macphail

Physical Literacy: Activity and Engagement Throughout the Lifecourse
Edited by Margaret Whitehead

Disability and Youth Sport

**Edited by
Hayley Fitzgerald**

Routledge
Taylor & Francis Group

LONDON AND NEW YORK

First published 2009
by Routledge
2 Park Square, Milton Park, Abingdon, Oxon, OX14 4RN

Simultaneously published in the USA and Canada
by Routledge
270 Madison Avenue, New York, NY 10016

*Routledge is an imprint of the Taylor & Francis Group,
an Informa business*

Typeset in Times New Roman by
Florence Production Ltd, Stoodleigh, Devon
Printed and bound in Great Britain by
TJ International Ltd, Padstow, Cornwall

British Library Cataloguing in Publication Data
A catalogue record for this book is available
from the British Library

Library of Congress Cataloging-in-Publication Data
Disability and youth sport/edited by Hayley Fitzgerald.
    p. cm.
  Includes index.
  1. Sports for people with disabilities—Cross-cultural studies.
  2. Youth with disabilities—Recreation—Cross-cultural studies.
  I. Fitzgerald, Hayley.
  GV709.3.D57 2009
  796′.087—dc22   2008029017

ISBN10: 0–415–47041–2 hbk
ISBN10: 0–415–42353–8 pbk
ISBN10: 0–203–88973–8 ebk

ISBN13: 978–0–415–47041–4 hbk
ISBN13: 978–0–415–42353–3 pbk
ISBN13: 978–0–203–88973–2 ebk

Contents

Illustrations

Figures

Tables

Contributors

Aspley Wood School is located in Nottingham, England. Six pupils attending the school participated as co-researchers in a project exploring the physical education and youth sport experiences of pupils at the school. Although the pupils will remain anonymous the story about their research is told through a 'pictured report'. Barbara Mole, the Head Teacher, has written the forword to the chapter.

Len Barton is Emeritus Professor of Inclusive Education at the Institute of Education, University of London, England. In 2007, Len received the Senior Scholar Award for outstanding contributions to international disability studies from the Disability Studies in Education (Special Interest Group) of the American Educational Research Association.

Karen DePauw is the Vice Provost for Graduate Studies and Dean of the Graduate School at Virginia Polytechnic Institute and State University and tenured Professor in the Departments of Sociology and Human Nutrition, Foods and Exercise. Prior to this she served 22 years at Washington State University.

Hayley Fitzgerald is a Senior Lecturer in Sport, Leisure and Culture at the Carnegie Faculty of Sport and Education, Leeds Metropolitan University, England. Prior to taking this position Hayley worked as a researcher at Loughborough University and managed the evaluation of a range of national and regional projects focusing on youth sport and disability. She has also worked for a number of disability sport organizations in England.

Donna Goodwin is the Executive Director of The Steadward Centre for Personal and Physical Achievement and an Associate Professor within the Faculty of Physical Education and Recreation at the University of Alberta, Canada. Donna's research focuses on health promotion for persons with disabilities through physical activity. She is currently on the Editorial Board of *Adapted Physical Activity Quarterly*.

Anne Jobling is an Adjunct Professor at the University of Queensland, Australia. Until recently Anne was the Co-Director of the Down syndrome

Research Programme and managed a Literacy and Technology Course – Hands On (LATCH-ON). Anne's major research covers lifelong aspects of development related to motor development and health as well as education and self-regulation.

David Kirk is currently Dean of the Carnegie Faculty of Sport and Education at Leeds Metropolitan University and Professor of Physical Education and Youth Sport. David also holds an Honorary Chair in Human Movement Studies at the University of Queensland. David received the International Olympic Committee President's Prize in 2001 for his contribution to research in physical and sport education.

Catherine Morrison is a Lecturer in Health and Physical Education at the College of Education, University of Otago, New Zealand. Her current research involves an examination of the cultural, social and gender influences on young males with Developmental Disorder Coordination (DCD) and their engagement in physical education and sport.

Andy Smith is a Lecturer in Sociology of Sport and Exercise at the Chester Centre for Research into Sport and Society and Department of Sport and Exercise Sciences, University of Chester, England. He is a co-author of *Disability, Sport and Society: An Introduction* and *An Introduction to Drugs in Sport: Addicted to Winning* (both with Routledge).

Pam Stevenson is a full-time consultant, prior to this she worked as a Lecturer in Equal Opportunities in Physical Education at Liverpool Community College, England. Pam has been involved in the development of a range of training courses such as 'Including disabled pupils in PE' (EFDS) and 'The Active Play' programme in Liverpool for Foundation stage children.

Annette Stride is a Ph.D. student in the Carnegie Faculty of Sport and Education, Leeds Metropolitan University, England. Within the contexts of physical education and physical activity her research focuses on gender, difference and intersectionality. When Curriculum Leader for Sport and Public Services at Bradford College, Yorkshire, she initiated a successful partnership between non-disabled sports students and the Personal and Community Skills course.

Acknowledgements

I would like to offer my sincere gratitude to a number of people, all of whom made this edited collection possible. First, many thanks go to the authors who agreed to contribute to this edited collection. For a number of years I have enjoyed reading their work and it has been a pleasure working on this project with all of them. Second, much of the collection includes insights from young disabled people, teachers and coaches and I would like to acknowledge with appreciation all these research participants who agreed to share their views about physical education and youth sport. Third, I would like to recognize the encouraging and positive support I received from colleagues at Leeds Metropolitan University. Particular thanks go to Anne Flintoff and Julie Harpin who provided valuable comments on the structure and content of a number of chapters. I would also like to express thanks to Anthony Bourne who generated the drawings included in Chapter 8.

Abbreviations

ALT-PE	Academic Learning Time – Physical Education
BCDP	British Council for Disabled People
CCPR	Central Council for Physical Recreation
CISS	International Committee of Sports for the Deaf
CPD	Continuing Professional Development
CP-ISRA	Cerebral Palsy-International Sports and Recreation Association
DCD	Developmental Coordination Disorder
DCMS	Department for Culture, Media and Sport
DES	Department of Education and Science
DfEE	Department for Education and Employment
DfES	Department for Education and Skills
DPI	Disabled Peoples' International
EBD	Emotional and behavioural difficulties
EFDS	English Federation of Disability Sport
EHRC	Equality and Human Rights Commission
IAs	instructional assistants
IBSA	International Blind Sports Association
ICC	International Coordinating Committee of the World Sports Organizations
ICPS	International Cerebral Palsy Society
IDP	Including Disabled Pupils in Physical Education
INAS-FMH	Organizations International Federation for Sports for Persons with Mental Handicap
IOC	International Olympic Committee
IPC	International Paralympic Committee
ISOD	International Sports Organization for the Disabled
ISMWSF	International Stoke Mandeville Wheelchair Sports Federation
ITT	Initial Teacher Training
LEA	Local Education Authority
LSAs	learning support assistants
NCPE	National Curriculum for Physical Education
NWBA	National Wheelchair Basketball Association

OAA	outdoor and adventurous activities
OFSTED	Office for Standards in Education
OT	Occupational Therapist
PE	physical education
PESSCL	Physical Education, School Sport and Club Links
QCA	Qualifications and Curriculum Authority
SEN	special educational needs
SENCOs	SEN Co-ordinators
SEU	Social Exclusion Unit
SPARC	Sport and Recreation New Zealand
SSCo	School Sports Co-ordinator
SSCs	Specialist Sports Colleges
UNESCO	United Nations Educational, Scientific and Cultural Organization
UPIAS	Union of the Physically Impaired Against Segregation and the Disability Alliance
WO	Welsh Office
YST	Youth Sport Trust

1 Bringing disability into youth sport

Hayley Fitzgerald

Disability and the goals of youth sport

It is estimated that there are 650 million disabled people in the world, approximately 10 per cent of the population.[1] Over the past thirty years, the life chances and opportunities for many disabled people have dramatically changed, particularly in the areas of education, health and employment. To a large extent the political action instigated by disability activists and human rights advocates has heightened awareness of the inequalities and oppression that disabled people experience in social life. Although positive developments have resulted from these movements it should be acknowledged that internationally the pace of change has not been uniform and many disabled people remain institutionalized, discriminated against and continue to experience social isolation (Filmer 2005; Watermeyer *et al.* 2006; Loeb *et al.* 2008). Sport for some will never be significant and instead concerns are likely to focus on getting through daily life. I make this important point because although this edited collection is about disability and youth sport there should be a recognition that as scholars, students and practitioners we have a responsibility to not only advocate for young disabled people in sport but also need to do this in broader dimensions of life. After all, sport is inextricably connected to wider social and cultural practices and norms and we need to engage with these debates if we are serious about enhancing the sporting opportunities and experiences of young disabled people.

Sport has been, and will undoubtedly continue to be, an important part of the fabric of society. Whatever a person's disposition and response towards sport, we should be mindful that initial youth sport experiences provide the platform from which thinking about sport is moulded and this subsequently influences future choices and engagement in sport (Kirk 2005; MacPhail and Kirk 2006). Initial participation in youth sport, or as Côté and Hay (2002) describe the 'sampling years', takes place in a variety of contexts including informal recreational settings, physical education and organized community sport. Within these settings the 'goals' of youth sport will differ and Siedentop (2002) usefully reminds us that they centre on a combination of educative, public health, elite development and preserving goals. For example, if the educative goal dominates a youth sport programme 'it would be as inclusive as possible, attractive to diverse children and youths, modified physically and emotionally to fit developing bodies, talents, and spirits' (Siedentop, 2002: 394). In part, Siedentop's (2002) talk of 'inclusion' and 'modification' signals an aspiration to include many young people in youth sport. Indeed, some time ago Hellison and Templin (1991) alerted us to the variety of young people who may be the recipients of youth sport.

> Billy wants to be there, Mary doesn't. Suzi is an exceptionally skilled athlete, Joey has difficulty with any physical activity. Danny is back in school after two suspensions, Karen has a perfect attendance record. Pam is epileptic, Larry is learning disabled, and Dave has a congenital heart defect. Tom constantly complains, and Don brings the teacher an apple every day. Andrew is a 4-foot, 5-inch ninth grader, and Jack is a 6-foot, 5-inch ninth grader. Kay's father is the CEO of one of the country's largest companies, and they live in the suburbs; Sue lives with her divorced mother in the inner city, and they are on welfare.
>
> (Hellison and Templin, 1991: 27)

This discussion about the goals of youth sport and the diversity of young people engaging in sport raises a number of interesting questions concerning the extent to which these goals are *equally* relevant and attainable by *all* young people. Are the goals of youth sport, in fact, unrealistic and not conceived in a manner that will enable the majority of young disabled people to achieve in youth sport? This argument is supported, for example, when consideration is given to understandings of 'disability' and 'sport', both emphasize physicality. However, sport is underpinned by precision in movement whereas disability often signifies deficiency. How can or does youth sport reconcile what would seem to be a fundamental contradiction? How is this manifest through the experiences of young disabled people and youth sport practitioners? In what ways do broader discourses within society contribute to the value(s) afforded to young disabled people participating in youth sport? Has youth sport been challenged in any way and how have alternative constructions been rearticulated?

In this chapter I suspend judgment on these particular questions as the other contributors to this edited collection help to explore these issues. What I would suggest though is that there is immense value in using the vantage point of disability to interrogate the constitution and practices of youth sport. On this issue, DePauw argues that, 'The lens of disability allows us to make problematic the socially constructed nature of sport and once we have done so, opens us to alternative constructions, and solutions' (DePauw 1997: 428). For instance, through this lens we can uncover the most revealing stories about life and feelings towards sport. Many of these stories are not found within 'sporting texts' but rather incorporated into rich biographical accounts of disabled people. In Paul Hunt's seminal edited collection *Stigma: The*

Experience of Disability, Margaret Gill recollects her childhood and impressions of sport.

> The 'I wants' of childhood become 'I want to be normal'; 'I want to run in the races, play football, netball, tennis, like the others'. The reply from his classmates is invariably the hard truth: 'We don't want you; you are too slow; we shall never win if *you* are with us; and when it is time to 'pick teams' the disabled child is always left until last.
>
> (Gill 1966: 100)

More recently, Luke Jackson gives another insightful account of physical education:

> The familiar hustle and bustle murmuring and giggling that follow the instruction 'Get into teams' are always accompanied by the predictable 'Aw Sir, do we have to?' Or 'No way are we having him' as the games teacher allocates me to a random team rather like a spare piece of luggage that no one can be bothered to carry.
>
> (Jackson, 2002: 129)

In both accounts, there is a sense that physical education is not a happy place – the prospect of doing physical education evokes thoughts of dread, isolation and desires to be 'normal'. So what of my life and the other contributors to this edited collection? How would we reflect upon our youth sport experiences and in what ways have these experiences contributed to our outlook, disposition towards sport and interest in disability sport? As a way of providing an insight into such experiences I offer a brief reflection about my sporting encounters and journey into disability sport.

An outsider's journey into youth sport and disability

As a very 'able' sports performer, I lived for youth sport. In fact, school for me revolved around physical education; without this subject I would have found school quite unbearable. In my mind, the purpose of being at school became apparent when I was doing physical education or other extra-curricular sports-related activities. My memories of school focus on these experiences and I chose to put at the back of my mind all the other horrible subjects I endured in order to get my weekly kick of sport. At college and university I continued to surround myself with other 'sporty' people. Sport has played, and continues to play, an important part in my life. It was a long time before I recognized that not everyone shares the feelings I have towards sport. The panic I felt in every English lesson at the thought of the teacher saying, 'Hayley, your turn to read' or 'your spelling results are . . .' was horrible, and I had not realized that some of my classmates felt like this about sport. When I began to work with different groups of young disabled people I began to reflect on, and compare, my experiences of life to those of the young participants I was working with. Why was it that at my school I could not remember any disabled people being there? Where did they go? What sort of youth sport did they experience? Did sport figure in any way in their lives? Over time, I got to know many young people and found out more about them and their experiences. I began to understand how the liberating sporting experiences I received were not necessarily evident in the recollections and stories I heard.

Just over ten years ago, when I became a researcher, I remember conducting numerous interviews and developing various questionnaires with teachers and coaches that aimed to find out about the experiences of young disabled people in youth sport. While doing this research and drawing on the experiences of my advocacy background, I became increasingly aware that there was something important missing from the research I was doing – the views of the young disabled people. At this point, I was intrigued to find out more. Was it just our research that was positioned in this way? How had other research included young disabled people? What was already known about the youth sport experiences of young disabled people? As I began to explore these issues I discovered a body of literature focusing on 'disability studies' and this continues to help me develop and guide my thinking. When I read *Doing Disability Research* (Barnes and Mercer 1997), I could not put it down (something I have managed to do very easily with many other texts). I spent a week reading and re-reading this book and it helped me to begin to see research in a different light and ask critical questions about 'why' and 'how' we all do research. At this time, I also began to read youth sport literature and was at a loss to understand why the majority of these works failed to recognize disability as a form of social oppression requiring the same kind of debate and discussion that is afforded to other inequalities.[2] At worst issues relating to disability do not feature in some socio-critically underpinned sport texts that claim to be exploring equity. At other times, disability gets an arbitrary mention – usually at the end of the line of other equity issues or is sidelined as an '*etc.*' issue where readers are left to guess what in fact this encompasses. These omissions, I suggest, illustrate how scholars continue to be complicit in marginalizing young disabled people's needs and interests in youth sport.

I have now spent more than fifteen years working or researching around disability and youth sport. This edited collection forms part of my ongoing commitment and belief that researchers within youth sport have a responsibility to include, and listen to, the voices of young disabled people.

Structure of the book

Disability and Youth Sport attempts to provide an innovative and critical way of exploring the relationship between disability and youth sport. This edited collection develops a socially critical dialogue by focusing on key historical, theoretical and policy developments concerned with disability and youth sport. This text also explores the ways in which these kinds of developments have impacted on the pedagogy practised in youth sport and in particular centralizes the experiences of young disabled people. Our contributors draw on a breadth of literature from sports pedagogy, sociology of sport, disability studies, inclusive education and adapted physical activity. By utilizing this diverse literature we seek to address Aitchison's (2003) call to move beyond the discursive boundaries of our field and engage in wider discourse. Although the contributors to this text come from different fields and hold a range of views regarding theory, policy and practice we have come together with an overarching commitment to sharing and extending understandings about disability and youth sport.

This edited collection is divided into three major parts. The first of these, 'Theoretical and contextual background', focuses on key historical and contemporary policy and theoretical developments informing youth sport and disability. This section begins in Chapter 2 with Karen DePauw mapping out the historical development of sport for disabled people. This chapter highlights how these origins were underpinned by a medical imperative and how in more recent times emphasis has been placed on agendas associated with inclusion and competitive disability sport pathways. After this, in Chapter 3, Andy Smith further conceptualizes recent policy developments in physical education and youth sport related to discourses of inclusion and equity. This chapter emphasizes the complexities of policy-making in this area and the ongoing challenges of moving policy forward through developments in practice. Chapter 4 explores disability, social theory and youth sport. Here Len Barton draws on writing found within disability studies relating to medical and social model understandings of disability and considers how these understandings can be used to critique normalized conceptions and practices within youth sport. The chapters included in this part of the edited collection are foundational and in many ways should be seen as setting the scene for the discussions that develop in the preceding chapters.

The second part of this collection is entitled 'Youth sport insights from young disabled people' and focuses on the views and insights of youth sport from young disabled people. By including this substantive theme, I wanted to highlight the importance of engaging with young disabled people about their experiences – their absence from research and decision-making is unacceptable. In Chapter 5, Donna Goodwin provides a review of the research on student experiences in inclusive physical education and provides a critique of how these experiences align against recommended pedagogical practices in inclusive physical education. Following this broad review the remaining chapters in this part of the edited collection focus on specific examples of recent empirical research. In Chapter 6 Annette Stride explores experiences of extra-curricular sport and she focuses on the development of football opportunities for girls with learning disabilities attending a special school. After this, in Chapter 7 David Kirk and myself draw on data generated from on interview-based study and make problematic the position, place and value of disability sport within physical education. Chapter 8 is the final part of this section and represents a contribution from Aspley Wood School. In this chapter the findings from a research project in which students worked as co-researchers are reported through a 'pictured report'. This largely visual contribution serves as an important illustration of how research can be disseminated in a meaningful and accessible way to young participants and the recipients of research.

The final part of this collection is entitled 'Inclusion in practice' and, in different ways, focuses on practitioners' experiences of working towards inclusive youth sport. In Chapter 9 Pam Stevenson discusses the pedagogy of inclusive youth sport and outlines the development of the 'inclusion spectrum' and how this model can help in a very practical sense work towards inclusive youth sport. This chapter presents a challenge to academics and practitioners to provide 'real solutions' for teachers and coaches rather than preoccupying ourselves with the ongoing debates about the theoretical and conceptual meanings of inclusive youth sport. After this, in Chapter 10 Catherine Morrison presents a personal narrative as a female, teacher, educator and athlete and reflects upon her journey of 'difference' with her son Leo. Through the narrative of 'Leo' the chapter explores his position in discourses of child development, medicine and education. As an educator, Catherine questions many of the unexamined assumptions that have guided her work and urges us all to be more reflective about the consequences that our practice has on young disabled people. In Chapter 11 I move on by critiquing research practice in youth sport and explore the ways in which young disabled people have traditionally been positioned as unreliable sources of research information. I challenge youth sport researchers to question this kind of disabilist position and in doing this review a number of examples of youth sport research that has attempted to engage in an inclusive and meaningful way with young disabled people. This collection concludes with Chapter 12 where Anne Jobling and I reflect upon the key developments in youth sport and disability discussed throughout this edited collection. In particular, we consider the inroads that have been made and signpost future directions in research and theorizing that would enable us to better understand experiences of youth sport and disability.

I hope this book challenges your thinking and serves as a catalyst to stimulate further dialogue and debate focusing on youth sport and disability.

A word about language

I acknowledge that the international audience of this edited collection will have different expectations regarding the way in which disability and disabled people are talked about and understood. At times, differences in the use of language can be related to the process of translation. On other occasions, more fundamental beliefs and understandings underpin the way in which someone speaks of disability. In this text, you will see that authors 'speak' of disability in different ways. For example, some contributors have chosen to use 'person first' terminology and refer to 'people with disabilities'. This position is taken to emphasize the individual first and disability as something that does not define the person. Other contributors refer to 'disabled people' and in doing this may be seeking to 'avoid the phrase "people with disabilities" because it implies that the impairment defines the identity of the individual, blurs the crucial conceptual distinction between impairment and disability and avoids the question of causality' (Barnes *et al*. 1999: 7). In my view, we should let the conversations flow – in whatever form. This means respecting different positions and recognizing that to preclude from discussions would be a loss to our debates. It is a shame that some key sports related journals do not take this position and by doing this, I would argue, are limiting the nature of their scholarly contributions.

Notes

1   This is a global estimate and based on partial data available. It should be acknowledged that within specific national contexts there are often different measures of disability (see Purdam *et al*. 2008) and ongoing debates about how disability is defined within research (see Pfeiffer 2000; Barnes *et al*. 1999; and Hurst 2000).

2   There are some notable exceptions and it should be acknowledged that a small group of scholars writing from a socially critical perspective have made some significant contributions in this area including Hayes and Stidder (2003), Vickerman (2007) and Howe (2008).

References

Aitchison, C. (2003) 'From Leisure and Disability to Disability Leisure: Developing Data, Definitions and Discourses', *Disability and Society*, 18 (7): 955–69.

Barnes, C., Mercer, G. and Shakespeare, T. (1997) *Exploring Disability: A Sociological Introduction*, Cambridge: Polity Press.

Barnes, C. and Mercer, G. (eds) (1997) *Doing Disability Research*, Leeds: The Disability Press.

Côté, J. and Hay, J. (2002) 'Children's Involvement in Sport: A Developmental Perspective', in J.M. Siva and D. Stevens (eds), *Psychological Foundations of Sport*, Moston: Merrill, pp. 484–502.

DePauw, K.P. (1997) 'The (In)Visibility of DisAbility: Cultural contexts and Sporting Bodies', *Quest*, 49 (4): 416–30.

Filmer, D. (2005) 'Disability, Poverty, and Schooling in Developing Countries: Results from 11 Household Surveys' (December), *World Bank Policy Research Working Paper No. 3794*, available from: http://ssrn.com/abstract=874823 (accessed 21 March 2007).

Gill, M. (1966) 'No Small Miracle', in P. Hunt (ed.), *Stigma: The Experience of Disability*, London: Geoffrey Chapman, pp. 99–107.

Hayes, S. and Stidder, G. (eds) (2003) *Equity and Inclusion in Physical Education and Sport: Contemporary Issues for Teachers, Trainees and Practitioners*, London: Routledge.

Hellison, D.R. and Templin, T.J. (1991) *A Reflective Approach to Teaching Physical Education*, Champaign, IL: Human Kinetics.

How, P.D. (2008) *The Cultural Politics of the Paralympic Movement Through an Anthropological Lens*, Routledge: London.

Hurst, R. (2000) 'To Revise or Not to Revise?', *Disability and Society*, 15 (7): 1083–7.

Jackson, L. (2002) *Freaks, Geeks and Asperger Syndrome: A User Guide to Adolescence*, London: Jessica Kingley Publishers.

Kirk, D. (2005) 'Physical Education, Youth Sport and Lifelong Participation: The Importance of Early Learning Experiences', *European Physical Education Review*, 11 (3): 239–55.

Loeb, M., Eide, A.H., Jelsma, J., Toni, M. and Maart, S. (2008) 'Poverty and Disability in East and West Cape Provinces, South Africa', *Disability and Society*, 23 (4): 311–21.

MacPhail, A. and Kirk, D. (2006) 'Young People's Socialisation into Sport: Experiencing the Specialising Phase', *Leisure Studies*, 25 (1): 57–74.

Pfeiffer, D. (2000) 'The Devils Are in the Details: The ICIDH2 and the Disability Movement', *Disability and Society*, 15 (7): 1079–82.

Purdam, K., Afkhami, R., Olsen, W. and Thornton, P. (2008) 'Disability in the UK: Measuring Equality', *Disability and Society*, 23 (1): 53–65.

Siedentop, D. (2002) 'Junior Sport and the Evaluation of Sport Cultures', *Journal of Teaching in Physical Education*, 21 (4): 392–401.

Vickerman, P. (2007) *Teaching Physical Education to Children with Special Educational Needs*, London: Routledge.

Watermeyer, B., Swartz, L., Lorenzo, T., Schneider, M. and Priestley, M. (2006) *Disability and Social Change: A South African Agenda*, Cape Town: HSRC Press.

Part I

Theoretical and contextual background

2 Disability sport

Historical context[1]

Karen DePauw

Introduction

Physical activity and sport have been present in some form throughout history. These physical activity forms can be traced across the ages and include early representations as work, curative exercise and physical training and evolved into movements forms including physical education, sport, therapy, and recreation. Sport as we know it today has its roots from the rich history of physical activity and human movement. Sport is a highly visible entity in today's society and seems most visibly represented through the Ancient and Modern Olympics. As sport has evolved across the centuries, new sport forms and opportunities emerged. Prior to the mid-twentieth century, those with physical, sensory or intellectual impairments had limited opportunities to participate in formal programmes of physical activity, physical education and organized sport competition. But contemporary society offers sport, including disability sport, as a viable option for youths and adults with disabilities; the opportunities span the social, educational, recreational, competitive and community-based purposes of physical activity and sport.

Historical context for physical activity

As Table 2.1 illustrates physical activity has been an important component of human life throughout history. The roots can be traced back to antiquity, when early humans needed strength and endurance for basic survival, hunting, fishing and fighting. Training one's body was simply part of one's education.

A curative use of physical activity was found in records and drawings representing life in China approximately 2700 BC. Additionally, exercise, massage and baths were used by early Egyptians, Hindus, Greeks and Romans. Individuals exercised to prevent and alleviate physical disorders and illnesses. Specific exercises were developed for the sick, convalescent and sedentary. Physical activity for the development of a beautiful and well-proportioned body was prevalent in the fifth century BC when Athenian education was contrasted with the Spartan brutality. Greek society emphasized balance among mental, social and physical forms of training.

Table 2.1 Historical periods and physical activity

Time periods	Uses of physical activity
Antiquity	Strength and endurance for survival
2700 BC China	Curative period for prevention and alleviation of physical disorders
Fifth century BC (Greek society)	Development of beautiful and harmonious body – balance of mental, social and physical training
Sixteenth- and seventeenth-century Europe	Sound mind and sound body through medical gymnastics
1850s (US)	Medical gymnastics used by US physicians
Early 1900s	Physical education to improve physical condition of youth
After the First and Second World Wars	Rehabilitation through physical activity and sport educational model for physical education
Twenty-first century	Sport as empowerment and social change

After this early emphasis upon physical activity, it was not until the Reformation of the sixteenth and seventeenth centuries that physical activity received serious attention again. The development of a 'sound mind in a sound body' was promoted by English philosopher John Locke during this time. The European influences were many and varied, and they have had a lasting effect upon physical activity today. Specifically, two particular systems of medical gymnastics emerged. The German system and the Swedish system of physical education were both aimed at developing the body, mind and character of youth using gymnastics, mass drills and games of skill. Accordingly, exercise was thought to be the best medicine, and physicians were the main advocates for medical gymnastics. These physical educational systems, also referred to as medical gymnastics, were transported to the United States during the nineteenth century. By the 1850s, American physicians, like those in Britain and Australia, had begun to use these programmes. As a result, specialized programmes and facilities were developed to correct postural defects, alleviate organic conditions and improve physical strength and stamina.

Physical education evolved before, and emerged more prominently after, the world wars. The growth was experienced because many of the youth were unfit for war; thus, physical education programmes were developed to address their physical condition. Physicians, who had been long involved with physical activity, became involved in physical education programmes prior to the First World War and remained so long after the Second World War. Their involvement after the wars included remedial applications of physical activity, specifically rehabilitation. Physical education continued to flourish and was embraced within an educational model of provision. In contrast, rehabilitation and therapy (recreation, physical, corrective) remained positioned under a medical model imperative.

Historical context for sport; exclusion but moving toward inclusion

Individuals who did not or could not conform to the prescribed norm of the time in either appearance or behaviour tended to experience differential treatment often, but not always, resulting in exclusion. According to Hewett and Forness (1974), those who were perceived as 'different' were destroyed, tortured, exorcized, sterilized, ignored, exiled, exploited, pitied, cared for, categorized, educated and even considered divine. This historical treatment varied based upon the individual, the perception of the nature of the impairment and the cultural values and norms of the time (see DePauw and Gavron 2005; Hewett and Forness 1974).

In the primitive and ancient periods (3000 BC to 500 BC) survival of the fittest and superstition were the key elements. Survival of the fittest for individuals impacted on those who were found to be obviously physically deformed and/or not physically capable of hunting for food or defending themselves and so faced the consequences of the harsh environment. Superstition of those individuals born with physical deformities as being evil meant they were therefore isolated from the family unit.

In the Greek and Roman period (500 BC to 400 AD), several perspectives were prevalent. Persons born with impairments were faced with a harsh physical environment and the doctrine of the survival of the fittest was applied not only to the environmental conditions but to the harsh discipline and punishment often inflicted upon children with disabilities. The Greeks and the Romans were quite concerned about the physical capability of their citizens and war was the catalyst for building strong bodies and developing advanced skills for war. In this environment, those with impairments were not valued and often were put to death. Initially, superstition of those with mental impairments existed during this period and the treatments included purification, exorcism and other demonological practices. But toward the end of this period, Hippocrates and Plato proposed different conceptualizations of mental illness and care that included physical activity or exercise, hydrotherapy, massage and exposure to sunshine.

The early Christians (AD 400–1500) had an even greater impact on individuals with disabilities because of the strong emphasis placed on the concept that taking a life was a sinful act. Infanticide was no longer an accepted practice. Despite the fact that infants born impaired were allowed to live, many were still not able to survive in their harsh physical and social environments.

During the Middle Ages, individuals with physical and mental impairments were often able to survive in the protective environments of monasteries and royal courts. Their status was limited, but their quality of life was much improved over previous periods. Although the religious influences of the period did much to foster acceptance, understanding and humanitarian treatment, differential treatment exists between those with 'mental retardation' and those with 'mental illness'. Those with mental retardation, the 'blessed', were often employed in the courts of kings and queens as court jesters. For those considered mentally ill, occasionally exorcism, torture, witch burning and other demonological practices persisted.

The science and medicine era (sixteenth and seventeenth centuries) continued and expanded the differential treatment. The demonological tradition persisted; individuals with mental illness were still tortured and/or burned at the stake. In contrast, those with hearing impairments and mental retardation received more humanitarian treatment. In institutions designed specifically for them, deaf children were taught reading, writing, arithmetic, astronomy, Greek and other subjects. Both oral language and finger spelling were used to educate these individuals. Due to their privileged status, children with hearing impairments were provided with a high standard of living. Individuals with mental retardation were still considered idiots and simpletons, but attempts were made to understand them from psychological and educational perspectives. They were often segregated from society, and although some were employed in workhouses, most remained unemployed and were perceived as a burden on society.

During the eighteenth century, the society that had been significantly influenced by belief in demons and 'evil spirits' finally became overshadowed by the movement toward the rights (and dignity) of humans – a transition from fear, superstition and hostility toward individuals with impairments to compassion and a decision to educate these individuals. The treatment during this period involved the use of asylums, hospitals or schools as residential institutions. Schools for children who were blind and deaf also appeared by the end of the period. The French Revolution awakened the sense of individual responsibility and led to more humane treatment of individuals.

Education treatment was a focus of the nineteenth century. Among the major events of this period was the work of Jean Marc Itard with the 'wild boy' (1962) named Victor. Itard was the first to show that severely retarded individuals could be taught and that improved functioning could result. The notion of the residential institutions found in Europe crossed the Atlantic and found a stronghold in the United States where institutions were established throughout the country. Institutional segregation tended to be viewed as the most effective treatment for those individuals with disabilities.

The twentieth century can be viewed as a period of social reform, war, increased governmental concern for individuals with disabilities and the emergence of concern about disability, especially in the fields of education, psychology and medicine. Legislation was enacted to address the issues of education, nondiscrimination, accessibility and equal opportunity and the disability rights movement began in the last half of the twentieth century (DePauw 1997; Shapiro 1993). The large number of injured world war veterans and the need for rehabilitation posed challenges for society in general and created opportunities in sport and education in particular.

Current societal perceptions about disability have historical roots in the medical profession (Chappell 1992; Oliver 1990; Linton 1998), which tended to view disability as a 'physical or psychological condition considered to have predominately medical significance' (Linton 1998: 10) and primarily, a problem found within the individual and not with society (Oliver 1990). This 'medicalization of disability casts human variation as deviance from the norm, as pathological condition, as deficit' (Linton 1998: 11). But the emergence of the disability rights movement has challenged professionals to reconceptualize disability in the context of social relationships (see Chappell 1992; Davis 1995; Linton 1998) and social theory (see Abberley 1987; Oliver 1990; Barnes *et al.* 2002). As discussed in Chapter 4, at the core of this movement is the simple belief that disability, of itself, is not tragic or pitiable. Further, many individuals with disabilities tend not to view themselves as 'deviant' and do not view their bodies as weak or frail, or even imperfect. However, in a society where individuals are judged by their appearance and valued for their youth, physical prowess and physical beauty, individuals with disabilities have often been shunned by society and treated as social inferiors (Shilling 2003). This is most vividly illustrated by Sandy Slack who reflects upon her life and experiences of disability. As a young non-disabled person she recalls how negative cultural meanings associated with disability were embedded within the talk of the school playground:

> Gathered in the school playground which seemed harmless in a simple sense echoed back to me in memory with most painful force. Words like 'cripple', 'spas', 'mental', 'stupid', 'clumsy', 'blind as a bat', and 'deaf as a post'. I could go on, but even reviving and actually writing these words feels abusive.
>
> (Slack 1999: 28)

For Sandy, physicality was central to how she understood herself and was viewed by others.

> Gymnastics, dance, athletics, swimming and team games – they are more than the surface observation. To those who take part they are a language. They require focused concentration, skill and knowledge, but all these without the internal spirit which drives you forward are meaningless. To use the body to its maximum capabilities is like painting that picture or writing that book or playing that music – it is almost spiritual. That was

my language. I communicated with the world and myself through the
medium of perpetual motion. It was who I was.

(Slack 1999: 30)

After acquiring a disability there was a sense that part of her 'self' – who
she was and how she was defined had been lost.

The language I knew and felt so at easy with is no longer accessible to
me. My language was the one of movement. The sheer heaven and joy
of expression through movement gave me all the language I thought I
would ever need.

(Slack 1999: 29)

Sandy, like other people with disabilities became defined by others:

Disabled people frequently become the property of many authorities.
Except this is not a positive status, it is an official statement which can
mean you need someone or something in order to live your life. The
creation of dependency begins with this process. It has little to do with
choice and much to do with how structures are organized. Disabled
people variously become 'clients', 'patients' or 'service users'. They are
then filed on computer (permission for this is rarely sought), and they
belong to that department. Disabled people became property in order to
beget property.

(Slack 1999: 34)

Throughout history, sport has tended to reflect dominant societal values related
to disability and in this way reproduces social inequalities (Donnelly 1996).
However, as women and individuals with disabilities have entered the sporting
arena, sport has begun to change. We know that sport can provide a context
for resistance to the status quo and a site for social change (Donnelly 1996;
DePauw 1997; Hargreaves 2000). People with disabilities can participate in
sport in a variety of contexts including mainstream community sport, disability
sport supported through mainstream sporting organizations and dedicated
disability sport pathways. In the following section attention is given to the
historical development of disability sport.

Early history of disability sport

Deaf individuals were the first grouping of individuals to participate in
organized sport. The first Sports Club for the Deaf was founded in Berlin
in 1888. By 1924, six national sport federations for the deaf had emerged:
Belgium, Czechoslovakia, France, Great Britain, Holland and Poland. In
1924, the first International Silent Games were held in Paris, France.
Competitors came from these six countries as well as Hungary, Italy and

Romania. On the occasion of these games, the International Committee of Sports for the Deaf (CISS) was founded. Competitions were held every four years initially as Summer Games but were expanded to provide summer and winter competitions for deaf athletes. These games became known as the World Games for the deaf and are now identified as the Deaflympics.

In addition to deaf individuals, amputees enjoyed early sport opportunities. The British Society of One-Armed Golfers was founded in 1932, and annual golf tournaments for amputees have since been held throughout England. Today, there are golf associations and sporting opportunities for amputees in countries throughout the world.

The world wars of the early twentieth century significantly influenced western societal views of individuals with physical impairments and brought rehabilitation to the forefront (Huber 1984; Shapiro 1993). Many veterans returned to their home countries with physical impairments and psychological needs that could not be accommodated by traditional techniques. And thus, sport rehabilitation programmes were developed to assist these individuals, primarily males, to make the transition back into society.

The British government is credited with being the first to recognize these needs by opening the Spinal Injuries Centre at Stoke Mandeville Hospital in Salisbury, England in 1944. Sir Ludwig Guttmann, director of this centre, first introduced competitive sports as an integral part of the rehabilitation of disabled veterans. The competitive sports of the time included punchball exercises, rope climbing and wheelchair polo (Guttmann 1976). Under Guttmann's tutelage, the First Stoke Mandeville Games for the Paralyzed were held in 1948. At these games, 26 British veterans (including three women) competed in archery.

In the late 1940s, sport as a part of medical rehabilitation spread throughout Europe and ultimately to the United States. The earliest known athletic event for athletes with disabilities in the United States was a wheelchair basketball game played by war veterans at southern California's Corona Naval Station in 1945. In 1947 and 1948, wheelchair basketball teams emerged: the 'Pioneers' from Kansas City; the 'Whirlaways' from Brooklyn; the 'Gophers' from Minneapolis; the 'Bulova Watchmakers' of Woodside, New York; the 'Chairoteers' of Queens; and the 'New York Spokesmen' from Manhattan.

Since 1946, wheelchair basketball in the United States has increased so much in popularity that a wheelchair basketball tournament was desired. Tim Nugent, director of student rehabilitation at the University of Illinois, organized the first wheelchair basketball tournament in 1949 in Galesburg, Illinois. During the preparations for the tournament, it became necessary for Nugent to form a planning committee to oversee administrative aspects. This evolved into the National Wheelchair Basketball Association (NWBA), the first governing body for wheelchair basketball in the United States.

In 1952, Guttmann organized the first international competition for wheelchair athletes. These games were held at Stoke Mandeville, and the British competed against a team from the Netherlands: 130 athletes with spinal cord injuries competed in six wheelchair sports. To honour the social and human value derived from the wheelchair sports movement, the International Olympic Committee recognized Guttmann's work in 1956 and awarded him and his associates the Fearnley Cup.

Since the early beginnings at the Stoke Mandeville Games, wheelchair sport has expanded and become an international entity. In addition to wheelchair archery, the sports of lawn bowling, table tennis, shot-put, javelin and club throw were added to the growing list of wheelchair sports. In the 1960s, wheelchair basketball, fencing, snooker, swimming and weightlifting were introduced. South America and the United States sent teams to the Stoke Mandeville Games competitions held in 1957 and 1960, respectively. By 1960, the International Stoke Mandeville Wheelchair Sports Federation (ISMWSF) had been formed to sanction all international competitions for individuals with spinal cord injuries. Although originally sanctioned for those with spinal cord injuries, these games were expanded in 1976 to include other physical and visual impairments and would evolve and eventually be referred to as the Paralympics (Gold and Gold 2007).

The middle years (mid-twentieth century)

During the 1960s, international sport competitions were expanded to include other disability groups not eligible for the World Games for the Deaf or the International Stoke Mandeville Games. The leadership for these additional disability sport competitions came in the form of the International Sports Organization for the Disabled (ISOD). In 1964, the ISOD was officially formed to provide international sport opportunities for the blind, amputee, and other locomotor disabilities (Lindstrom 1984). Its founders intended that ISOD would become an entity parallel in structure and functions to the International Olympic Committee (IOC).

In part due to dissatisfaction with existing competitions, the International Cerebral Palsy Society (ICPS) was founded in 1968 to sponsor the first international games for individuals with cerebral palsy. ICPS continued this competition every two years until 1978 when the Cerebral Palsy-International Sports and Recreation Association (CP-ISRA) became recognized by ISOD as the official sanctioning body for cerebral palsy sports.

In a similar fashion, the International Blind Sports Association (IBSA) was formed in 1981 in response to increasing interest and expanding opportunities for competitions for athletes with visual impairments including blindness. These two groups (IBSA, CP-ISRA) became the last disability sport groups to seek and attain recognition from ISOD.

Joint interest in expanding the opportunities for international sport for athletes with a disability brought the CP-ISRA, IBSA, ISMWSF and ISOD together in 1982 to form a new umbrella organization. The International Coordinating Committee of the World Sports Organizations (ICC) was formed to coordinate disability sport worldwide and to negotiate with the International Olympic Committee (IOC) on behalf of athletes with a disability. CISS (Deaf sports) and International Federation for Sports for Persons with Mental Handicap (INAS-FMH) joined the ICC in 1986.

Inasmuch as the ICC served as a fragile alliance of international sport federations and experienced an uneasy history from 1982 to 1987, representatives of 39 countries and representatives from the six international federations met to determine the future of international disability sport. This meeting, known as the 'Arnhem Seminar', was held on 14 March 1987, in Arnhem, the Netherlands. Seminar participants decided that a new international sports organization should be created to represent disabled sportsmen and sportswomen around the world, and they appointed an ad hoc committee to draft the constitution. As specified during the Arnhem Seminar, the new organization was to have national representation from every nation with a disability sport programme and was to govern itself through a council of nations. Athletes and disability sport organizations were to have a voice in the governance of disability sport on an international level. The new structure was also charged with responsibility for developmental and recreational activities in addition to international and elite sport. The existing members of the ICC were recognized and were to become an integral part of this new organization. In Düsseldorf, Germany, on 21 and 22 September 1989, the International Paralympic Committee (IPC) was born. At this meeting, officers were elected and the governance structure was adopted, along with a draft of the constitution. The IPC began a most significant chapter in the history of sport and disability. Initial efforts were devoted to streamlining operations, coordinating international sport, and securing communication between the IPC and IOC.

Inasmuch as the 1992 Paralympics in Barcelona were to be held under the auspices of the ICC, the final exchange of power from the ICC to the IPC was set to occur at the conclusion of the 1992 Paralympics. Thus, since September 1992, the IPC has been recognized as the sole international coordinating entity for athletes with disabilities.

Recognizing the need for a professionally run organization and acknowledging the increasing growth and complexity of its operations, the IPC selected Bonn, Germany as the site for its headquarters. The German Federal Government and the City of Bonn were instrumental in identifying an appropriate location and providing funding for the IPC headquarters. The early 1900s once-private residence turned office building was renovated and made wheelchair accessible and the official opening of the headquarters was held on 3 September 1999. In attendance at the Grand Opening were dignitaries, officials, athletes with disabilities, coaches and professionals throughout the world. Then IOC President Samaranch presented IPC President Robert Steadward with a sculpture depicting a wheelchair athlete in motion that is displayed prominently at IPC Headquarters.

The relationship between the IPC and IOC has strengthened throughout the years. The practice of holding the Olympic Games followed shortly thereafter by the Paralympics Games in the same host city has been in effect since 1988 (Summer Games – Seoul, 1988; Barcelona, 1992; Atlanta, 1996; Sydney, 2000; Athens, 2004; Beijing, 2008 and Winter Games – Lillehammer, 1994; Nagano, 1998; Salt Lake City, 2002). This practice has now become more formalized and incorporated into the bid process for hosting the Olympic Games. In 2000, a cooperation agreement was signed by then IOC President (S.E.M. Juan Antonio Samaranch) and then IPC President (Dr. Robert D. Steadward) in Sydney, Australia. The agreement acknowledged that the IPC and IOC shared a 'common belief in the right of all human beings to pursue their physical and intellectual development', identified specific areas of cooperation including representation of the IPC on the IOC commissions and working groups and co-opted then IPC President Steadward as a member of the International Olympic Committee. Further confirmation of the solid relationship was demonstrated in the election of Phil Craven, current IPC President, as the 123rd member of the IOC.

Contemporary opportunities and challenges for athletes with disabilities

International competitive sport opportunities for athletes with disabilities have increased significantly since the mid-twentieth century. Today, there are major international competitions for athletes with disabilities, numerous national and regional competitions and many recreational opportunities found in local sporting contexts. Multisport, multidisability international competitions, world championships and single-sport, single-disability international competitions are held on a regular basis. Examples are plentiful and include major competitions that have events for athletes with disabilities as well as disability sport specific competitions such as international wheelchair archery tournaments, world goalball championships, international wheelchair marathons, Pan American Wheelchair Games, World Cup Alpine disabled skiing championships, European championships for athletics and swimming, as well as multisport, single-disability events such as the European Special Olympics and national competitions for deaf athletes.

As the number and range of sporting opportunities for athletes with disabilities has increased so too have the challenges in relation to facilitating such provisions. For example, the multitude of local, regional, national and international organizations supporting disability sport can be a source of confusion for potential participants or other associated support workers (including teachers, coaches, family members) (Sport England 2001). In some ways, this is compounded by the policies and strategies discussed later by Andy Smith that promote inclusion. Consequently, a young person with a disability may opt to engage in sport in a mainstream rather than dedicated disability sport setting. Or this young person could crosscut within and between mainstream and disability sport. A complex infrastructure of sport for people with disabilities has emerged and can be the cause of confusion for participants or those charged with supporting opportunities.

Another associated challenge for people with disabilities when participating in sport concerns the differential value that society places on this experience. This is particularly evident through the media where normalized conceptions of sporting ability and performance are promoted through the mass media (Evans 2004). According to Hughes *et al.* (2005: 5) this situation is not surprising and they argue that: 'objects of consumption tend to be sold by mobilizing the signifiers of youth and perfection. The signifiers of disability do not appeal to advertisers who wish to market a product or service.' Within the context of the Paralympics Thomas and Smith (2003) have argued that the media under-represents athletes with disabilities and this reinforces an inferior position of disability sport in comparison to mainstream sport.

The Paralympics is one of the largest sporting events in the world and in recent years has courted similar levels of controversy as those found in the Olympics and sport more generally. An ongoing issue across disability categories concerns the role of classification and the debate continues about how athletes should best be classified and where the boundaries between classifications should be drawn (Vanlandewijck and Chappel 1996; Doyle *et al.* 2004; Tweedy 2002). Following the Sydney Paralympics, this debate intensified for athletes with intellectual disabilities. In part, this resulted because a number of ineligible Spanish basketball players participated without having an intellectual disability. All athletes with intellectual disabilities have subsequently been banned from competing in ICP sanctioned events, including the Paralympics (Darcy 2003). While not denying that significant rule-breaking led to the exclusion of these athletes, their absence raises further questions about who is considered to be a Paralympic athlete and how society considers those athletes that are excluded.

Concluding comments

Physical activity and sport are important in the lives of youth and adults with disabilities. Today, many opportunities exist – in schools, community centres and clubs, at local, national and international levels. Youth participation in disability sport and preparation for international competitions are among the priorities of the major disability sport organizations. Many of these disability sport organizations sponsor developmental programmes for youth, training and coaching opportunities and of course, local, regional and national competitions.

Physical activity and sport have changed over time, most notably in the late twentieth century providing for the disability sport as we know it in the twenty-first century. The perspective of sport as rehabilitation has given way to sport as sport. Sport, including disability sport, will continue to evolve and become more inclusive. Sport will provide the opportunity for many to explore physical abilities. Empowerment through sport can become a reality especially for those once excluded.

Healthful living, physical fitness and competitive sport programmes can now be accessed by those individuals with disabilities of all ages who are interested and willing to participate thanks to those whose efforts created a change. Society in the twenty-first century provides numerous opportunities not enjoyed by the previous generations. It is the responsibility of professionals to share the benefits and pleasures of being physically active with the youth with disabilities of today and for those of tomorrow.

Note

1   This chapter was adapted from DePauw and Gavron (2005).

References

Abberley, P. (1987) 'The Concept of Oppression and the Development of a Social Theory of Disability', *Disability, Handicap and Society*, 2 (1): 5–19.

Barnes, C., Oliver, M. and Barton, L. (2002) *Disability Studies Today*, Cambridge: Polity.

Chappell, A.L. (1992) 'Towards a Sociological Critique of the Normalization Principle', *Disability, Handicap and Society*, 7 (1): 35–50.

Darcy, S. (2003) 'The Politics of Disability and Access: The Sydney 2000 Games Experiences', *Disability and Society*, 18 (6): 737–57.

Davis, L.J. (1995) *Enforcing Normalcy: Disability, Deafness, and the Body*, London: Verso.

DePauw, K.P. (1997) 'The (In)Visibility of DisAbility: Cultural Contexts and Sporting Bodies', *Quest*, 49 (4): 416–30.

DePauw, K.P. and Gavron, S.J. (2005) *Disability Sport*, Champaign, IL: Human Kinetics.

Donnelly, P. (1996) 'Approaches to Social Inequality in the Sociology of Sport', *Quest*, 48, 221–42.

Doyle, T., Davis, R., Humphries, B., Shim, J.K., Horn, B. and Newton, R.U. (2004) 'Further Evidence to Change the Medical Classification System of the National Wheelchair Basketball Association', *Adapted Physical Activity Quarterly*, 21 (1): 63–70.

Evans, J. (2004) 'Making a Difference? Education and "Ability" in Physical Education', *European Physical Education Review*, 10 (1): 95–108.

Gold, J.R. and Gold, M.M. (2007) 'Access for All: The Rise of the Paralympic Games', *The Journal of the Royal Society of the Promotion of Health*, 127 (3): 133–41.

Guttmann, L. (1976) *Textbook of Sport for the Disabled*, Oxford: H.M. & M. Publishers.

Hargreaves, J. (2000) *Heroines of Sport. The Politics of Difference and Identity*, London: Routledge.

Hewett, F.M., and Forness, S.R. (1974). *Historical Origins*, Boston: Allyn & Bacon.

Huber, C.A. (1984) 'An Overview and Perspective on International Disabled Sport: Past, Present, Future', *Rehabilitation World*, 8: 8–11.

Hughes, B., Russell, R. and Patterson. K. (2005) 'Nothing To Be Had "Off the Peg" Consumption, Identity and the Immobilization of Young Disabled People' *Disability and Society*, 20 (1): 3–17.

Lindstrom, H. (1984) 'Sports for Disabled: Alive and Well', *Rehabilitation World*, 8 (1): 16.

Linton, S. (1998) *Claiming Disability: Knowledge and Identity*, New York: NYU Press.

Oliver, M. (1990) *The Politics of Disablement*, London: Macmillan.

Shapiro, J. (1993) *No Pity: People with Disabilities Forging a New Civil Rights Movement*, New York: Random House.

Shilling, C. (2003) *The Body and Social Theory*, London: Sage Publications.

Slack, S. (1999) 'I Am More Than My Wheels', in M. Corker and S. French (eds), *Disability Discourse*, Buckingham: Open University Press, pp. 28–37.

Thomas, N. and Smith, A. (2003) 'Pre-occupied with Able-bodiedness? An Analysis of the British Media Coverage of the 2000 Paralympic Games', *Adapted Physical Activity Quarterly*, 20: 166–81.

Tweedy, S. (2002) 'Taxonomic Theory and the ICF: Foundations for a Unified Disability Athletics Classification', *Adapted Physical Activity Quarterly*, 19 (2): 220–37.

Vanlandewijck, Y.C. and Chappel, R.J. (1996) 'Integration and Classification Issues in Competitive Sports for Athletes with Disabilities', *Sport Science Review*, 5 (1) 65–88.

3 Disability and inclusion policy towards physical education and youth sport

Andy Smith

Introduction

The term social inclusion is a relatively new one first used in French government policy in 1974. Along with social exclusion, it has come increasingly to dominate the policy agenda of many Western governments, and especially those in Europe. In Britain, social inclusion became a cornerstone of social policy following the election of the Labour Government in May 1997, with particular attention being focused upon those considered vulnerable to social exclusion, namely, young people (particularly, 13- to 19-year-olds); the elderly; those on low incomes and those living in areas of high deprivation; ethnic minorities; people with disabilities; the long-term unemployed; the homeless; and prisoners. The achievement of greater social inclusion of these groups has come to be seen as achievable only through 'joined up government', that is, through cross-departmental strategies leading to 'the construction of a comprehensive policy response to a complex and multi-dimensional problem' (Houlihan and White 2002: 84). Among a plethora of initiatives designed to achieve social welfare policy goals in Britain have been policies predicated on the assumption that the provision of educational and cultural activities (including the arts and sport and physical activities) can facilitate social inclusion by reducing crime and drug use; promoting educational attainment and community integration; breaking down racial barriers; and increasing the acceptance of minority groups such as people with disabilities in the wider society (Coalter 2001, 2005, 2006; Coalter *et al.* 2000; Department for Culture, Media and Sport (DCMS) 1999; Long *et al.* 2002; Sport England 2006).

Set in this context, the purpose of this chapter is to examine the increasing use of physical education and youth sport as vehicles of social policy targeted at promoting the inclusion of young people with disabilities and those with special educational needs (SEN) in mainstream (or regular) schools. In particular, it will draw upon the 2000 National Curriculum for Physical Education (NCPE) for England, which featured for the first time a detailed statutory statement on inclusion (Department for Education and Employment (DfEE)/Qualifications and Curriculum Authority (QCA) 1999), as a case study through which to demonstrate how 'inclusion' and 'inclusive practices' have become increasingly central to government policy related to education and physical education (PE) (Penney 2002).

Sport and social inclusion policy

However, before examining these issues, it is important to note how the increasing emphasis on issues of inclusion in policy related to NCPE and youth sport has emerged, in part, out of the broader sport policy priorities of the Labour Government in Britain. Upon entering office, New Labour established the Social Exclusion Unit (SEU) to examine how it could achieve its social inclusion and welfare policy objectives. The SEU subsequently established the PAT 10 Working Group to report on the potential contribution that the arts and sport might make to the promotion of greater social inclusion. The findings of the PAT 10 report have been outlined in greater detail elsewhere (see Collins with Kay 2003; DCMS 1999; Houlihan and White 2002; Long *et al.* 2002). It is apparent, however, that together with the review of the England National Lottery Strategy in 1998, the PAT 10 report provided the foundation for a focus on social inclusion in future sport policy (Houlihan and White 2002). For example, in *A Sporting Future for All* published by the DCMS in 2000, it was claimed that 'Sport can make a unique contribution to tackling social exclusion in our society' (DCMS 2000: 39) and local authorities (together, for example, with schools and local sports clubs) were identified as playing a crucial role in developing 'creative and innovative ways of using sport to help re-engage people and to equip them with the skills and confidence to rejoin the mainstream of society' (DCMS 2000: 39). In the educational context, *A Sporting Future for All* created the expectation that those involved in the development and delivery of PE and youth sport in schools, especially those working in Specialist Sports Colleges (SSCs),[1] would 'commit themselves to putting social inclusion and fairness at the heart of everything they do' (DCMS 2000: 20). In relation to the experiences of PE and school sport among young people with disabilities, it was suggested that:

> All pupils should have access to physical education and disability should not be a barrier to inclusion in sport programmes. Appropriate arrange-ments, including teacher support and development if needed, should be in place to support young people with physical and learning disabilities to have good access to physical education and sport, in both mainstream and special school settings.
>
> (DCMS, 2000: 31)

Social inclusion was also a core policy theme of *Game Plan* (DCMS/Strategy Unit 2002), which features a list of benefits that participation in sport and physical activities is alleged to have in the promotion of social inclusion and the development of young people in schools. More recently, Sport England (2006) released a series of publications entitled *Sport Playing Its Part* which pointed to the ways in which sport is said to aid the delivery of the desired community, health and environmental outcomes, as well as meeting the needs of young people (especially educationally).

These views regarding the supposed social benefits of sport are, of course, not new. They have been repeatedly articulated in policy statements and other semi-official pronouncements since the 1960s (Central Council for Physical Recreation (CCPR) 1960; Coalter 2006; Green 2006; Houlihan and Green 2006; Houlihan and White 2002). Nevertheless, the growing expectation from the mid-1990s that sport-related policy interventions can achieve a vast array of desired social objectives is merely one expression of the ways in which government ministers in Britain – as elsewhere – have become increasingly interventionist in setting the sport policy agenda (Green and Houlihan 2006). As the above summary of recent inclusion policy developments indicates, one consequence of this growing involvement of government in sport policy-making has been that sport policy priorities have shifted away from the development of sport and achievement of sport-related objectives, towards the use of sport to achieve other desired social objectives. It is also the case that – whilst a myriad of 'disadvantaged groups' are identified in much of the New Labour political rhetoric regarding social inclusion – it is young people and school-aged children who are the principal target group of sport-related interventions where proactive responses to a range of social problems and the achievement of social policy goals are emphasized (Green 2006). Indeed, as Houlihan and Green (2006: 78) have noted, 'from the late 1990s onwards sport and physical activity for young people has emerged as one of the central policy themes within the government's wider social inclusion agenda', with schools and local communities considered central to the achievement of that overall objective.

It is within this developing social inclusion policy context that the recent re-emphasis on the inclusion of young people, particularly those with disabilities, SEN and those from other minority groups, has emerged. Accordingly, a recognition of these issues and an appreciation of broader changes in educational policy are vital prerequisites for developing an understanding of the ways in which growing concern with inclusion, and the provision of positive worthwhile educational experiences for young people with disabilities and SEN, have come to be a feature in contemporary PE policy. In this context, the next section provides a brief review of recent developments in educational policy and takes as its focus the revision of the 2000 NCPE for England. It does so in order to examine how the rhetoric of inclusion has come to be expressed in the policy and practice of PE and youth sport, and to identify some of the outcomes emanating from the constraints on teachers to make a contribution to the achievement of greater social inclusion in schools.

Educational policy and the inclusion of young people with disabilities and special educational needs

Although the inclusion of young people with disabilities and SEN in mainstream schools is a process the roots of which can be traced back to the 1800s, it was during the mid-1990s that growing political commitment to the provision of 'inclusive education' came increasingly to be expressed in the social policies of many governments. Indeed, there is now hardly any form of government social policy that does not contain at least some reference to issues of 'equal opportunity', 'equity' and 'inclusion'. In educational policy, the Salamanca Statement on inclusive education, for example, which was influenced by a growing human rights and social inclusion agenda, expressed the ostensible commitment by governments worldwide to providing a more inclusive education system and 'equalizing opportunities' for all pupils in mainstream education (United Nations Educational, Scientific and Cultural Organisation (UNESCO) 1994). A survey of government legislation relating to SEN in 52 countries following the publication of the Salamanca Statement noted that underpinning the educational policies of the majority of countries was the perceived *prima facie* right of a child with SEN and disabilities to be educated in mainstream schools, on the condition that those schools had the capacity to meet pupils' needs (UNESCO 1996). In the USA, PL 94–142, the Education for All Handicapped Children Act of 1975, Section 504 of the Rehabilitation Act (PL 93–112) which was passed in 1973 but not implemented until 1977, PL 105–17 and PL 108–446, have also all stressed the need to promote a shift away from educating young people with SEN and disabilities in segregated settings (such as special schools) towards 'including' them in mainstream schools (Fitzgerald 2006; UNESCO 1996). Political commitment to inclusion in Australia also came to be explicitly expressed in the steady flow of government policies published from the 1980s onwards (see, for example, Australian Labor Government 1988; Victorian Ministerial Review Committee 1984). The same was also true in France, where the shift towards educating pupils with disabilities in regular schools under the jurisdiction of the Ministry of Education was repeatedly emphasized in a plethora of national legislation and policy-related initiatives published since the mid-1970s (UNESCO 1996).

In Britain, the principle of educating pupils with SEN and disabilities in mainstream schools has gained growing political support since the introduction of the 1944 Education Act in which these pupils were assigned to medically-defined categories such as the physically handicapped, blind and educationally sub-normal (Halliday 1993; Thomas 2008). Following a medical or psychological assessment pupils were often placed into (segregated) special education in predetermined categories of impairment which, Halliday (1993) suggests, did not consider their individual needs or competencies. By the mid-1960s however, there was growing support for the desire to undo the segregation of young people with disabilities and those who received their education in special schools towards encouraging their ability to 'access' and be educated alongside their age-peers in mainstream schools. While this was due in part to educational policy developments at this time, the move towards the integration of these pupils in mainstream education needs to be understood in the context of changing power differentials between disability activist groups (for example, the Union of the Physically Impaired Against Segregation), people with disabilities generally and other groups within the wider society since the 1960s. More specifically, in conjunction with the gradual long-term change in the overall distribution of power from greater to smaller power differentials, the campaigning between these groups helped focus attention upon the need for people with disabilities to have similar opportunities to access, and participate in, education and social life more generally (Smith and Thomas 2005).

The growing policy emphasis on the desirability of educating pupils with SEN and disabilities in mainstream schools was further consolidated by the 1978 Warnock Report and the 1981 Education Act. Based on the recommendations of the Warnock Report, the medically defined categories through which the individual child was perceived as the 'problem' some thirty years previously, were replaced with the concept of SEN in the 1981 Education Act to prevent the sharp distinction between two groups of pupils: the handicapped and the non-handicapped (Halliday 1993; Thomas 2008). The introduction of the legally-defined term 'SEN' resulted in a move away from using rigid categories of handicap that had previously been the basis for the provision of special educational services for those pupils who needed them. In this regard, the concept of SEN now refers to the school-based learning needs of pupils that arise from a wide range of difficulties – including cognitive, physical, sensory, communicative or behavioural difficulties as well as those who are perceived to be specially 'gifted and talented' – and is used to identify (typically in a statement of SEN) those pupils for whom some kind of special educational provision needs to be made (Audit Commission 2002; Department for Education and Skills (DfES) 2001). More specifically, while pupils with SEN – like all pupils – are not a homogenous group and 'are part of a continuum of learners' (Garner and Dwyfor Davies 2001: 26) they are typically considered to have a learning difficulty of one kind or another if they:

(a) have a significantly greater difficulty in learning than the majority of children of the same age; or
(b) have a disability which prevents or hinders them from making use of educational facilities of a kind generally provided for children of the same age in schools within the area of the local education authority; or
(c) are under compulsory school age and fall within the definition at (a) or (b) above or would so do if special educational provision was not made for them.

(DfES, 2001: 6)

While the previous categories of handicap applied to approximately 2 per cent of the school population – many of whom were educated in special schools – this re-classification of pupils, which apparently focused more fully on their individual needs, led to the identification of as many as 20 per cent of children considered to have SEN (some of whom may have disabilities) (DES 1978). Although there are real difficulties in trying to arrive at a precise estimate of the number of pupils with SEN and disabilities currently being educated in mainstream schools, recently published data indicates that approximately one in five school children with SEN of one kind or another continue to receive their education in mainstream settings (Audit Commission 2002; Vickerman 2007).

According to Halliday (1993), the constraints imposed upon teachers and schools by the 1981 Act further encouraged what has been a 'partial and gradual transference' of pupils from special to mainstream schools and thus mainstream PE. It has been partial inasmuch as it was typically those pupils with less severe difficulties who were being educated in mainstream schools, whilst those with more severe difficulties tended to remain in the special school sector (Halliday 1993; Thomas 2008). By the mid-1990s however, the commitment towards integrated education (as it had come to be known by this time) and the debate surrounding its feasibility was further expressed by the publication of the 1993 and 1996 Education Acts, the introduction of the *Code of Practice* and the 1996 *Disability Discrimination Act*. The political commitment by the current Labour Government to endorsing the recommendations of the Salamanca Statement and developing a 'more inclusive education system' is also made clear in the Green Paper *Excellence for All Children: Meeting Special Educational Needs* (DfEE 1997). In particular, it was suggested that:

> We want to see more pupils with SEN included within mainstream primary and secondary schools. We support the United Nations Educational, Scientific and Cultural Organization (UNESCO) Salamanca World Statement on Special Needs Education. This calls on governments to adopt the principle of inclusive education, enrolling all children in regular schools, unless there are compelling reasons for doing otherwise. That implies the progressive extension of the capacity of mainstream schools to provide for children with a wide range of needs.
>
> (DfEE, 1997: 44)

The commitment to ensuring that all pupils who were formerly educated in segregated special schools alongside their peers in mainstream schools unless this is incompatible with the wishes of the pupil's parents or 'the provision of efficient education for other children' (Stationery Office 2001), continues to form a mainstay of educational policy in Britain. For example, the *White Paper Meeting Special Educational Needs: A Programme of Action* (DfEE 1998), *SEN Revised Code of Practice* (DfES 2001), *Special Educational*

Needs and Disability Act (Stationery Office 2001), and the publication of *Removing Barriers to Achievement* (DfES 2004) are all predicated on the assumption that mainstream schools should not refuse a pupil with SEN or a disability on the basis that they cannot meet their needs. In this regard, inclusive education policy in many countries is said to be centrally concerned with the 'development of strategies that seek to bring about a genuine equalization of opportunity' (UNESCO 1994: 11) and improvement in the educational experiences and achievement of young people.

National Curriculum Physical Education and inclusion

Given the growing policy emphasis that has come to be placed on inclusion and the provision of equal opportunities for pupils with SEN and disabilities alongside their age-peers in mainstream schools, it is unsurprising that PE and youth sport in schools have become an increasing focus for achieving broader social policy goals. In particular, the introduction of the National Curriculum for Physical Education (NCPE) established a 'broad and balanced' curriculum as a statutory entitlement for all pupils educated in all state schools and was, like other areas of the National Curriculum (NC), 'heralded as a significant step towards, if not a guarantee of, equal opportunities' (Penney 2002: 110). This having been said, while it is intended that all pupils should experience a broad range of involvement in each of the activity areas that comprise the NCPE (namely, team games, athletics, gymnastics, swimming, dance and outdoor and adventurous activities (OAA)), the NC Working Group recognized prior to the implementation of the NCPE that teachers would experience difficulty in 'fully integrating children with (SEN and disabilities) into all aspects of a physical education programme' (Department of Education and Science/Welsh Office (DES/WO) 1991: 36). The Working Group also acknowledged that 'traditional' team games, rather than more individualized pursuits (such as dance, swimming and OAA), are activities in which teachers might experience particular difficulty in incorporating some pupils with SEN and disabilities (DES/WO 1991). More specifically, it was suggested that:

> Modifications to conventional games sometimes facilitate access, but the placing of a child with a visual impairment, or with a severe locomotor disability, in a class learning netball or rugby are not likely to be successful.
>
> (DES/WO, 1991: 38)

Despite this early recognition of some of the constraints that the presence of pupils with SEN and disabilities might have on teachers' practices, it was the revision of the NCPE 2000 for England (DfEE/QCA 1999) where the perceived contribution that PE and youth sport could make to the achievement of greater social inclusion of these pupils was explicitly identified. More particularly, in the NCPE 2000 for England the British Government formally emphasized the alleged centrality of 'inclusion' and 'inclusive practices' in PE and created an expectation that teachers would ensure that all pupils were 'enabled to participate as fully and effectively as possible within the National Curriculum and the statutory assessment arrangements' therein (DfEE/QCA 1999: 33). Of course, teachers have always been expected to employ differentiated strategies that are appropriate and challenging to all pupils regardless of how diverse their needs and abilities are. The emphasis on inclusion in current NCPE policy, however, reaffirms the expectation that teachers should 'ensure that all pupils have the chance to succeed, whatever their individual needs and the potential barriers to their learning may be' (DfEE/QCA 1999: 3). It also creates the expectation that teachers will design and deliver PE curricular with 'due regard' to three principles of inclusion, namely, setting suitable learning challenges; responding to pupils' diverse learning needs; and overcoming barriers to learning and assessment for individuals and groups of pupils (DfEE/QCA 1999). The expectation that PE and youth sport can make an important contribution to the inclusion of young people with disabilities and those with SEN also formed part of the underlying rationale for establishing SSCs in the late 1990s (Houlihan and Green 2006; Smith 2008), while in several publications the Youth Sport Trust (YST) has repeatedly emphasized the ways in which teachers should, and can, provide a more inclusive curriculum for pupils (YST 2004). But to what extent has the NCPE achieved its stated objective of greater inclusion in schools? In other words, has the inclusion of pupils with SEN and disabilities in mainstream PE lessons helped to enhance the educational experiences of these pupils? Or have these policies also resulted in consequences that, in the event, may well be the very reverse of what was intended?

Including young people with disabilities and special educational needs in physical education: some unplanned outcomes

Smith and Thomas (2005, 2006) have noted that whilst there is a large body of literature that has explored the reality of young disabled peoples' experiences of PE and youth sport in schools in the USA (for a review, see Block and Obrusnikova 2007), until recently few attempts have been made to examine the outcomes associated with the introduction of policies designed to promote the inclusion of these pupils in mainstream PE in Britain and elsewhere in Europe. Despite this dearth of literature, on the basis of research conducted largely with teachers, but increasingly with pupils, it seems that whilst the NCPE 2000 was intended to bring about, among other things, more equitable and positive experiences of PE and youth sport for pupils with disabilities and SEN, for many – though certainly not all – of those pupils it would appear to have been particularly limited in achieving these desired objectives. It should be noted in this regard that the failure of social policies such as the NCPE to achieve their declared objectives, and to have outcomes that were unplanned and which may even be the opposite of what was intended, is by no means unusual. Indeed, insofar as the formulation and implementation of policy is a complex process, it is a process that almost inevitably has consequences that are not only unplanned but which, as may be the case here, are held to be undesirable by the relevant parties involved (Dopson and Waddington 1996).

The findings of several studies conducted in Britain (Fitzgerald 2006; Fitzgerald *et al.* 2003; Fitzgerald and Kay 2004; Morely *et al.* 2005; Smith 2004; Smith and Green 2004), Ireland (Meegan and MacPhail 2006), the USA (Block and Obrusnikova 2007; Goodwin and Watkinson 2000; Hodge *et al.* 2004) and European countries such as Sweden (Kristen *et al.* 2003), for example, have all revealed that whilst there is a basic belief in the desirability of inclusion and a commitment by teachers to providing 'equal opportunities' for young people with disabilities and SEN in mainstream PE, this appears in practice to have created the opportunity for the experience of PE to become even more unequal. In particular, insofar as policy towards inclusion in PE and youth sport amounts almost to a statement of faith in its effectiveness in promoting pupils' educational experiences, it seems that when young people with disabilities and those with SEN are educated in the same learning contexts as their age-peers, there is a tendency for them to be taught *separately* (usually with the help of a non-PE qualified teaching assistant) from one another within the same PE class. Thus, the tendency for such inclusion policy to be driven largely by the ideological agendas of policy-makers has meant that the trend towards inclusion in PE has, in fact, resulted in the existence of *de facto* integration whereby pupils with disabilities and SEN are required to 'fit into' existing curricula as they are already planned by teachers (Barton 1993; Morley *et al.* 2005; Smith 2004; Smith and Green 2004). One corollary of the existence of integration in PE has been a *reduction* in pupils' opportunities to experience a 'broad and balanced' NCPE, rather than the 'genuine equalization' hoped for, somewhat optimistically, by policy-makers and organizations such as OFSTED (2003) and UNESCO (1994). Indeed, much of the available evidence points towards the ways in which, when compared to their age-peers, young people with disabilities and those with SEN typically receive a more narrowly focused PE curriculum in which they tend to participate in more individualized physical activities (such as swimming, gymnastics, badminton and dance) and adapted versions of team sports.

In this regard, although it depends upon the particular needs and abilities of pupils, it seems that the further we move away from more individualized physical activities towards more complex, competitive performance-oriented team sports, the greater the likelihood that *some* pupils with SEN and disabilities will be excluded from all or some aspects of those activities, but particularly those with more severe emotional and behavioural difficulties (Hodge *et al.* 2004; Meegan and MacPhail 2006; Morley *et al.* 2005; Penney and Evans 1995; Smith 2004; Smith and Green 2004). It is particularly noteworthy, however, that for some – perhaps even a majority – of young people, their limited experience of the breadth of activities available as part of NCPE in mainstream schools is something that has come to have a negative impact on their self-esteem and confidence in PE and sport (Fitzgerald 2006; Fitzgerald *et al.* 2003; Goodwin and Watkinson 2000). More specifically, it is not uncommon to find that the tendency for these pupils to be taught different activities separately from others in the class has the effect of isolating them from other members of the class, and of reinforcing, rather than breaking down, barriers between pupils with different abilities. This informal divide between pupils in mainstream PE classes also appears to have helped construct an implicit hierarchy of acceptable activities in PE where the status of those undertaken by young people with disabilities are at times perceived, both by teachers and pupils, as inferior compared to those done by others in the class (Fitzgerald 2006; Fitzgerald *et al.* 2003; Goodwin and Watkinson 2000).

A final problem of the strong ideological commitment to the policy of inclusion in schools has been the perceived failure of government and policy-makers to provide adequate resources to realize the desired objectives. In particular, there has been growing criticism of the perceived inadequacy of teachers' experiences of the overly-theoretical nature of initial teacher training (ITT) and continuing professional development (CPD) programmes in preparing them for meeting the PE and sporting needs of pupils (OFSTED 2003; Robertson *et al.* 2000; Vickerman 2002, 2007), and for assessing them according to the criteria set out in the NCPE (Smith and Green 2004). In this context, OFSTED (2003) has noted recently that notwithstanding the trend towards inclusion in mainstream schools, it is not uncommon for many teachers to claim that they 'were being asked to teach children with significant learning needs and manage difficult situations without enough learning' (OFSTED 2003: 24) and without sufficient confidence to do so. The achievement of greater inclusion in PE and school sport has allegedly been compromised further by the associated tendency for learning support assistants (LSAs), many of whom are not specialists or qualified to teach PE, to place a significant degree of constraint upon the everyday activities of teachers (Hodge *et al.* 2004; Morley *et al.* 2005; Smith and Green 2004). Among other things, this has had a whole series of consequences for the experiences of those pupils with whom LSAs work ranging, on the one hand, from the alleged benefits this can have for them in terms of their individual learning and, on the other, the perceived lack of support they receive from LSAs compared to other ostensibly more academic subjects such as English, maths and science to help enhance their experiences of the subject (see Fitzgerald *et al.* 2003; Hodge *et al.* 2004; Morley *et al.* 2005; Smith and Green 2004). In relation to the latter, the findings of several recent studies have indicated how, as a consequence of the growing political commitment towards inclusion, PE teachers are becoming increasingly constrained to work with LSAs and other SEN-related staff (such as SEN

Co-ordinators (SENCOs)). The ways in which these groups seek to dissem-inate, where it is available, information regarding the particular abilities of pupils has, however, been a source of concern for PE teachers, not least because much of that information tends to tell them very little about the specific needs of young people with disabilities and those with SEN in PE (Morley *et al.* 2005; Smith and Green 2004).

This having been said, and despite the tendency for teachers to be rather critical of the kind and amount of support they receive from LSAs, one study has demonstrated how teachers have been particularly receptive to the involvement of LSAs in lessons, not least because of the practical benefits this had for them (Smith and Green 2004). Indeed, Smith and Green (2004) observed that although the teachers in their study appeared committed to working with LSAs to meet pupils' needs, their primary concern appeared to be one of pragmatism; that is to say, by supporting ostensibly less-able pupils, LSAs let teachers 'off the hook', as it were, and enabled them to 'get on with teaching the other pupils'. One further way in which LSAs might be viewed as playing a crucial role in this regard is that of assisting teachers with ensuring the safety of pupils generally, and those with SEN and disabilities in particular. In policy terms this is significant, for the constraint on teachers to include pupils with emotional and behavioural difficulties (EBD) and severe learning difficulties alongside those who use mobility devices (such as wheelchairs), for example, is likely to further intensify the pressures experienced by teachers in ensuring the safety of all pupils in lessons, whilst meeting the expectation of them to include pupils of all needs and abilities in PE (Hodge *et al.* 2004; Morley *et al.* 2005).

Conclusion

This chapter has attempted to establish the developing policy context within which the political commitment towards including pupils with disabilities and SEN in PE and youth sport in mainstream British schools has emerged. In this regard, it was argued that while inclusion has been uncritically accepted and considered as an unambiguously good and desirable policy response designed to improve young people's experiences of PE and sport, the trend towards educating young people with disabilities and SEN in mainstream schools has been accompanied by what might be held to be a series of un-intended, unforeseen outcomes. In particular, the alleged 'privileging' of sport over more individualized physical activities (Penney and Evans, 1999) in NCPE, alongside the provision of a limited and somewhat narrow range of activities for some pupils, appears to raise serious questions about the extent to which pupils with disabilities and SEN *are* being included in any meaningful sense within sport-based PE curricula originally designed for 'able-bodied' young people (Barton 1993). Furthermore, in contrast to the expectations of policy-makers and government ministers, the emphasis on inclusion appears to have had the effect of further alienating some pupils (particularly those with more severe needs) from others in PE lessons. Simultaneously, from the perspective of pupils and teachers, this appears to have had the effect of limiting the extent to which young disabled people and those with SEN can derive satisfying experiences from PE and sport in schools.

However, even though the revised NCPE 2000 has been met with, at best, only very limited success and does not seem to have yet generated the desired impact on improving pupils' experiences of PE and sport in mainstream schools, it should *not* necessarily be interpreted as an abject policy failure. Indeed, it would be churlish to deny that the introduction of NCPE 2000 has not had *any* impact on challenging dominant perceptions of pupils' abilities, or on improving the experiences and participation of pupils. Indeed, there is some – albeit limited – evidence which indicates that the emphasis on inclusion in NCPE 2000 has enjoyed a measure of success in helping to develop positive experiences of, and participation in, PE and sport among some young people with disabilities. This is particularly the case where pupils have been able to choose which activities they are able to participate in at school, and especially when they are able to do so in activities such as swimming, dance and other more recreational activities as part of NCPE (Atkinson and Black 2006; Fitzgerald and Kay 2004; Smith 2004). However, given the lack of empirically-grounded studies of the ways in which inclusion exists *in practice* in mainstream schools, it will be the task of future research to examine whether the continued policy commitment to inclusion can, in fact, help make a greater contribution to the promotion of young peoples' experiences in PE and sport than has been the case hitherto.

Note

1 SSCs are maintained secondary schools that receive additional funding from the government in order to: (i) increase participation and raise standards in PE and sport in a 'family' of elementary and secondary schools in their vicinity; and (ii) identify and develop young sporting talent in partnership with sports clubs in their communities (DfES/DCMS 2003). SSCs lie at the heart of 'families of schools' – known as School Sport Partnerships – required to work together to develop PE and sporting opportunities for young people.

References

Atkinson, H. and Black, K. (2006) *The Experiences of Young Disabled People Participating in PE, School Sport and Extra-Curricular Activities in Leicestershire and Rutland*, Loughborough: Institute of Youth Sport/Peter Harrison Centre for Disability Sport, Loughborough University.

Audit Commission (2002) *Special Educational Needs: A Mainstream Issue*, London: Audit Commission.

Australian Labor Government (1988) *Towards a Fairer Australia: Social Justice Under Labor*, Canberra: Australian Government Publishing Service.

Barton, L. (1993) 'Disability, Empowerment and Physical Education', in J. Evans(ed.), *Equality, Education and Physical Education*, London: Falmer Press, pp. 43–54.

Block, M. and Obrusnikova, I. (2007) 'Inclusion in Physical Education: A Review of the Literature from 1995–2005', *Adapted Physical Activity Quarterly*, 24 (2): 103–24.

Central Council of Physical Recreation (CCPR) (1960) *Sport and the Community*, London: CCPR.

Coalter, F. (2001) *Realising the Potential of Cultural Services: The Case for Sport*, London: Local Government Association.

Coalter, F. (2005) *The Social Benefits of Sport: An Overview to Inform the Community Planning Process*, Edinburgh: SportScotland.

Coalter, F. (2006) *Sport-in-Development. A Monitoring and Evaluation Manual*, London: UK Sport.

Coalter, F., Allison, M. and Taylor, J. (2000) *The Role of Sport in Regenerating Deprived Urban Areas*, Edinburgh: Scottish Office Central Research Unit.

Collins, M. with Kay, T. (2003) *Sport and Social Exclusion*, London: Routledge.

Department of Culture, Media and Sport (DCMS) (1999) *Policy Action Team 10 (Arts and Sport): A Report to the Social Exclusion Unit*, London: DCMS.

Department for Culture, Media and Sport (DCMS) (2000) *A Sporting Future for All*, London: DCMS.

Department for Culture, Media and Sport (DCMS)/Strategy Unit (2002) *Game Plan: A Strategy for Delivering Government's Sport and Physical Activity Objectives*, London: DCMS/Strategy Unit.

Department for Education and Employment (DfEE) (1997) *Excellence for All Children: Meeting Special Educational Needs*, London: Stationery Office.

Department for Education and Employment (DfEE) (1998) *Meeting Special Educational Needs: A Programme of Action*, London: DfEE.

Department for Education and Skills (DfES) (2001) *Special Educational Needs Code of Practice*, London: DfES.

Department for Education and Skills (DfES) (2004) *Removing Barriers to Achievement: The Government's Strategy for Special Educational Needs*, London: DfES.

Department for Education and Skills (DfES)/Department for Culture, Media and Sport (DCMS) (2003) *Learning through PE and Sport*, London: DfES/DCMS.

Department for Education and Employment/Qualifications and Curriculum Authority (DfEE/QCA) (1999) *Physical Education: The National Curriculum for England*, London: HMSO.

Department of Education and Science (1978) *Special Educational Needs: Report of The Committee of Enquiry into the Education of Handicapped Children and Young People (The Warnock Report)*, London: HMSO.

Department of Education and Science/Welsh Office (DES/WO) (1991) *Physical Education for Ages 5–16. Proposals of the Secretary of State for Education and the Secretary of State for Wales*, London, DES/WO.

Dopson, S. and Waddington, I. (1996) 'Managing Social Change: A Process-Sociological Approach to Understanding Change within the National Health Service', *Sociology of Health and Illness*, 18(4): 525–50.

Fitzgerald, H. (2006) 'Disability and Physical Education', in D. Kirk, D. MacDonald and M. O'Sullivan (eds), *The Handbook of Physical Education*, London: Sage, pp. 752–66.

Fitzgerald, H. and Kay, T. (2004) *Sports Participation by Disabled Young People in Derbyshire. A Report for the Derbyshire and Peak Park Sport and Recreation Forum*, Loughborough: Institute of Youth Sport, Loughborough University.

Fitzgerald, H., Jobling, A. and Kirk, D. (2003) 'Valuing the Voices of Young Disabled People: Exploring Experiences of Physical Education and Sport', *European Journal of Physical Education*, 8 (2): 175–201.

Garner, P. and Dwyfor Davies, J. (2001) *Introducing Special Educational Needs: A Companion Guide for Student Teachers*, London: David Fulton.

Goodwin, D. and Watkinson, E. (2000) 'Inclusive Physical Education from the Perspective of Students with Physical Disabilities', *Adapted Physical Activity Quarterly*, 17 (2): 144–60.

Gorard, S., Taylor, C. and Fitz, J. (2003) *Schools, Markets and Choice Policies*, London: Routledge/Falmer.

Green, M. (2006) 'From "Sport for All" To Not About "Sport" at All: Interrogating Sport Policy Interventions in the United Kingdom', *European Sport Management Quarterly*, 6 (3): 217–38.

Green, M. and Houlihan, B. (2006) 'Governmentality, Modernisation and the "Disciplining" of National Sporting Organisations: Athletics in Australia and the United Kingdom', *Sociology of Sport Journal*, 23(1): 47–71.

Halliday, P. (1993) 'Physical Education within Special Education Provision', in J. Evans (ed.), *Equality, Education and Physical Education*, London: Falmer Press, pp. 205–16.

Hodge, S., Ommah, J., Casebolt, K., LaMaster, K. and O'Sullivan, M. (2004) 'High School General Physical Education Teachers' Behaviours and Beliefs Associated with Inclusion', *Sport, Education and Society*, 9 (3): 395–420.

Houlihan, B. and Green, M. (2006) 'The Changing Status of School Sport and Physical Education: Explaining Policy Change', *Sport, Education and Society*, 11(1): 73–92.

Houlihan, B. and White, A. (2002) *The Politics of Sports Development: Development of Sport of Development Through Sport?*, London: Routledge.

Kristen, L., Patriksson, G. and Fridlund, B. (2003) 'Parents' Conceptions of the Influences of Participation in a Sports Programme on their Children and Adolescents with Physical Disabilities', *European Physical Education Review*, 9(1): 23–41.

Long, J., Welch, M., Bramham, P., Hylton, K., Butterfield, J. and Lloyd, E. (2002) *Count Me In: The Dimensions of Social Inclusion through Culture and Sport*, London: Department of Culture, Media and Sport.

Meegan, S. and MacPhail, A. (2006) 'Irish Physical Educators' Attitudes Toward Teaching Students with Special Educational Needs', *European Physical Education Review*, 12(1): 75–97.

Morley, D., Bailey, R., Tan, J. and Cooke, B. (2005) 'Inclusive Physical Education: Teachers' Views of Teaching Children with Special Educational Needs and Disabilities in Physical Education', *European Physical Education Review*, 11(1): 84–107.

Office for Standards in Education (OFSTED) (2003) *Special Educational Needs in the Mainstream*, London: HMSO.

Penney, D. (2002) 'Equality, Equity and Inclusion in Physical Education and School Sport', in A. Laker (ed.), *The Sociology of Sport and Physical Education: An Introductory Reader*, London: Routledge/Falmer, pp. 110–28.

Penney, D. and Evans, J. (1995) 'The National Curriculum for Physical Education: Entitlement for All?', *The British Journal of Physical Education*, 26(1): 6–13.

Penney, D. and Evans, J. (1999) *Politics, Policy and Practice in Physical Education*, London: E. & F.N. Spon.

Robertson, C., Childs, C. and Marsden, E. (2000) 'Equality and the Inclusion of Pupils with Special Educational Needs in Physical Education', in S. Capel and S. Piotrowski (eds), *Issues in Physical Education*, London: Routledge/Falmer, pp. 47–63.

Smith, A. (2004) 'The Inclusion of Pupils with Special Educational Needs in Secondary School Physical Education', *Physical Education and Sport Pedagogy*, 9(1): 37–54.

Smith, A. (2008) 'Specialist Sports Colleges', in D. Malcolm (ed.), *The Sage Dictionary of Sport Studies*, London: Sage, pp. 235–6.

Smith, A. and Green, K. (2004) 'Including Pupils with Special Educational Needs in Secondary School Physical Education: A Sociological Analysis of Teachers' Views', *British Journal of Sociology of Education*, 25(5): 593–608.

Smith, A. and Thomas, N. (2005) 'Inclusion, Special Educational Needs, Disability and Physical Education', in K. Green and K. Hardman (eds), *Physical Education: Essential Issues*, London: Sage, pp. 220–38.

Smith, A. and Thomas, N. (2006) 'Including Pupils with Special Educational Needs and Disabilities in National Curriculum Education: A Brief Review', *European Journal of Special Needs Education*, 21: 69–83.

Sport England (2006) *Sport Playing Its Part: The Contribution of Sport to Meeting the Needs of Children and Young People*, London: Sport England.

Stationery Office (2001) *Special Educational Needs and Disability Act (2001)*, London: Stationery Office.

Thomas, N. (2008) 'Sport and Disability', in B. Houlihan (ed.), *Sport and Society: A Student Introduction*, London: Sage, pp. 205–29.

United Nations Educational, Scientific and Cultural Organization (UNESCO) (1994) *The Salamanca Statement and Framework for Action*, Paris: UNESCO.

United Nations Educational, Scientific and Cultural Organization (UNESCO) (1996) *UNESCO Survey on Special Needs Education Law 1996*, Paris: UNESCO.

Vickerman, P. (2002) 'Perspectives on the Training of Physical Education Teachers for the Inclusion of Children with Special Educational Needs – Is There an Official Line View?', *The Bulletin of Physical Education*, 38(2): 79–98.

Vickerman, P. (2007) *Teaching Physical Education to Children with Special Educational Needs*, London: Routledge.

Victorian Ministerial Review Committee (1984) *Integration in Victorian Education. Report of the Ministerial Review of Educational Services for the Disabled*, Melbourne: Education Department of Victoria.

Youth Sport Trust (2004) *Ten Years of Building a Brighter Future for Young People Through Sport: Annual Review 2003/2004*, Loughborough: Youth Sport Trust, Loughborough University.

4 Disability, physical education and sport

Some critical observations and questions

Len Barton

Introduction

In this brief paper, I am going to revisit, to some degree, something I wrote over ten years ago (Barton 1993). This will involve drawing on more recent debates and ideas within disability studies as well as material relating to sport. The intention is to be informative, provide supportive illustrations for my developing arguments, and to raise questions for discussion. This must not be seen as a final, authoritative statement on these complex issues, but rather some critical observations, which I hope the reader will actively engage with. In this process, we are all learners.

The social model of disability

In this opening section, I want to outline some of the key ideas and issues that have informed how disability is being conceived in this chapter. In doing this, the voices of disabled people are of paramount importance. Their perspectives, interests and concerns are of central significance.

How we define disability is extremely important because the language we use to describe and think about disabled people will influence our expectations and interactions with them. Too often the language we use and the assumptions informing such discourses have been disablist and deficit-based. The challenge that disabled people are involved with is that of the politics of recognition in which the politics of identity is of central importance. Listen to Anya Souza (1997), a person labelled as having learning difficulties:

> It takes a lot of courage and strength to fight against people who have the power to define who you are. People who think they can define you also assume they can tell you what your rights are and, because of who they think you are, specify what you should do with your life. They don't specify this by telling you what to do with your life only. It's worse than that. They put you in situations where there are only a limited range of things you can do with your life.
>
> (Souza 1997: 4)

Disabled people are, through their organizations and individually, seeking to gain more choices and rights in their lives. This demand for participation needs to be viewed in a positive way as Morris (1991) so powerfully reminds us:

> Our anger is not about having 'a chip on our shoulder', our grief is not a 'failure to come to terms with our disability'. Our dissatisfaction with our lives is not a personality defect, but a sane response to the oppression which we experience.
>
> (Morris 1991: 9)

These voices are connected to a wider set of issues involving the development and maintenance of a social model of disability. This model has been developed from within struggles against discrimination and the pursuit of a better life. It is concerned with the demand by disabled people, in the sphere of policy and practice in all service provisions that, the implications of the slogan 'Nothing About Us Without Us' should be recognized and acted upon.

Disability has meant different things, in different historical periods and cultural contexts. This is reflected in the shift of official categories and their meaning including, 'moron', 'imbecile', 'idiot', 'insane', 'feebleminded', 'mentally deficient', 'mentally retarded', 'subnormal', 'mentally handicapped', 'people with learning disabilities' and 'learning difficulties'. These categories are themselves a reflection of particular socio-economic and cultural developments and the different ways in which policy and service provision are associated with particular conceptions.

A social model approach to disability raises serious questions about the nature of the existing society we live in and the kind of society we desire or hope for. Why and how a society excludes particular individuals and groups involves processes of categorization, in which the inferior, the inabilities, unacceptable aspects of a person's makeup, are highlighted and legitimated. Which definitions are seen as significant, why and with what consequences, must therefore, be the subject of serious critical scrutiny.

In his seminal paper on examining the concept of oppression in relation to the development of a social theory of disability, Abberley (1987) argues, that viewing disability as oppression provides a basis for disabled people to both understand and transform their own situation. He contends that:

> To claim that disabled people are oppressed involves, however, arguing a number of other points. At an empirical level, it is to argue that on significant dimensions disabled people can be regarded as a group whose members are in an inferior position to other members of society because they are disabled. It is also to argue that these disadvantages are dialectically related to an ideology or group of ideologies which justify and perpetuate this situation. Beyond this it is to make the claim that

such disadvantages and their supporting ideologies are neither natural nor inevitable. Finally, it involves the identification of some beneficiary of this state of affairs.

(Abberley 1987: 7)

Advocating that disabled people are oppressed necessitates engaging with the issue of power. In this approach power is not viewed as a form of property, which some people possess, but rather, as a set of relations involving the exercise of decision-making. This encourages particular forms of questioning including how, why and with what consequences does the exercise of power take place within particular sets of social conditions and relations? How are such developments justified and maintained? Finally, who benefits from this state of affairs?

Recognizing the centrality of institutional, ideological, structural and material disabling barriers within society is fundamental to a social model of disability. It is an unadaptive, unfriendly and hostile set of material conditions and social relations that cumulatively contribute to the marginalization, disempowerment and exclusion of disabled people. This is where the critical analysis has to focus and the changes have to take place.

The definitional support for the social model is to be found in the statement on Fundamental Principles of Disability, which resulted from a discussion between The Union of the Physically Impaired Against Segregation and The Disability Alliance (UPIAS). The UPIAS (1976) position is quite clear:

Disability is something imposed on top of our impairment by the way we are unnecessarily isolated and excluded from full participation in society. Disabled people are therefore an oppressed group in society.

(UPIAS 1976: 3–4)

This statement, as Barnes (1997) notes, has since been broadened to include all impairments, physical, sensory and intellectual and is the official position of the British Council of Disabled People and the Disabled Peoples' International. Thus Oliver (1990) contends:

All disabled people experience disability as social restriction, whether these restrictions occur as a consequence of inaccessible built environments, questionable notions of intelligence and social competence, the inability of the general public to use sign language, the lack of reading material in Braille or hostile public attitudes to people with non-visible disabilities.

(Oliver 1990: xiv)

By emphasizing the collective dimensions of these issues, the importance of the position and future of the disability movement is raised. The disability movement is concerned with the establishment and support of organizations created and managed by disabled people. They are concerned with critiquing organizations for disabled people that have historically tended to disseminate and legitimate individual, charity-based conceptions. Such an approach produces pity and dependency with the underlying message being, as Hevey (1992: 26) a disabled person maintains, 'that important charities speak for disabled people and that disabled people cannot speak for themselves'. This whole issue is fundamentally about control and as Morris (1992: 11) contends, it raises the questions: 'Who has the right to say how we should be presented to the public?' and 'Who has the right to say how money raised in our name should be spent?'

The movement is also concerned with establishing various forms of peer support, self-help and encouragement in a range of relevant areas, through the use of seminars, conferences, websites, in-house publications, consultations and newsletters. Annual conferences are a further means of support. All these forms of engagement are attempting to establish the importance and realization of empowerment, self-determination, participation and active citizenship, in terms of the value of the contribution that disabled people can offer to economic and social life.

The Disability Movement clearly encourages a recognition of the voices of disabled people as an absolute necessity in the struggles for change and improvement in disability services. In England a Report from the Prime Minister's Strategy Unit (2004) clearly outlines the scope of change that is required:

> Disabled people should be at the heart of how relevant public services are designed and delivered.
>
> Services for disabled people should be personalized to reflect the range of needs of individual disabled people.
>
> Service providers should be held to account by disabled people wherever possible. Disabled people should also be involved in the design and planning of services – but should maintain the ability to provide strong critical challenge.
>
> Disabled people should have increased choice regarding the services and benefits they receive, with specific support available to archive informed choice.
>
> (Prime Minister's Strategy Unit 2004: 25)

This approach to disabled people is based on human and civil rights, which raises such significant questions as, 'who should speak for disabled people?' and 'whose definition of disability is important?' This struggle for recognition challenges the extent to which civil society and governments recognize the legitimacy of these demands. The various forms of political engagement required are concerned on the one hand, with protecting disabled people, and on the other, a means of developing accountability in terms of a public commitment to establishing an inclusive, non-discriminatory society.

It is essential that we do not underestimate the seriousness with which this task is viewed by disabled people. There are no quick, slick, easy answers to what are fundamental issues, as Rachel Hurst (1996) vividly reminds us:

> For disabled people in particular, the interaction between our right to individual freedom and choice and control over our own lives and our rights to non-discrimination and inclusion measures is crucial. Our exclusion has been so systematic and rigorous that there is a need for fundamental changes to society in order to support our inclusion.
>
> (Hurst 1996: no page numbers)

Indeed, in terms of a global dimension through, for example, the impact of wars and famine 'the lifestyle of the overwhelming majority of disabled people is characterized by poverty and social isolation' (Barnes 1996: 10).

The social model approach provides a radical alternative to other dominant perspectives. Disability is not viewed as a tragedy, a punishment, or the result of some sin(s) of the parent(s), or the individual concerned, it is not a sickness in need of a cure, it is not a subject for charity and sentimental, patronizing and dependency creating attitudes and relationships. It is a human rights issue. From this perspective, disabled people including children and adults experience varying degrees of discrimination, exclusion and stigmatization. This includes being treated as less than human, being viewed as objects of charity, being excluded from the workforce and living on or below the poverty line, being unable to experience the entitlements of citizenship resulting in a lack of real participation in social encounters and decisions over issues affecting their lives (Barnes 1991; Barnes and Mercer 2003).

It is important to be clear as to what a commitment to a social model of disability means and involves for individuals and organizations of disabled people. They are not arguing for sameness, or to become as normal as possible, nor are they seeking an independence without assistance. Their vision is of a world in which discrimination and injustice are removed, including stereotypes, ignorance and fear. They are desirous of the establishment of alternative definitions and perceptions based on a dignified view of difference.

In our attempts to write and talk about these crucial issues we need to be cautious and resist portraying disabled people as passive, incomplete, unfortunate recipients of overwhelming constraints and controls, in that this underplays the active agency of disabled people in their struggle for change. Alternatively, portraying disabled people as heroines, or heroes minimizes the very real costs of oppression and gives an impression that they can do it alone. Both of these perspectives are unacceptable and counter-productive to the realization of a non-oppressive way of defining and interacting with disabled people.

By seeking to question the impact of dominant ideologies on policy and practice in all spheres of service provision, disabled people at an individual level and importantly through their organizations nationally and internationally, are involved in varying degrees of oppositional politics. This includes pro- viding alternative definitions, insights and understandings relating to disability. They are refusing to accept a deficit dependency role and are engaged in a struggle to capture the power of naming. An emancipatory meaning of difference is one example of a more general goal of developing dignified and empowering perspectives. Personal and collective pride and motivation are essential features of this process.

One of the major aims of the Disability Movement has been that of establishing a policy of 'independent living' and encouraging governments to support this approach. In a paper on 'What Price Independence?', Zarb and Evans (1998) contend that moral arguments emanating from the principles of equality and rights need to be supported by economic arguments. He maintains that there is a major contradiction between 'care' as expressed in health and social service provision and 'independent living'.

> Developing alternative forms of thinking and practice entails a recognition of several restrictive barriers including: that the funding of long term care is . . . premised on the assumption that residential care will continue to be presented as the option of 'first choice', for the majority of older and disabled people requiring high levels of support.
>
> (Zarb 1999: 2)

Furthermore, there is no serious commitment and recognition underpinning service policy and provision that independence is a basic human and civil right. Finally, that the costs involved in the development of independent living are not viewed as a form of social and economic investment.

The ultimate concern of independent living is for disabled people to be at the centre of the planning, implementation and evaluation of services that involve the quality of their lives. It is about the benefits and responsibilities of having control, choices and rights in their lives. Various organizations run by disabled people have developed in order to support these significant changes to policy and practice. The National Centre for Independent Living is a key agency, and they publish a newsletter called 'Independently', and also have an excellent website providing a range of free and accessible material, information and news.

In one of their publications by Hasler (2004) a helpful overview of evidence on direct payments is carefully set out. The reasons for the necessity of the development of independent living are outlined as well as some of the key benefits. The general consensus is that direct payments provide for disabled people a more reliable service delivery; greater flexibility in support provision; high quality support which maximizes choice and centralizes a means of recognizing and experiencing the value of peer support (Zarb 1999; Mercer 2004; Hasler 2004). These user-led initiatives offer as Evans (1996: 224) so succinctly and powerfully notes 'the freedom to make decisions about your own life, and to participate fully in your community'. This is clearly a process of learning in which there is no room for complacency because of the need to see more disabled people involved in these developments and to improve the practices that are in existence.

In a project undertaken by Barnes *et al.* (2001) disabled users of services were interviewed, and whilst they acknowledged the benefits of such developments including choices and control, they also noted some areas for improvement. For example, the need for better publicity; more involvement in the assessment, designing and evaluation of services; improved/more accessible premises and better-paid workforce.

If 'nothing about us without us' is to be an assumption informing all service policy and practice, then it will be essential to pursue the demands for human and civil rights. It will also be crucial as Goble (2004) contends that to be independent requires challenging the discriminatory perspective that assumes that the presence of functional impairment inevitably means that such individuals are not normal, and are dependent on professional expertise, for which they need to be grateful.

One of the dangers of offering a brief analysis, is that of providing a homogenized and overly romantic, linear series of insights and understandings. In an important paper, Barnes (2005) is conscious of this possibility and provides a carefully supported overview of developments relating to the impact of disability activism in the British context. He outlines the varied ways in which disabled people and their organizations have contributed to changes concerning how disability is defined, the impact on legislation, social services, welfare, educational provision and practice. Importantly, he also identifies the barriers that still need to be critically challenged if more disabled people are to experience the benefits of these changes in their daily lives. One of his main worries centres on the danger of incorporation, in which government concerns become more significant than those of disabled people. Looking back over the history of the disability movement, Oliver and Barnes (2006) highlight the ways in which the British Council of Disabled People and other local coalitions have increasingly become politically isolated and damaged by the lack of core financial support. They also highlight the damaging impact of the intensity of the struggles involved in terms of the health and leadership within the movement. They maintain that the pursuit of a single aim or goal in disability politics is counter-productive in the struggle for effective change, and powerfully contend that the 'only viable long-term political strategy for disabled people, is to be part of a far wider struggle to create a better society for all' (Oliver and Barnes 2006).

Disabled pupils, education and sport

Inclusive Education raises the contentious issue of the extent to which education can contribute to the realization of a non-discriminatory, non-oppressive society. This involves the necessity of identifying and challenging barriers to inclusive conditions, relations and practices (Barton and Armstrong

2007). Education must not be conceived in a vacuum, but rather understood within a wider inter-related range of socio-economic and political factors. From this perspective, education is viewed as a human rights issue. This means that all pupils are entitled to quality education and no child is ineducable. Educators thus need to approach teaching with the highest form of expectations with regard to pupil learning and experience. The culture of schools needs to be increasingly characterized by zero-tolerance in relation to all forms of exclusion and discrimination internally, as well as those in the local community and society generally (Barton and Armstrong 2007).

Inclusive education is committed to transformative change, involving, for example, the curriculum, assessment, teacher attitudes, the nature of learning and teaching styles, in order for the maximum participation of all pupils in the life of schools to take place and be maintained. This commitment encourages the development of such critical questions as: What are schools for? What do pupils need to learn? In what context should this learning take place? What do schools and teachers need in order for them to become more inclusive?

In an important analysis, Evans (2004) raises the issue of the connection between the pursuit of social democratic ideals and the benefits to all children in schools. This engagement, he maintains, involves a critical interrogation of how 'ability' is 'recognized, conceptualized, socially configured, nurtured, and embodied through the practice of PE as well as those of sport and health' (Evans 2004: 95). He further contends that a great deal of the interests and practices underpinning PE are increasingly defined in terms of 'compensatory education'. Such a deficit approach is supported by the language of 'special needs', which assumes that the difficulties or deficiencies are essentially located within-the-child (Corbett 1996). Evans believes that such factors have contributed to PE remaining:

> a conservative force, building on and reproducing rather than challenging and changing the 'ability' deficits and (where appropriate) the differences children develop outside the school.
>
> (Evans 2004: 101)

The importance of understanding disability as a significant means of social differentiation and the need to develop a critical analysis which challenges the barriers to inclusion within society and particularly in terms of PE and sport can be seen as an urgent and serious necessity for the following reasons. The extent to which PE recognizes the importance of disability is still an issue of serious concern. Within the literature it is often viewed in tokenistic ways conceived as a bolt-on addition to more significant factors such as class, race and gender (Fitzgerald and Gard 2007). Even more offensive is the absence of any reference to disability within what are otherwise valuable and thoughtful analyses (Azzarito and Solomon 2005). A further issue concerns the distinction between laudable rhetoric within official documents and actual practices within classrooms and schools. For example, it is suggested that high quality PE and sport will 'enable all young people, whatever their circumstances or ability, to take part in and enjoy PE and sport' (DfES 2004: 1). Whilst this is a commendable claim, it would seem that the nature of changes required to enable this to be realized have not taken place, and inequalities relating to access and opportunities continue to be experienced by disabled pupils (Fitzgerald 2005). A further issue surrounds the question of an 'acceptable sporting body' and the extent to which disabled athletes strive for the 'able-bodied ideal'. This perspective Hardin (2003) contends, is a reflection of wider social values and norms, and in particular those which are inherent in capitalist hegemonic ideals and standards. The position and role of the media and advertising in communicating these standards is seen as significant and as Hardin (2003: 112) maintains, disabled people '(who lack the capitalist ideal-body) have been excluded or marginalized in advertising and thus society'. Those who manage to succeed often become known as 'supercrips', which reflects a hierarchical view of impairments and a weak conception of discrimination and change (Hardin and Hardin 2004). Finally, there is the danger of an uncritical emulation of non-disabled standards diverting attention from, and the struggle for changes in, the social relations and conditions of society. Hahn (1984), a disabled scholar, raises some crucial questions on these issues including:

> the extent to which disabled persons wish to strive to emulate the values of the non-disabled portion of society through extensive participation of sports;
>
> the extent to which growing involvement in athletic competition might contribute to the inequality rather than to the equality of the disabled citizens without widespread efforts to modify the environment in which they live;
>
> the extent to which sports play a 'gate-keeping' role in society that may be detrimental to the interests of disabled men and women.
>
> (Hahn 1984: 3)

Whilst these questions were raised over two decades ago, they still remain of fundamental relevance and need to be integral to discussions of all those involved in a professional capacity in the field of PE and sport.

Conclusion

In this brief chapter, I have endeavoured to identify some of the key ideas and issues relating to the social model of disability. This approach has its roots in the struggles of disabled people for human rights, social justice and independent living. The intention has been to provide a stimulus for further explorations and discussions. Nor should this approach be viewed as an unexamined orthodoxy in that disabled people are continually engaged in re-examining and critically reflecting on these ideas (Barnes and Oliver 2006). In the light of the previous analysis several questions can be raised demanding urgent and serious attention including: To what extent is the definition of disability a fundamentally significant issue? What is the relationship between your pre-existing conception and understanding of disability and that outlined in this chapter? What challenges to both personal and professional values and practices do you now recognize?

In seeking to grapple with these issues I want to suggest the following forms of engagement and responsibility. While legislation is not a sufficient factor in and of itself to produce inclusion, it is nevertheless an essential aspect of the pursuit of transformative change. Since December 2007 all maintained schools and local authorities in England and Wales have to produce their own Disability Equality Schemes. The Disability Equality Duty is now a new positive duty covering all public bodies requiring the promotion of disability equality. This includes, for example, the elimination of unlawful discrimination, disability-related harassment and the promotion of positive attitudes towards disabled people (Disability Rights Commission 2006).[1] One of the implications of this development is the responsibility on all educators to obtain an informed understanding of current legislation and its implication for their practices with disabled students. This is not a matter of personal choice, it is now a duty enshrined in law. Secondly, given these developments the language of entitlement now needs to be clearly established when thinking about and engaging in educational practices relating to disabled students. Thirdly, the question of teachers and teaching and the implementation of legislative requirements is a matter of immense importance. But what is being advocated in this chapter is not the establishment of special teachers/ teaching, but rather good teachers who are able to use their imaginative and creative skills to meet the diversity of pupils' learning requirements. Finally, where there is a serious attempt to constructively engage with these issues, time and opportunity will need to be provided for debate within schools and other institutions which will enable learning and change to take place and be maintained. Such an approach will be of benefit to all learners and participants in this exciting process.

Acknowledgement

I am grateful for some helpful correspondence from Hayley Fitzgerald, which she sent me during the preparation of this chapter.

Note

1   A code of practice and various forms of guidance can be found at www. dotheduty.org.

References

Abberley, P. (1987) 'The Concept of Oppression and the Development of a Social Theory of Disability', *Disability, Handicap and Society*, 2 (1): 5–19.

Azzarito, L. and Solomon, M.A. (2005) 'A Reconceptualisation of Physical Education: The Intersection of Gender/Race/Social Class', *Sport, Education and Society*, 10 (1): 25–47.

Barnes, C. (1991) *Disabled People in Britain and Discrimination*, London: Hurst and Co. in association with the British Council of Organisations of Disabled People.

Barnes, C. (1996) 'Theories of Disability and the Origins of the Oppression of Disabled People in Western Society', in L. Barton (ed.), *Disability and Society: Emerging Issues and Insights*, Harlow: Addison Wesley Longman.

Barnes, C. (1997) 'A Legacy of Oppression: A History of Disability in Western Culture', in L. Barton and M. Oliver (eds), *Disability and Society: Emerging Issues and Insights*. Harlow: Addison Wesley Longman.

Barnes, C. (2005) 'Disability, Activism and the Voice of Success: A British Experience', paper presented at the Institute of Advanced Studies, University of Western Australia, Perth.

Barnes, C. and Mercer, G. (2003) *Disability*, Cambridge: Polity Press.

Barnes, C., Morgan, H. and Mercer, G. (2001) *Creating Independent Futures: An Evaluation of Services Led by Disabled People. Stage Three Reports*, Leeds: The Disability Press.

Barton, L. and Armstrong, F. (eds) (2007) *Policy, Experience and Change: Cross-Cultural Reflections on Inclusive Education*, Dordrecht: Springer Books.

Barton, L. (1993) 'Disability, Empowerment and Physical Education', in J. Evans (ed.), *Equality, Education and Physical Education*, London: Falmer Press, pp. 43–54.

Corbett, J. (1996) *Bad Mouthing*, London: Falmer Press.

Department for Education and Skills (2004) *High Quality PE and Sport for Young People. A Guide to Recognizing and Achieving High Quality PE and Sport in Schools and Clubs*, Annesley: Department for Education and Skills.

Disability Rights Commission (2006) *The Disability Duty*, Stratford-upon-Avon: Disability Rights Commission.

Evans, J. (1996) 'Direct Payments in the UK', paper presented at European Network on Independent Living Conference, Stockholm: National Institute for Independent Living, June. Quoted in F. Hasler (2004) 'Direct Payments', in J. Swain, S. French, Barnes, C. and Thomas, C. (eds), *Disabling Barriers – Enabling Environments*, London: Sage, pp. 219–25.

Evans, J. (2004) 'Making a Difference? Education and "Ability" in Physical Education', *European Physical Education Review*, 10 (1): 95–108.

Fitzgerald, H. (2005) 'Still Feeling Like a Spare Piece of Luggage? Embodied Experiences of (Dis)Ability in Physical Education and School Sport', *Physical Education & Sport Pedagogy*, 10 (1): 41–59.

Fitzgerald, H. and Gard, M. (2007) 'Physical Education, the Elite Development Goal, and Disabled Students', paper presented in the Research on Learning & Instruction in Physical Education SIG at the American Educational Research Association Annual Meeting, Chicago, April.

Goble. C. (2004) 'Dependence, Independence and Normality', in J. Swain, S. French, C. Barnes and C. Thomas (eds), *Disabling Barriers – Enabling Environments*, London: Sage, pp. 41–6.

Hahn, H. (1984) 'Sports and the Political Movement of Disabled Persons: Examining Non-Disabled Social Values', *Arena Review*, 8 (1): 1–15.

Hardin, M. (2003) 'Marketing the Acceptably Athletic Image: Wheelchair Athletes, Sports-Related Advertising and Capitalist Hegemony', *Disability Studies Quarterly*, 23 (1): 108–25.

Hardin, M.M. and Hardin, B. (2004) 'The "Supercrip" in Sport Media: Wheelchair Athletes Discuss Hegemony's Disabled Hero', *Sociology of Sport* (Internet), 7 (1), available from: http://physed.otago.ac.nz/sosol/v7i1/v7i1 1.html (accessed 20 July 2007).

Hasler, F. (2004) *Clarifying the Evidence on Direct Payments into Practice*, London: National Centre for Independent Living, available from: www.ncil.org.uk/evidence_paper.asp (accessed 14 February 2007).

Hevey, D. (1992) *The Creatures Time Forgot: Photography and Disability Imagery*, London: Routledge.

Hurst, R. (1996) 'Disability and Policy – Survival of the Fittest', paper presented at an Economic and Social Research Council Seminar, City University, London.

Mercer, G. (2004) 'User-Led Organisations: Facilitating Independent Living', in J. Swain, S. French, C. Barnes and C. Thomas (eds), *Disability Barriers – Enabling Environments*, London: Sage, pp. 176–82.

Morris, J. (1991) *Pride Against Prejudice: Transforming Attitudes to Disability*, London: The Woman's Press.

Morris, J. (1992) *Disabled Lives: Many Voices, One Message*, London: BBC.

Oliver, M. (1990) *The Politics of Disablement*, Basingstoke: Macmillan.

Oliver, M. and Barnes, C. (2006) 'Disability Politics and the Disability Movement in Britain: Where Did It All Go Wrong?', *Coalition Magazine of Greater Manchester Coalition of Disabled People*, Manchester: Greater Manchester Coalition of Disabled People.

Prime Minister's Strategy Unit (2004) *Improving the Life Chances of Disabled People*, London: Cabinet Office.

Souza, A. (1997) 'Everything You Ever Wanted to Know About Down's Syndrome, But Never Bothered to Ask', in P. Ramcharan, G. Roberts, G. Grant and J. Borland (eds), *Empowerment in Everyday Life*, London: Jessica Kingsley Publishers.

Sport England (2003) *Making English Sport Inclusive: Equity Guidelines for Governing Bodies*, London: Sport England.

Union of the Physically Impaired against Segregation (1976) *Fundamental Principles of Disability*, London: Union of the Physically Impaired against Segregation.

Zarb, G. (1999) *What Price Independence?*, London: National Centre for Independent Living.

Zarb, G. and Evans, J. (1998) 'What Price Independence?', paper presented at Shaping Our Futures, A Conference on Independent Living, London: European Network of Independent Living (Internet), pp. 32–50, available from: www.independent living.org/docs2/enilfuture3.html#anchor1 (accessed 15 September 2007).

Part II

Youth sport insights from young disabled people

5 The voices of students with disabilities

Are they informing inclusive physical education practice?

Donna Goodwin

Introduction: the voices of students with disabilities

Inclusion has been defined as 'a place where everyone belongs, is accepted, supports and is supported by his or her peers' (Stainback and Stainback 1990: 3) and has been a prominent ideology in western education since the 1980s. Research on inclusive physical education has increased significantly in the past ten years over the previous ten. A review by Block and Vogler in 1994 found only ten studies that focused specifically on students with disabilities in general physical education.[1] A review of the literature from 1995–2005 (Block and Obrusnikova 2007) revealed 38 studies focusing on students with disabilities in general physical education in six areas of focus: (a) support, (b) affects on peers without disabilities, (c) attitudes and intentions of children without disabilities, (d) social interactions, (e) ALT-PE of students with disabilities (Academic Learning Time-Physical Education) and (f) training and attitudes of general physical education teachers. Of the 38 articles reviewed, only five reported the actual experiences of students with disabilities.

The purpose of this chapter is threefold: (a) to review the research on student experiences in inclusive physical education, (b) to align student experiences against recommended pedagogical practices in inclusive physical education and (c) to identify synergies and divergences that may reinforce current practice or suggest areas for change. At the time of the writing of this chapter, a search of physical education related databases resulted in the identification of nine studies in which students with disabilities depicted their experiences of inclusive physical education in their own voices. The concept of voice has several meanings, including the literal voice (representing the intent of the speaker), the metaphorical voice (the messages within the speaker's words) and the political voice (the right to speak and to be represented) (Britzman 1989). The voices of the students will be reviewed against proposed best practices in inclusive physical education. The closing discussion of the chapter will juxtapose the experiences of students against the proposed best practices, highlighting synergies and divergences pertaining to the literal, metaphorical and political voices of the students.

Many physical education contexts have been criticized for not translating policies of inclusion and equitable opportunities for students with disabilities into tangible opportunities (Fitzgerald *et al.* 2003). As Chapter 9 illustrates, teachers are key agents of inclusive physical education and therefore have been the focus of considerable research attention. Moreover, as Chapter 3 indicates, lack of teacher preparation, knowledge and experience of including students with disabilities in their programmes has been well documented (e.g. Chandler and Green 1995; Hodge *et al.* 2004; Lieberman *et al.* 2002; Lienert *et al.* 2001; Smith and Green 2004). LaMaster *et al.* (1998) explored elementary school teachers' effectiveness when including students with disabilities in general physical education and concluded that teachers felt unsupported, unable to accommodate students with disabilities, and inadequately prepared. These findings were supported by Hodge *et al.* (2004) in a study of high school teachers who although positively disposed to inclusion as an educational philosophy, held differential efficacy in achieving successful inclusion and encountered challenges in establishing inclusive practice, feeling at times inadequately prepared or lacking supports to effectively teach students with severe disabilities.

The relationship between attitudes of teachers toward students with disabilities and such variables as teaching, university course work, nature of practicum experiences, gender of teachers, nature of student disabilities, and perceived competence have been investigated (e.g. Block and Rizzo 1995; Folsom-Meek *et al.* 2000; Rizzo and Vispoel 1991). A review of the literature on teacher attitude towards students with disabilities by Hutzler (2003) concluded: (a) previous contact with children with disabilities has resulted in conflicting findings as to its importance in attitude development, (b) course preparation seems to be a significant factor in the development of positive attitudes, (c) teachers' perceived competence is a significant predictor of positive attitudes, and (d) attitudes towards students based on the nature of their disabilities is inconclusive. The support networks required for teachers to implement inclusive programmes have not progressed in any real way in twenty years (Welch 1996). The result of not acknowledging definitively that the educational system has failed teachers is that the burden of learning in this deficient environment has been placed on the student (Soodak *et al.* 1998).

Those who are proponents of inclusive physical education have been slow to seek information about the experiences of students with disabilities. Understanding the perspective of students can provide a unique vantage point from which to view the inclusive physical education environment and student perceived educational outcomes (Blinde and McCallister 1998; Sanders 1996). Students with disabilities have valuable insights and opinions that should be heard and celebrated (Fitzgerald *et al.* 2003). Furthermore, children comprehend the world differently from adults and may be inhabiting and constructing profoundly different subjective worlds (Sanders 1996).

Not embracing the perspective of students with disabilities may be due in part to insecurity in our lack of pre-service preparation for teachers (LaMaster *et al.* 1998); not having empirical models for effective instructional strategies (Goodwin 2003); teacher assumptions about students with disabilities and their desire to be involved (Blinde and McCallister 1998; Sanders 1996); the perpetuation of the dualism of the mind and body caused by the medicalization of disability (Grenier 2007); lack of administrative support such as resource allocation, staffing, information flow and operating procedures (Praisner 2003); and finally, the general lack of importance given by teachers to the evaluation of their own programmes (Smith and Green, 2004).

Voices of students

Blinde and McCallister (1998) interviewed 20 students, aged 10–17 years, with various physical disabilities about their physical education experiences. Their participation ranged from full inclusion to full exclusion. Although the students indicated that they were like other students in their enjoyment of physical activity, games and sports, the resulting themes: (a) limited participation in activities and (b) negative emotional responses highlighted the disappointing nature of their physical education experiences. Betty, who had cerebral palsy, was involved the largest degree but was the exception. The other students more typically indicated that their limited participation resulted from being relegated to non-participatory roles such as being the observer ('I'd sit up on the stage from when I first got there until the end of class every day'), a line judge, cheerleading for classmates, or simply being a physical boundary marker (e.g. replacing a pylon). Limited participation was reported to be due to concern for student safety, teacher liability, lack of modification or adaptations to activities, and general lack of encouragement for the students to participate.

The students' negative emotional responses were triggered by exclusion from activities in which they would have liked to participate and unpleasant social interactions with classmates. Having to sit and watch others play left the students feeling sad or angry. They also felt like outsiders ('I felt different, like uh, there was something wrong with me') and unwanted by their peers ('They just don't ask me to play'). The students were subjected to ridicule and embarrassment due to their perceived ability, suggesting to the authors that teachers may be inadequately monitoring the social dynamics within their programmes. The authors further concluded that no student should leave physical education having experienced the limited participation and negative emotional responses that were experienced by these students.

Goodwin and Watkinson (2000) revealed the physical education experience of nine elementary school-aged students, aged 10–12 years, with physical disabilities through focus group interviews and student drawn illustrations. The students' experiences were presented as *good days* and *bad days*. Good days were accentuated by feelings of belonging that came with companionship and support to complete activities ('When you are doing relays they cheer you on'), being able to partake in the benefits of physical education ('It builds my strength'), and skillful participation for its intrinsic rewards of self-efficacy, as well as the external acknowledgement by others of their skill proficiency ('It's nice when they see me in with the Grade 6 kids swimming at their level and ahead of them sometimes').

Bad days were characterized as ones where the participants were socially isolated, had reason to question their competence, or had active participation in class restricted. On bad days, social isolation took the form of being rejected, neglected, or seen as an object of curiosity ('there's always one or two kids that are making fun of you'). The physical competence of the students was assumed lacking because of the mere presence of a disability ('You can't do this, you have a disability'), and which was manifest when students did not pass to students with disabilities in game play ('They won't let me be in net or anything'). Teachers' uncertainty about performance expectations and activity adaptations also resulted in exclusion ('My teacher won't let me do anything'), as did physical barriers ('I can only go on the tarmac'). The authors concluded that the students' insights into what contributes to good and bad days in physical education provides cause for reflection on the pedagogical sensitivity afforded students with disabilities in general physical education.

Goodwin (2001) described the meaning of help from classmates in general physical education expressed by 12 students, aged 7–13 years, with physical disabilities. Using the threat to self-esteem model to facilitate the interpretation of the students' interviews, it was found that peer support was positively received when it was instrumental, consensual, and caring. Help from peers was self-threatening when it resulted in a loss of independence, was reckless, interfered with participation, or threatened self-esteem. Positive peer support was reported through peer actions such as: 'They see I that I can't pick it up because I can't reach it . . . they get the ball for me' and 'He appreciates me and never gets mad at me'. Peer support that was not well received caused the students with disabilities to become defensive or feel badly about themselves. The students recalled instances when 'I don't need help, they just come and help me no matter what', 'Sometimes people assume I can't do stuff when I really can', and finally, 'Sometimes . . . they'll take my handlebars and push me out of the way'. Although peer support can facilitate participation goals and enhance social outcomes, the author suggested that unmonitored peer support (help) may interfere with the completion of tasks, be unwanted, and be offered because of perceived incompetence and lack of ability. Moreover, the unmonitored application of peer support can undermine the benefits that genuine instrumental help can provide.

Place and Hodge (2001) completed a case study of three Grade 8 girls with physical disabilities and their classmates in general physical education. The themes that resulted from the analysis of the student interviews were *segregated inclusion* and *social isolation*. Segregated inclusion referred to the times when the students were separated from their classmates without disabilities in terms of proximity and engaged in activities within their own group, or were excluded from activities altogether ('sometimes we don't get to go [on field trips] because they don't have any transportation for us. They forget about us'). Social isolation referred to times when the students were neglected, viewed as objects of curiosity, or a sense of awkwardness existed between them and their classmates ('They act like we are different'). These findings are not surprising given the researchers found almost no social interaction occurred among the students with and without disabilities in the classes that were observed. The average percentage of time that classmates gave to social talk with student with disabilities was 2 per cent. The students with disabilities interacted with each other to a greater extent than they did with their other classmates. The authors concluded that social interaction will be an outcome of inclusion only if curricular adaptations, instructional modifications, human resources (e.g. peer tutors), and informed decision making occurs.

Kristen *et al.* (2003) described the experiences of twenty children and adolescents, aged 9–15 years, with physical disabilities, regarding their participation in integrated sports programmes (i.e. orienteering, golf, and archery). The programmes ran one to two hours weekly for a period of one year. Although this study addressed programmes outside of the school system, it is worthy of review as the findings were universally positive. Six categories emerged from the analysis of the interviews: (a) finding new friends socially and companions for sport participation, (b) learning concrete and experience-based knowledge, (c) strengthening one's physique and gaining physical improvement, (d) becoming someone by being accepted in the group and gaining confidence, (e) experiencing nature and gaining inner satisfaction as well as skills in moving freely in woods and fields, and (f) having a good time understanding and assimilating the formal and informal rules associated with the activities. The children and youths' experiences reflected the themes respectively in their comments, 'I get to know new friends', 'One gets better and better at it the more one shoots', 'I already feel fitter and happier', 'I'm becoming a bit more self-confident', 'It's a great sport; one gets to be out in the countryside', and 'When you have learnt how to do it, it's great fun'. The authors concluded that when sport is used as a means of achieving social support and well-being, belief in oneself and the ability to be assertive increases. The authors concluded that inclusive sport can provide many positive factors for children and youths with disabilities, both at individual and societal levels.

Hutzler *et al.* (2002) completed a study that explored the personal experiences of ten children with physical disabilities, aged 9–14, in physical education and other inclusive physical activity settings to identify supporting and limiting mechanisms to their sense of empowerment. Criteria for empowerment were defined as social competence and problem solving, sense of self-efficacy and self-respect, social competence and leadership, and active learning. The comparative qualitative analysis of student interviews revealed five themes: (a) *assistive devices*, (b) *physical activity*, (c) *peers*, (d) *important adults*, and (e) *self*. The descriptions of the themes reflected both positive and negative experiences of the participants. The presence of a brace or wheelchair was sometimes a source of distress and embarrassment ('I'm saying that I broke my arm and now I have to wear it [arm brace] – I lie to them'). In contrast, the wheelchairs could provide opportunities for positive social interactions as classmates vie for the role of pushing the wheelchair. Some peers teased and ridiculed the students with disabilities ('I'm disappointed'), while others encouraged their participation in games and exercises ('I feel one of the group' and 'I feel something in common'). Physical activity caused distress to some students to the point of crying, and they were left to do what they could. Some who were not included responded by being emotionally tough, stating, 'I accept it' and 'It doesn't bother me'. Other students reported 'It is hard for me' and 'It makes me cry'. Although the students preferred to be involved in physical education, the physical education teachers' roles in mediating their involvement were minor. The students turned to classroom teachers and other staff members when they had difficulties coping with a situation. The theme of self was reflected in the students' internal resources to cope and find solutions. The students stated, 'I don't let them have pity for me' and 'I suggest to the teacher which exercises I should do'. The authors concluded that inclusive physical education revealed no general trend towards supporting or limiting empowerment.

Doubt and McColl (2003) interviewed three female and four male high school students with cerebral palsy and spina bifida, aged 15–19 years, about their high school experiences. Participation in physical education and athletics were prominently featured in their narratives. Three of the students avoided taking physical education by substituting other classes. They did not expect that adaptations would be made to accommodate them in physical education ('I wouldn't expect them to change the whole course because of one student') and to do so would have highlighted their disabilities at a time when masking their disabilities was a preferred strategy to facilitate social inclusion ('at lunch hour . . . I'll just grab another chair and sit in it, instead of sitting in the wheelchair').

The findings included internal and external factors that both facilitated and limited inclusion. Extrinsic factors included negative peer reactions and inaccessible activities. The students were treated as younger than their ages, illustrating perceptions of being less competent ('They talk to me like I'm really young . . . It's mostly their tone of voice probably more than what they're saying'). The participants felt that the athletics programme was not accessible to them because they get 'blown away' by the competition (e.g., track team); however, some sought out secondary roles to facilitate inclusion. David and Evan were officials for the school hockey team but recognized that their roles were peripheral. David said: 'I'll sit down at my spare if some of them are there and I don't say too much as I'm not really one of them ... They don't tell me to get lost or anything.' Evan stated: 'I guess I'm part of the team. I just got to hang out with the guys and go to the games and help out wherever I could.'

Intrinsic factors included the disability itself, masking the disability, finding a niche, making fun of the disability and educating peers. Assuming a less desirable game position in physical education was a way of establishing a participation niche. Liam stated: 'In floor hockey I'll be the first one picked ... Everyone else is reluctant to put on the pads because there's more glory in scoring.' Liam even went so far as to hide his national level disability sport success ('The kids could tease me or put down my sport saying it's not real sports or something'). David, in contrast, wrote an article for the school paper explaining the sport of sledge hockey and organized a sledge hockey game against the school hockey team. Self-deprecation was a strategy the students use to put others at ease. For example, a student might laugh along with a student who referred to him as 'crippled' when he dropped an object. Whereas Liam did not want to expose his disability sport success to ridicule by those he felt wouldn't understand David used disability sport as a way to educate his peers. The authors concluded that education should be accompanied by support if adolescents are to avoid viewing themselves as secondary citizens within their own high schools, and within physical education classes in particular.

Suomi *et al.* (2003) investigated the factors that had positive and negative effects on the social experiences of 12 elementary students, four of whom had learning and/or mild cognitive impairments. Two of the students were in kindergarten and two were in Grade 4. Observational and interview data with students and teachers were collected. Only the findings specific to the interviews with the students with disabilities are reported here. Two physical education specialists followed an established curriculum that promoted cooperation while minimizing competition. The school staff reported that they had a three-R focus – responsibility, reliability and respect that was also reflected in their developmentally and instructionally appropriate physical education programme. All students indicated that they enjoyed coming to the gym because it was fun and a time to learn. All students also indicated that they liked their teachers; however, it became clear in discussions with the students with disabilities that there were hidden negative social situations. Negative social situations were predicated, for example by the 'find your own partner' strategy used by the teachers. The students with disabilities found themselves in the *leftover* category, as they could not find partners as quickly as other students and had to be paired up by the teachers. The strained social interactions were also evident during game play. Tag games led to hurt feelings and students with disabilities were not *unfrozen* or not picked at all in Duck Duck Goose. The kindergarteners with disabilities said, for example: 'I feel like no one likes me because I get tagged and then I don't move' and 'I felt left out I didn't get a turn to run. It made me sad'.

The teachers were unaware that the games they selected and the 'finding your own partner' strategy had negative social consequences on the students with disabilities. As early as kindergarten, students avoid students with disabilities if they perceive them to hold a lower social status than themselves. One of the Fourth-Graders stated that she would work with anyone in the class, but later she said: 'I would be a partner with Gail (classmate with disability) only if the teacher asked me.'

Observational data also recorded instances when classmates were mean spirited and encouraged a classmate with a disability to engage in a socially inappropriate behaviour (e.g. kiss me) that would subsequently be reprimanded by the teacher. Some of the behaviours of the students with disabilities reflected socially immature behaviours relative to their peers (e.g. hugging, touching of hair, laughing) that were not attended to by the teachers. These behaviours had a deleterious effect on social interactions with their kindergarten peers – 'I don't like to play with Suzan . . . she kisses and hugs me. She kind of embarrasses me.' The authors remarked that it is only through persistent observation that hidden social consequences can be identified emphasizing the importance of observation time and opportunities for students to discuss their experiences in physical education. The authors concluded, 'a developmentally appropriate curriculum and the utilization of a socially responsible curriculum model does not necessarily dictate positive social experiences for all students' (Suomi *et al.* 2003: 200).

Butler and Hodge (2004) using a qualitative case study method described the social interactions of a 13-year-old girl with Down syndrome concomitant with a mild intellectual impairment and a 13-year-old boy with scoliosis and their sixteen Sixth-Grade classmates in general physical education. Four themes emerged from the field notes and interviews with the students with impairments (a) fun and cooperative interaction, (b) friendships, (c) aggressive male classmates without disabilities created feelings of uneasiness, and (d) favourite class. The theme of fun and cooperation reflected the students' feelings of belonging and the help they received from classmates in some activities. Best friends were found among their classmates and physical education was reported to be one of their favourite classes. There were occasions, however, when Ben and Rita indicated that they limited their interactions with classmates when the boys were aggressive. The results of this study have been included in the review, even though the words of the students were not presented in the article.

In summary, the nine inclusive physical education studies reviewed presented the literal voices of children and youth between the ages of 5 and 19 years with physical and developmental disabilities. The studies also represent student experiences from Canada, the USA, Sweden, Israel and the UK. There are discernible and international similarities in the experiences of inclusive physical education. Children and youths with disabilities enjoy physical activity and want to be involved alongside their classmates without disabilities. Moreover, classmates can provide important instrumental support that facilitates successful and meaningful involvement. Metaphorically, inclusive physical education can provide a sense of belonging, social acceptance, and the opportunity to enjoy the companionship of friends. The knowledge they gain about performance supports their skilful participation in activities and provides the opportunity to demonstrate their physical competence.

In contrast, inclusive physical education can be socially isolating when students are ridiculed and embarrassed or conversely neglected or ignored by their classmates. Ironically, when peers did choose to interact with their classmates with disabilities, the help they provided was often unsolicited resulting in loss of independence or the help was reckless and therefore unwelcome. Participation can be further restricted when teachers do not encourage involvement or when activity adaptations were not provided. It should be noted that not all students experienced the full breadth of the positive and negative occurrences described. Given the similarities of experiences described however, for students with disabilities inclusive physical education was marked by distinctly good days and bad days (Goodwin and Watkinson 2000).

Pedagogical practices in inclusive physical education

David Lusted (1986: 3) defined pedagogy as: 'the transformation of consciousness that takes place in the intersection of three agencies – teacher, the learner and the knowledge they together produce.' It could be argued that without an understanding of how students with disabilities experience physical education, that learning together to create knowledge is not possible. This section of the chapter will provide an overview of the pedagogical practices promoted in inclusive physical education settings. Pedagogical practices of inclusion of students with disabilities in physical education include three major categories: (a) curricular adaptations, (b) instructional strategies, and (c) other teaching supports (e.g. DePauw and Goc Karp 1994; Goodwin 2003; Vogler *et al.* 2000).

Curricular Adaptations

Stein (1987) wrote about the myth of the adapted physical education curriculum, challenging the adapted physical activity community to set aside its preoccupation with creating or assigning physical activities according to the students' perceived activity limitations. His challenge was in response to the curriculum guides, text books and articles of the 1970s that advocated corrective, therapeutic or remedial physical education programmes for students with disabilities that were to be implemented by teachers with specialized skills. Stein (1987: 34) posed the question: 'Have you ever seen adapted physical education activities that are different from activities found in a good, appropriate, individualized, and developmental physical education programmes?' That being said, unless there is flexibility in the interpretation and application of the curriculum, students with disabilities may be subject to marginalized participation.

The acquisition and improvement of motor skills and the improvement of physical fitness are of primary importance for student with disabilities (Sherrill and Montelione 1990). Equally important is socialization and the application of a solid knowledge base and movement skill to games and sports that support a physically active lifestyle. However, as Chapters 3 and 9 outline, traditional games are perceived to be difficult to adapt for students with disabilities and may contribute to teachers' reluctance to include students with disabilities in their physical education programmes. Chandler and Greene (1995: 272) state that 'shifting emphasis away from traditional games and sports skills instructions may in fact allow all students access to knowledge and leisure skills'.

Although students have been asked, albeit to a limited extent, what they think, feel and know about their inclusive physical education experiences students play a minimal role in curriculum innovation. Their political voices have not been represented in the process of curriculum-making (Brooker and MacDonald, 1999). At the system level, curricula are centrally developed by people deemed by educational authorities to have relevant expertise and usually include teachers, university educators and representatives from the ministry of education (bureaucrats). Students are rarely consulted in curriculum making, even though they are considered to be central to schooling (Brooker and MacDonald, 1999).

Instructional strategies

Various approaches to instruction have guided the teaching of adapted physical activity, each holding underlying assumptions that have implications for their application (Goodwin 2003).

Task analysis

Task analysis has been used to analyze complex motor skills and identify their component parts for the purpose of teaching them in sequential order toward the achievement of the final performance. Often these sequences are based on developmentally determined motor milestones. Teaching the component parts or sub-skills can be supported by changing task and/or environmental variables such as weight, size, length of implements and surface, dimensions and location of playing areas. In addition to analyzing a motor skill by subtasks, the complexity of the skill can be further regulated by modifying the environment such that skills are learned in a closed (predictable self-paced e.g. kicking a stationary ball) or open (changing externally paced e.g. running and kicking a rolling ball) environment (Goodwin 2003).

An assumption of developmental task analysis is that students follow typical stages of motor development and that the mastery of sub-skills is required before students can progress to more complex performances. For students with neurological impairments, traditional task analysis may not be appropriate as the underlying assumption of typical motor development does not apply. The experiences of the students from the studies reviewed indicated that the task analysis principles of changing task and environmental variables to facilitate success, and the breaking down of complex tasks were not necessarily applied within some of their learning environments. It may be that teachers are unaware of the potential efficacy of task analysis as an instructional tool.

Ecological task analysis

Davis and Burton (1991) presented an alternative model of instruction, that took into account the interaction of the motor task, the environment and the capabilities of the student. Although the efficacy of the Ecological Task Analysis model has yet to be fully reported in the research literature, the approach promotes individualized instruction, student choice, and collaborative decision-making while also being applicable within the general physical education curriculum.

There are four steps to ecological task analysis. The first is to select and present the motor task specific to its function. Secondly, provide choice such that the learner determines the skill and movement form that will be executed to achieve the task. The third step involves the identification of relevant task dimensions and performer variables to determine the optimal performance level. Finally, the instructor provides direct instruction and manipulates the task variables such as rules or equipment to vary the complexity of the task and enhance learning (Rizzo *et al.* 1994).

A study by Grenier (2006) highlighted the use of a cooperative learning approach for inclusive physical education that also included elements of ecological task analysis. A cooperative learning approach was utilized as the teacher felt it promoted peer support, connection and communication. The case study was of a Third-Grade physical education class that included Jack, a student with cerebral palsy with a visual impairment. The students were sensitively grouped in a dance unit and given task sheets to complete (e.g. with a partner, slide across the room) and asked to problem-solve solutions. In this instance, Jack's participation involved beating out the rhythm with a drum and stick while his classmates skipped and slid as they created their dances. Although the student was not participating using the same movement forms as his classmates he stated that his movement was 'like a butterfly . . . My hands can feel what your legs are feeling'. His statement was not one of exclusion or embarrassment, but reflected an understanding of the motor tasks and choice in movement form.

Although the student was meaningfully involved in the activity, ironically, the teacher acknowledged that her approach was unusual, yet questioned whether others would think it was physical education as she did not assume a command style of teaching. Furthermore, even at this young age, Jack's participation was not always accepted by his classmates, even when his role was modified to that of a support role. Not being able to turn the rope so his classmates could successfully complete the task sheet for jumping rope resulted in the rope being given to a classmate, him withdrawing and being eliminated from subsequent group discussions related to the activity. In this instance, unguided cooperative learning did not resolve a successful outcome for all members of the group.

Other teaching supports

Stainback and Stainback (1990) advocate support networking for teachers in inclusive educational settings. Among their suggested supports were parents, students, administrators, instructional assistants, specialists, and other educators. For the purposes of this discussion, students, instructional assistant and specialists will be reviewed.

Peer tutors

Peer tutoring relationships between students with and without disabilities have provided unique opportunities to individualize programmes, increase engaged instruction time, foster interdependence, promote social goals, decrease paraprofessional costs, and develop positive attitudes towards people with disabilities (Block *et al.* 1995).

Same age and cross-aged support from peers who received instruction on how to be effective peer tutors (e.g. minimal prompting, modelling, physical assistance, positive general and specific feedback), in advance of providing peer support to students with disabilities in general physical education has been demonstrated to enhance motor engagement (Lieberman Dunn *et al.* 2000; Lieberman *et al.* 1997), motor performance (Houston- Wilson *et al.* 1997) and/or attitude toward disability by non-disabled classmates (Block and Zeman 1996; Murata and Jansma 1997).

The impact of peer support on the recipient has received little research attention, in part because of the meritorious quality ascribed to helping others and the assumption that more is better in inclusive instructional settings (Goodwin 2001). The studies reviewed did not indicate the presence of peer tutor support, although interactions with classmates were foundational to experiences of students with disabilities. Researchers have recognized that the intentions and attitudes of classmates can play a role in the inclusion of students with disabilities (Hutzler 2003). The findings of studies addressing the attitudes of students without disabilities toward their classmates with disabilities have been somewhat disappointing. A study by Tripp *et al.* (1995) revealed that contact with students with disabilities in a general physical education class setting did not affect attitudes of students without disabilities. It should be noted that there was no systematic attempt to structure contact between students with and without disabilities. Similar findings were reported by Slininger *et al.* (2000) even though structured contact was implemented in a Fourth-Grade class which required two peers to stay within arm's length of two students who had intellectual disabilities and used wheelchairs. Following four weeks of structured contact, attitude changes were not noted.

Instructional assistants

The inclusion of students with disabilities in general education settings has changed the traditional role of teachers (Wallace *et al.* 2001). The solitary adult in charge of a group of relatively homogeneous students is the exception, rather than the rule (Giangreco *et al.* 2002). Instructional assistants (IAs), also referred to as teacher aides, support assistants or paraeducators, have become permanent additions to educational settings, hired to support the increasing number of students with disabilities. Although IAs have become the primary method for operationalizing inclusive education and are credited with being foundational to its success (Giangreco and Doyle 2002; Wolery *et al.* 1995), high turnover rates and increasing difficulty recruiting qualified people have been blamed on poorly defined job descriptions, lack of respect, lack of orientation and low pay (French and Chopra 1999; Kozleski *et al.* 2000).

Teachers have worked with instructional assistants since the early 1980s, yet little empirical research has been conducted to identify the skills teachers need to successfully supervise the support provided by IAs (French and Pickett 1997; Mueller and Murphy 2001). As a result, teachers have been left to determine for themselves how best to work with IAs (French and Pickett 1997). Moreover, massive hirings of IAs to meet the ideology of inclusive education outpaced the conceptualization of team roles and responsibilities (Giangreco *et al.* 1997). Much of the information pertaining to IA support is not grounded in data-based research but educational ideology which has a deep sense of 'what is right' (French 2001; Giangreco *et al.* 2001; Langone 1998).

It was only in the late 1990s that theoretically – and empirically – based studies began to raise questions about the efficacy and outcomes of IA education models (Freschi 1999; Jones and Bender 1993). While a better prepared, supervised and stable workforce is without question beneficial to students' programming, what have been labelled first generation issues have not given way to more central questions such as: Can IA support be counterproductive to students? Are IA dependent programmes appropriate? What is the efficacy of instructional assistants on skill competency, motivation or rates of participation? Does IA support contribute to social isolation? Are IA instructional models ethical given their possible link to dependency (French and Chopra 1999; Giangreco *et al.* 1997; Giangreco *et al.* 2001; Giangreco *et al.* 2003)?

IAs have been reported to present both physical and symbolic barriers to students with disabilities. Giangreco and colleagues (1997) found that IA proximity can interfere with programme ownership and responsibility for students with disabilities resulting in separation from classmates, dependence on adults and limited access to competent teacher instruction. Instructional assistants have also been observed to maintain physical contact by holding wheelchairs, sitting immediately next to the student, and accompanying the student to virtually every location in the school. The stigma that can be associated with being assigned an IA is evident. One can only infer the impact of this level of adult attention on the constructs of self-esteem, self-efficacy, and self-determination. Parents have also expressed concern over their children becoming passive recipients of unneeded, overindulgent and overprotective assistance, failing to attempt tasks of which they are capable (French and Chopra 1999). Undermining parent efforts to develop and reinforce self-determined behaviour creates home-school tensions (Field and Hoffman 1998). Suggestions for fading supports, relying on natural supports, and exploring differentiated teacher roles have only recently been proposed as alternatives to IA support (Mueller and Murphy 2001; Schepis *et al.* 2000).

The use of IAs is often recommended as being *fundamental* to the success of students with disabilities in physical education (Block 2000). The few studies that do focus on IA support in physical education are ideological musing on best practice, often citing 'do's and don'ts' (e.g. Hardy 1980; Horton 2001; Murata and Hodge 1997; O'Connor and McCuller 1997; Thompson and Edwards 1994). And yet, the mechanisms and efficacy of these recommendations are not well understood.

Murata and Jansma (1997) presented a model for paraprofessional support for high school students with intellectual and behaviour learning challenges in general physical education. The model involved paraprofessional and peer tutors who received an instructional programme prior to entering the general physical education setting. The resulting activity and knowledge time percentages were significantly higher when the students were assisted by the paraprofessional and peer tutor support than by teacher support in isolation. In one of the few studies that acknowledged the impact of paraprofessionals on general physical education, Lienert *et al.* (2001) noted that, of the fourteen teachers interviewed, 15 per cent of them delegated the instruction of the students with disabilities to the paraprofessionals. LaMaster *et al.* (1998) reported that paraprofessionals can carry high case loads and lack background information in physical education. The combination of deferring instruction and poorly prepared paraprofessionals is a less than ideal educational model of support.

As with peer tutors, the students of the studies reviewed did not speak of the support of paraprofessionals. It is unclear if they were present and not mentioned, or if the students participated in physical education without instructional assistant support. The utilization of adult instructional assistants and the experiences of students in inclusive physical education is an area in need of investigation.

Informing inclusive physical education practice

Phenomenological seeing of the lived experiences of students with disabilities, the listening to stories and making the stories of physical education meaningful to ourselves and others through student voice is not enough (Connelly 1995). There is the danger of celebrating their voices, after which we return to the everyday rather than being challenged to stimulate change (Brooker and MacDonald 1999). Biklen (2000: 351) very eloquently stated:

> The requested role of educators then is not to define who people are and aren't or, for that matter, what they can be expected to be, but to be supportive in seeking strategies that could foster an unfolding life.

Adapted physical education scholars are asking far-reaching questions. Are the traditions of inclusive physical education practice routed in/informed by the medical model of disability that pathologizes function against normative standards thereby creating a deficit model of disability that privileges developmentally determined motor competence over other abilities and outcomes of participation (Grenier 2006)? What are the inclusion practices that are effective for the inclusion of students with disabilities and how does this mesh with our current practice (LaMaster *et al.* 1998)? These questions and others can be answered by relational knowing that is sensitive to and responsive to the student experience.

Doubt and McColl (2003) concluded that although social acceptance is important, physical and psychological conformity is particularly challenging for students with disabilities. Physical conformity is an unrealistic goal and psychological conformity potentially promotes denial of disability which has negative implications on identity. Spending time in an environment oriented toward non-disabled students can reinforce that disability is a problem.

Students with disabilities may already have understandings of the social meaning of disability and they and their teachers, peers and curriculum makers would benefit from opportunities for the students to share their understanding of the social construction of disability alongside other important discussions of gender, race and ethnicity (Biklen 2000). Students may possess the experiences, skills and knowledge that enable them to be active learners. They may also have developed strategies for interacting with their world that can make them agents in their own learning should they be asked and provided with opportunities to explore and engage in the activities of physical education (Biklen 2000). The challenge is to create learning environments that honour the disability experience and seek to understand and incorporate disability knowledge in curriculum, instructional strategies and the application of other teaching resources.

Learning from the students

What have we learned from the students who shared their experiences through the nine studies that were reviewed?

1 Student experiences can serve as points of reflection for teachers in the evaluation of their own programmes (Blinde and McCallister 1999). It is only through the eyes of students that programmes can honour their learning. Talk to students, listen carefully and respond to what was learned together.
2 Students with disabilities enjoy physical activity and want to engage in the same activities as their peers without disabilities. This is particularly true when programmes promote social acceptance, a sense of belonging, provide instrumental support that encourages success and enable students to demonstrate their motor and social competence. Tactful pedagogy is required: 'the transformation of consciousness that takes place is the intersection of three agencies – teacher, the learner and the knowledge they together produce' (Lusted 1986: 3).
3 Listening to students may facilitate choice in movement forms that can be used to complete motor tasks thereby emphasizing individualized outcomes and de-emphasizing traditional approaches to the teaching of team sports (Blinde and McCallister 1999).
4 Numerous instructional strategies exist. Teachers need to be armed with a tool kit of approaches and strategies that can support individualization of programmes toward the success of students. Supporting teachers will ultimately support student success (Soodak *et al.* 1998).
5 The social dynamics of the physical education programme needs to be carefully monitored. Teacher strategies that encourage exclusion (e.g. student selected groups) should be minimized and peer to peer ridicule should be discouraged and used as an opportunity to address discrimination and ableism (Blinde and McCallister 1999). Disability awareness education, although demonstrating mixed results in the research may provide a mechanism for creating a sensitive learning environment. Contradictory findings on the benefits of disability awareness education on peer attitudes toward peers with disabilities are reported. In a non-control group study by Loovis and Loovis (1997) in which blindfolds, wheelchairs, and sign language were used to simulate disabilities for 430 Second- to Sixth-Graders, females showed statistically significant improvement in attitudes while the males did not. Lockhart *et al.* (1998) in marked contrast found that there were no changes in attitudes of females or males across three different intervention groups in: (a) cognitive empathy education (e.g. factual information on orthopedic disabilities), (b) affective empathy education prompted by disability simulations and (c) no disability education (control group). Parents, although not discussed in this chapter, are a resource that can be a source of information on

disability and a support to teachers and students alike (An and Goodwin 2007).

6 No student should be perceived to be an object of curiosity. It is only through persistent observation and listening to students that hidden social consequences can be identified. Hidden consequences emphasize the importance of observation time and opportunities for students to discuss their experiences in physical education (Suomi *et al.* 2003).

7 Peer support has a positive role to play when it is appropriately facilitated and supports specific goals (Goodwin 2001). However, peer support and peer tutoring should be monitored. Peer interactions can result in undesirable social outcomes when they detract from independence, are unwanted, or are provided because of perceptions of incompetence.

8 Engage students in curriculum making. They are experts in their own right. Childrens' worlds are not those of adults and they deserve to be more than passive learners in what should be a dynamic educational setting (Brooker and MacDonald 1999).

9 Teachers need to give themselves permission to bring innovation to their interpretation of the curriculum. Traditional teaching styles that reinforce rigid developmental sequences can exclude students from participation and reinforce differences.

10 Empirically based guidelines for determining when a student with a disability may need IA support and the potential drawbacks associated with one-on-one support are limited (Freschi 1999; Giangreco *et al.* 1999; Mueller and Murphy 2001). Understanding the experiences of students in this area are needed.

11 The student voice studies reviewed predominantly utilized phenomenological or phenomenological like approaches. Alternate research approaches are required to expand our current knowledge base. A student-led participatory research approach undertaken by Fitzgerald *et al.* (2003) holds promise for placing value on student voices, promoting dialogue between students and teachers, and enabling students to develop skills for enhancing their reflective capacity. The authors conducted two case studies and involved the students directly in conducting interviews, creating and administering surveys, taking photographs and the designing of posters.

Acknowledgement

This chapter was written with the support of The Social Sciences and Humanities Research Council of Canada.

Note

1 I use the notion of 'general physical education' throughout this chapter. By doing this I am referring to what some readers may term 'mainstream physical education'.

References

Allport, G.W. (1954) *The Nature of Prejudice*, Cambridge: Addison-Wesley.

An, J.I. and Goodwin, D.L. (2007) 'Physical Education for Students with Spina Bifida: Mothers' Perspectives', *Adapted Physical Activity Quarterly*, 24 (1): 38–58.

Balan, C.M. and Davis, W.E. (1993) 'Ecological Task Analysis: An Approach to Teaching Physical Education', *Journal of Physical Education, Recreation, and Dance*, 64 (9): 54–61.

Biklen, D. (2000) 'Constructing Inclusion from Critical Disability Narratives', *International Journal of Inclusive Education*, 4 (4): 337–53.

Blinde, M.E. and McAllister, S.G. (1998) 'Listening to the Voices of Students with Disabilities', *Journal of Physical Education, Recreation, and Dance*, 69, 64–8.

Block, M.E. (1996) 'Modify Instruction: Include All Students', *Strategies*, 9 (4): 9–12.

Block, M.E. (2000) *A Teacher's Guide to Including Children with Disabilities in General Physical Education*, Baltimore, MD: Brookes.

Block, M.E. and Obrusnikova, I. (2007) 'Inclusion in Physical Education: A Review of the Literature from 1995–2005', *Adapted Physical Activity Quarterly*, 24 (2): 103–24.

Block, M.E. and Rizzo, T.L. (1995) 'Attitudes and Attributes of Physical Education Teachers Towards Including Students with Severe and Profound Disabilities into Regular Physical Education', *Journal of the Association of Persons with Severe Handicaps*, 20: 80–7.

Block, M.E. and Vogler, E.W. (1994) 'Inclusion in Regular Physical Education: The Research Base', *Journal of Physical Education, Recreation, and Dance*, 65 (1): 40–4.

Block, M.E. and Zeman, R. (1996) 'Including Students with Disabilities into Regular Physical Education: Effects on Nondisabled Children', *Adapted Physical Activity Quarterly*, 13 (1): 38–49.

Block, M.E., Oberweiser, B. and Bain, N. (1995) 'Using Classwide Peer Tutoring to Facilitate Inclusion of Students with Disabilities in Regular Physical Education', *Physical Education*, 53 (1): 47–56.

Britzman, D.P. (1989) 'Who Has the Floor? Curriculum, Teaching, and the English Student Struggle for Voice', *Curriculum Inquiry*, 20 (2): 143–62.

Brooker, R. and MacDonald, D. (1999) 'Did We Hear You? Issues of Student Voice in a Curriculum Innovation', *Journal of Curriculum Studies*, 31 (1): 83–97.

Butler, R.S. and Hodge, S.R. (2004) 'Social Inclusion of Students with Disabilities in Middle School Physical Education Classes', *Research in Middle Level Education* (Internet), 27: 1–10, available from: www.nmsa.org/Publications/RMLEOnline/tabid/101/Default.aspx (accessed 16 February 2008).

Castaneda, L. and Sherrill, C. (1999) 'Family Participation in Challenger Baseball: Critical Theory Perspectives', *Adapted Physical Activity Quarterly*, 16 (4): 372–88.

Chandler, J.P. and Greene, J.L. (1995) 'A Statewide Survey of Adapted Physical Education Service Delivery and Teacher In-Service Training', *Adapted Physical Activity Quarterly*, 12 (3): 262–74.

Connolly, M. (1995) 'Phenomenology, Physical Education, and Special Populations', *Human Studies*, 18 (1): 25–40.

Davis, W. (1989) 'Utilizing Goals in Adapted Physical Education', *Adapted Physical Activity Quarterly*, 6 (3): 205–16.

Davis, W.E. and Burton A.W. (1991) 'Ecological Task Analysis: Translating Movement Behaviour into Practice', *Adapted Physical Activity Quarterly*, 8 (2): 154–77.

DePauw, K. (1996) 'Students with Disabilities in Physical Education', in S. Silverman and C. Ennis (eds), *Student Learning in Physical Education*, Champaign, IL: Human Kinetics, pp. 101–24.

DePauw, K.P. and Doll-Tepper, G. (2000) 'Toward Progressive Inclusion and Acceptance: Myth or Reality? The Inclusion Debate and Bandwagon Discourse', *Adapted Physical Activity Quarterly*, 17 (1): 135–43.

DePauw, K.P. and Goc Karp, G. (1994) 'Integrating Knowledge of Disability throughout the Physical Education Curriculum: An Infusion Approach', *Adapted Physical Activity Quarterly*, 11 (1): 3–13.

Doubt, L. and McCall, M. (2003) 'A Secondary Guy: Physically Disabled Teenagers in Secondary Schools', *The Canadian Journal of Occupational Therapy*, 70 (3): 139–51.

Downing, J.H. and Rebollo, J. (1999) 'Parents' Perceptions of the Factors Essential for Integrated Physical Education Programs', *Remedial and Special Education*, 20 (3): 152–9.

Field, S. and Hoffman, A. (1998) 'The Importance of Family Involvement for Promoting Self-Determination in Adolescents with Autism and other Developmental Disabilities', *Focus on Autism and Other Developmental Disabilities*, 14 (1): 36–41.

Fiorini, J., Stanton, K. and Reid, G. (1996) 'Understanding Parents and Families of Children with Disabilities: Considerations for Adapted Physical Activity', *Palaestra*, 12 (2): 16–23, 51.

Fitzgerald, H., Jobling, A. and Kirk, D. (2003) 'Valuing the Voices of Young Disabled People: Exploring Experience of Physical Education and Sport', *European Journal of Physical Education*, 8 (2): 175–200.

Folsom-Meek, S.L. (1984) 'Parents: Forgotten Teacher Aides in Adapted Physical Education', *Adapted Physical Activity Quarterly*, 1 (4): 275–81.

Folsom-Meek, S.L., Nearing, R.J. and Kalakian, L.H. (2000) 'Effects of an Adapted Physical Education Course in Changing Attitudes', *Clinical Kinesiology*, 5 (3): 52–8.

French, N.K. (2001) 'Supervising Paraprofessionals: A Survey of Teacher Practices', *Journal of Special Education*, 35 (1): 41–53.

French, N. and Chopra, R.V. (1999) 'Parent Perspectives on the Roles of Para-Professionals', *Journal of the Association for Persons With Severe Handicaps*, 24: 259–72.

French, N.K. and Pickett, A.L. (1997) 'Paraprofessionals in Special Education: Issues for Teacher Educators', *Teacher Education and Special Education*, 20 (1): 61–73.

Freschi, D.E. (1999) 'Guidelines for Working with One-to-One Aides', *Teaching Exceptional Children*, 31 (4): 42–7.

Giangreco, M.F. and Doyle, M.B. (2002) 'Students with Disabilities and Para-Professional Supports: Benefits, Balance, and Band-Aids', *Focus on Exceptional Children*, 34 (7): 1–12.

Giangreco, M.F., Broer, S.M. and Edelman, S.W. (1999) 'The Tip of the Iceberg: Determining whether Paraprofessional Support is Needed for Students with Disabilities in General Education Settings', *Journal of the Association for Persons with Severe Handicaps*, 24: 280–90.

Giangreco, M.F., Broer, S.M. and Edelman, S.W. (2001) 'Teacher Engagement with Students with Disabilities: Differences between Paraprofessional Service Delivery Models', *Journal of the Association of Persons with Severe Handicaps*, 26: 75–86.

Giangreco, M.F., Broer, S.M. and Edelman, S.W. (2002) '"That Was Then, This Is Now!" Paraprofessional Supports for Students with Disabilities in General Education Classrooms', *Exceptionality*, 10 (1): 47–64.

Giangreco, M.F., Edelman, S.W. and Broer, S.M. (2003) 'Schoolwide Planning to Improve Paraeducator Supports', *Exceptional Children*, 70 (1): 63–79.

Giangreco, M.F., Edelman, S.W., Luiselli, T.E. and MacFarland, S.C. (1997) 'Helping or Hovering? Effects of Instructional Assistant Proximity on Students with Disabilities', *Exceptional Children*, 64 (1): 7–18.

Goodwin, D.L. (2001) 'The Meaning of Help in PE: Perceptions of Students with Physical Disabilities', *Adapted Physical Activity Quarterly*, 18 (3): 144–60.

Goodwin, D.L. (2003) 'Instructional Approaches to the Teaching of Motor Skills', in R.D. Steadward, G.D. Wheeler and E.J. Watkinson (eds), *Adapted Physical Activity*, Edmonton, AB: University of Alberta Press, pp. 255–84.

Goodwin, D.L. and Staples, K. (2005) 'The Meaning of Summer Camp Experiences to Youth with Disabilities', *Adapted Physical Activity Quarterly*, 22 (2): 160–78.

Goodwin, D.L. and Watkinson, E.J. (2000) 'Inclusive Physical Education from the Perspective of Students with Physical Disabilities', *Adapted Physical Activity Quarterly*, 17 (2): 144–60.

Goodwin, D.L., Watkinson, E.J. and Fitzpatrick, D. (2003) 'Inclusive Physical Education: A Conceptual Framework', in R.D. Steadward, G.D. Wheeler and E.J. Watkinson (eds), *Adapted Physical Activity*, Edmonton, AB: University of Alberta Press, pp. 189–212.

Goodwin, D.L., Gustafson, P. and Hamilton, B.N. (2006) 'The Experience of Disability in Physical Education', in E. Singleton and A. Varpalotai (eds), *Stones in the Sneaker: Active Theory for Secondary School Physical and Health Educators*, London, ON: Althouse Press, pp. 223–53.

Grenier, M. (2006) 'A Social Constructionist Perspective of Teaching and Learning in Inclusive Physical Education', *Adapted Physical Activity Quarterly*, 23 (3): 245–60.

Grenier, M. (2007) 'Inclusion in Physical Education: From the Medical Model to Social Constructionism', *Quest*, 59 (3): 298–310.

Hall, J.P. (2002) 'Narrowing the Breach: Can Disability Culture and Full Educational Inclusion be Reconciled?', *Journal of Disability Policy Studies*, 13 (3): 144–53.

Hamilton, M., Goodway, J. and Haubenstricker, J. (1999) 'Parent-Assisted Instruction in a Motor Skill Program for At-Risk Preschool Children', *Adapted Physical Activity Quarterly*, 16 (4): 416–26.

Hardin, B. (2005) 'Physical Education Teachers' Reflections on Preparations for Inclusion', *The Physical Educator*, 62: 44–56.

Hardy, R. (1980) 'Paraprofessionals in Physical Education: Guidelines and Performance Responsibilities', *The Physical Educator*, 8: 97–98.

Horton, M.L. (2001) 'Utilizing Paraprofessionals in the General Physical Education Setting', *Teaching Physical Education*, 12 (6): 22–5.

Hodge, S.R., Ammah, J.O., Casebolt, K., LaMaster, K. and O'Sullivan, M. (2004) 'High School General Physical Education Teachers' Behaviors and Beliefs Associated with Inclusion', *Sport, Education and Society*, 9 (4): 395–419.

Houston-Wilson, C., Dunn, J.M., van der Mars, H. and McCubbin, J. (1997) 'The Effect of Peer Tutors on Motor Performance in Integrated Physical Education Classes', *Adapted Physical Activity Quarterly*, 14 (4): 298–313.

Hutzler, Y. (2003) 'Attitudes Toward Participation of Individuals with Disabilities in Physical Education: A Review', *Quest*, 55 (4): 347–73.

Hutzler, Y., Fliess, O., Chacham, A. and Van den Auweele, Y. (2002) 'Perspective of Children with Physical Disabilities on Inclusion and Empowerment: Supporting and Limiting Factors', *Adapted Physical Activity Quarterly*, 19 (3): 300–17.

Jones, K.H. and Bender, W.N. (1993) 'Utilization of Paraeducators in Special Education: A Review of the Literature', *Remedial and Special Education*, 14 (1): 7–14.

Kelly, L.E. (1994) 'Preplanning for Successful Inclusive Schooling', *Journal of Physical Education, Recreation and Dance*, 65 (1): 37–9.

Kozleski, E., Mainzer, R. and Deshler, D. (2000) 'Bright Futures for Exceptional Learners: An Action Agenda to Achieve Quality Conditions for Teaching and Learning', *Teaching Exceptional Children*, 32 (6): 56–69.

Kozub, F.M. and Lienert, C. (2003) 'Attitudes Toward Teaching Children with Disabilities: Review of Literature and Research Paradigm', *Adapted Physical Activity Quarterly*, 20 (4): 323–46.

Kristen, L., Patriksson, G. and Fridlund, B. (2003) 'Parents' Conceptions of the Influences of Participation in a Sports Programme on Their Children and Adolescents with Physical Disabilities', *European Physical Education Review*, 9 (1): 23–41.

LaMaster, K., Gall, K., Kinchin, G. and Siedentop, D. (1998) 'Inclusion Practices of Effective Elementary Specialists', *Adapted Physical Activity Quarterly*, 15 (1): 64–81.

Langone, J. (1998) 'Managing Inclusive Instructional Settings: Technology, Cooperative Planning, and Team-Based Organization', *Focus on Exceptional Children*, 30 (8): 1–15.

Lieberman, L., Houston-Wilson, C. and Kozub, F.M. (2002) 'Perceived Barriers to Including Students with Visual Impairments in General Physical Education', *Adapted Physical Activity Quarterly*, 19 (3): 364–77.

Lieberman, L.J., Newcomer, J., McCubbin, J. and Dalrymple, N. (1997) 'The Effects of Cross-Aged Peer Tutors on the Academic Learning Time of Students with Disabilities in Inclusive Elementary Physical Education Classes', *Brazilian International Journal of Adapted Physical Education Research*, 4 (1): 15–32.

Lieberman, L.J., Dunn, J.M., van der Mars, H. and McCubbin, J. (2000) 'Peer Tutors' Effects on Activity Levels of Deaf Students in Inclusive Elementary Physical Education', *Adapted Physical Activity Quarterly*, 17 (1): 20–39.

Lienert, C., Sherrill, C. and Myers, B. (2001) 'Physical Educators' Concerns about Integrating Children with Disabilities: A Cross-Cultural Comparison', *Adapted Physical Activity Quarterly*, 18 (1): 1–17.

Lockhart, R.C., French, R. and Gench, B. (1998) 'Influence of Empathy Training to Modify Attitudes of Normal Children in Physical Education toward Peers with Physical Disabilities', *Clinical Kinesiology*, 52: 36–41.

Loovis, E.M. and Loovis, C.L. (1997) 'A Disability Awareness Unit in Physical Education and Attitudes of Elementary School Students', *Perceptual and Motor Skills*, 84: 768–70.

Lusted, D. (1986) 'Why pedagogy', *Screen*, 27: 2–14.

Low, J. (1996) 'Negotiating Identities, Negotiating Environments: An Interpretation of the Experiences of Students with Disabilities', *Disability and Society*, 11 (2): 235–48.

Mueller, P.H. and Murphy, F.V. (2001) 'Determining When a Student Requires Paraeducator Support', *Teaching Exceptional Children*, 33 (6): 22–7.

Mulderij, K.J. (1996) 'Research in the Lifeworld of Physically Disabled Children', *Child: Care, Health and Development*, 22: 311–22.

Mulderij, K.J. (1997) 'Peer Relations and Friendship in Physically Disabled Children', *Child: Care, Health and Development*, 23: 379–89.

Murata, N.M. and Hodge S.R. (1997) 'Training Support Personnel for Inclusive Physical Education', *Journal of Physical Education, Recreation and Dance*, 68 (9): 21–5.

Murata, N.M. and Jansma, P. (1997) 'Influence of Support Personnel on Students With and Without Disabilities in General Physical Education', *Clinical Kinesiology*, 51: 37–46.

Murata, N.M., Hodge, S.R. and Little, J.R. (2000) 'Students' Attitudes, Experiences, and Perspectives on their Peers with Disabilities', *Clinical Kinesiology*, 54: 59–66.

O'Connor, J. and McCuller, S. (1997) 'Training Paraprofessionals to Work in an Inclusive Physical Education Setting', *LAHPERD Journal*, 61 (1): 9–11.

Place, K. and Hodge, S.R. (2001) 'Social Inclusion of Students with Disabilities in General Physical Education: A Behavioral Analysis', *Adapted Physical Activity Quarterly*, 18 (4): 389–404.

Praisner, C.L. (2003) 'Attitudes of Elementary School Principals Toward the Inclusion of Students with Disabilities', *Exceptional Children*, 16 (2): 135–46.

Rizzo, T.L., Davis, W.E. and Toussaint, R. (1994) 'Inclusion in Regular Classes: Breaking from Traditional Curricula', *Journal of Physical Education, Recreation and Dance*, 65 (1): 37–9, 56.

Rizzo, T.L. and Vispoel W.P. (1991) 'Physical Educators' Attributes and Attitudes Toward Teaching Students with Handicaps', *Adapted Physical Activity Quarterly*, 8 (1): 4–11.

Sanders, S.W. (1996) 'Children's Physical Education Experiences: Their Interpretations Can Help Teachers', *Journal of Physical Education, Recreation and Dance*, 67 (3): 51–6.

Schepis, M.M., Ownbey, J.B., Parsons, M.B. and Reid, D.H. (2000) 'Training Support Staff for Teaching Young Children with Disabilities in an Inclusive Preschool Setting', *Journal of Positive Behavior Interventions*, 2 (3): 170–8.

Sherrill, C. and Montelione, T. (1990) 'Prioritizing Adapted Physical Education Goals: A Pilot Study', *Adapted Physical Activity Quarterly*, 7 (4): 355–69.

Slininger, D., Sherrill, C. and Jankowski, C. (2000) 'Children's Attitudes Toward Peers with Severe Disabilities', *Adapted Physical Activity Quarterly*, 17 (2): 176–97.

Smith, A. and Green, K. (2004) 'Including Pupils with Special Education Needs in Secondary School Physical Education: A Sociological Analysis of Teachers' Views', *British Journal of Sociology of Education*, 25 (5): 593–607.

Soodak, L.C., Podell, D.M. and Lehman, L.R. (1998) 'Teacher, Student and School Attributes as Predictors of Teachers' Responses to Inclusion', *Journal of Special Education*, 31 (4): 480–97.

Stainback, S. and Stainback, W. (1990) 'Inclusive Schooling', in W. Stainback and S. Stainback (eds), *Support Networks for Inclusive Schooling: Interdependent Integrated Education*. Baltimore, MA: Brookes, pp. 2–23.

Stein, J.U. (1987) 'The Myth of the Adapted Physical Education Curriculum', *Palaestra*, 37 (3): 34–7.

Suomi, J., Collier, D. and Brown, L. (2003) 'Factors Affecting the Social Experiences of Students in Elementary Physical Education Classes', *Journal of Teaching in Physical Education*, 22 (2): 186–202.

Thompson, M.M. and Edwards, R.C. (1994) 'Using Paraprofessionals Effectively in Physical Education', *Teaching Elementary Physical Education*, 5 (2): 16–17.

Tripp, A. and Rizzo, T. (2006) 'Disability Labels Affect Physical Educators', *Adapted Physical Activity Quarterly*, 23 (3): 310–26.

Tripp, A., French, R. and Sherrill, C. (1995) 'Contact Theory and Attitudes of Children in Physical Education Programs Towards Peers with Disabilities', *Adapted Physical Activity Quarterly*, 12 (4): 323–32.

Vogler, W., Koranda, P. and Romance, T. (2000) 'Including a Child with Severe Cerebral Palsy in Physical Education: A Case Study', *Adapted Physical Activity Quarterly*, 17 (2): 161–75.

Wallace, T., Shin, J., Bartholomay, T. and Stahl, B.J. (2001) 'Knowledge and Skills for Teachers Supervising the Work of Paraprofessionals', *Exceptional Children*, 67 (4): 520–33.

Welch, M. (1996). 'Teacher Education and the Neglected Diversity: Preparing Educators to Teach Students with Disabilities', *Journal of Teacher Education*, 47 (4): 355–66.

Wolery, M., Werts, M., Caldwell, N., Snyder, E. and Liskowski, L. (1995) 'Experienced Teachers' Perceptions of Resources and Supports for Inclusion', *Education and Training in Mental Retardation and Developmental Disabilities*, 30: 15–26.

6 'We want to play football'

Girls experiencing learning disabilities and football

Annette Stride

Introduction

Internationally, issues relating to equity and inclusion continue to be embedded within legislation and policy and promoted in various arenas including education, welfare and employment. For example, in the United Kingdom, the advent of Every Child Matters (DfES 2004a) and the latest additions to the Disability Discrimination Act (2005) and the Special Educational Needs and Disability Act (2001) advocate inclusive and equitable practice (see Chapter 3 for a more detailed account of these developments). Within sport, issues concerning equity and inclusion are now prominent in many organizations' agendas (Sport England 2000; The Football Association 2002 and 2003), and the British government's national strategy, Physical Education, School Sport and Club Links (PESSCL)[1] also emphasizes this aspect of work. Discussions focusing on equity usually target a number of groups including females, minority ethnic communities, disabled people, older people and those with low socio-economic status, all of whom have low levels of participation in sport (Sport England 2001a; Women's Sport and Fitness Association 2007). Much research has focused on equity and inclusion in relation to 'single issues' such as disabled people's involvement in sport (Fitzgerald 2005; Goodwin and Watkinson 2000; Sport England 2001b). Similarly, other research has focused on specific issues concerned with gender and sport (Jinxia and Mangan 2002; Hall 2003; Williams 2003). Like poststructuralist feminists (Azzarito and Solomon 2005; Oliver *et al.* 2007), I recognize the importance of moving beyond single issue research that gives primacy to one social category, instead of focusing on the intersections. By intersections I refer to the interconnections and interdependence of one social marker, such as gender, with other categories including race, class and disability (Anthias and Yuval-Davis 1982). In this chapter, I focus on the intersection of gender *and* disability, within a football[2] specific intervention. In particular, I report on the outcomes of a small-scale research project that aimed to explore (a) the nature of football experiences encountered by the girls experiencing learning disabilities; (b) the extent to which the case study schools were supportive of the football interests of girls experiencing learning disabilities; and (c) the extent to which governing bodies of sport and other sport organizations facilitated opportunities for girls experiencing learning disabilities.

Intersecting gender, disability and football

In recent years, a number of high profile national development programmes have attempted to address inequalities in sports participation. In the United Kingdom, the Nike Girls in Sport Project (Institute of Youth Sport 2000), BSkyB Living for Sport Project (Holroyd and Armour 2003), and the Inclusive Fitness Initiative[3] have taken an issue specific approach in attempting to redress inequalities in sport. These programmes have undoubtedly contributed to our knowledge and understanding of various barriers and, in particular, highlighted the complexity of the challenges faced by those attempting to promote change in youth sport. On this issue Garrett (2004: 223) contends that: 'whilst the health implications of inactivity are well documented, the reasons for choosing these behaviours are complex, and related to the social, cultural and gender structure of society.'

In relation to young disabled people, research has repeatedly cited organizational, social, attitudinal and physical barriers as key contributors to low levels of participation and negative experiences of PE and youth sport. Enabling factors have also been cited that help to overcome, to some degree, negative experiences (Tregaskis 2003; Woolley *et al.* 2006). Meanwhile, concerns regarding female participation in youth sport continue to be raised and despite young women recognizing the benefits of regular activity, many do not actively engage in sport. Sleap and Wormald (2001) and Flintoff and Scraton (2001) found a range of factors adversely influencing participation including lack of time, employment, negative experiences of PE, being self-conscious of their bodies, lack of competence and confidence, transport difficulties and costs. Ennis (1999) suggests that it is not sports themselves that constrain young people's experiences but the environment in which they are undertaken. More specifically, it is claimed that sporting environments continue to be male dominated, with boys 'patrolling' girls who move into and encroach on 'their' space (McCallister *et al.* 2003).

Interestingly, in recent years football has experienced a rapid increase in participation by women and girls (The Football Association 2005). However, it is important to note that football has not always played such a significant role in their sporting lives. Williams (2003) noted a number of factors that have hindered the development of women's football including a ban on playing at the grounds used for men's games; insufficient numbers of women in decision-making roles; and lack of financial support. Moreover, it has been suggested that despite some change football is still 'a game that appears to be largely defined and controlled by White men' (Scraton *et al.* 2005: 79).

Over the past twenty years, research focusing on gender and sport has increasingly been influenced by feminist thinking and a number of 'waves' of feminism have evolved (Flintoff and Scraton 2006). Post-structuralist feminists have challenged earlier feminist thinking for being too simplistic and providing reductive explanations for women's oppression. Post-structuralists emphasize difference and diversity, moving beyond the homogenous term 'women' that fails to recognize that women are not a unified category but have multiple identities. They also view power as productive, exercised and existing in a multiplicity of sites rather than oppressive, top down and held by a single source. Furthermore post-structuralists recognize individuals as active agents who negotiate their own identities, within different contexts, transforming, resisting and challenging traditional power relations as opposed to their identities, realities and histories being defined by others (Azzarito and Solomon 2005; Flintoff and Scraton 2001).

Despite the call to recognize difference and diversity and to decentre white, middle class, heterosexual women's experiences, disability often remains at the margins of post-structuralist feminist research within PE and sport (Flintoff *et al.* 2008). Even when research has focused on disability it has often been undertaken in parallel with research exploring gender issues. There has been a limited attempt, in youth sport, to explore the interconnections between these categories and their different systems of oppression, ableism and patriarchy. West and Fenstermaker (1995: 9) call for:

> New models to rethink intersections of systems of oppression and how structures of power are organized around intersecting relations of race, class and gender to frame social positions of individuals . . . (and) to produce social locations for us all.

Their focus in rethinking intersectionality is *identity*, specifically how identities are accomplished through the interactions with others; the impact of powerful hegemonic cultures across different spaces; and how different identity markers are afforded more importance across multiple contexts and at certain times. West and Fenstermaker (1995) acknowledge that these interactions create clashes, conflicts, controversy, debates, disagreements and disputes. Thus identities are made and unmade, claimed and rejected. Valentine (2007) adds that theorizing about intersectionality in this way acknowledges that the intersections between multiple identity categories can be messy and are not always experienced in untroubled ways. Additionally, there is a recognition that individuals are active in the production of their own identities, dismissing earlier, more deterministic paradigms, that classified individuals into the fixed categories of oppressed and oppressor. Having briefly reviewed literature focusing on gender, disability and intersectionality I will move on by considering the football related programmes and pathways that are in place for girls, disabled people and girls experiencing learning disabilities.

Developments in football – pathways and programmes

The Football Association has produced a range of guidelines, policies and strategies addressing equity and inclusion. The *Opportunities For All* strategy (The Football Association 2001) identifies a number of specific initiatives targeting girls, including the 'Talent Development Programme', 'Active Sports Girls' Football Programme' and 'Girls' Football Campaign'. The Football Association has also given consideration to opportunities for disabled players and in partnership with the English Federation of Disability Sport (EFDS) and developed the 'Ability Counts' scheme (The Football Association 2004).[4] Amongst other things this scheme aims to increase local playing opportunities; improve the quality of coaching; establish a competitive structure; and develop a talent identification programme. Although the Football Association has separately recognized girls and disabled players there must also be a recognition that disabled girls are likely to be subjected to 'double oppression' as a result of the intersecting effects of patriarchy and ableism. Indeed, the challenges that this double oppression brings were illustrated in a recent Football Association Update (2006) which concluded that football for disabled women and girls has not developed as quickly as the men's game, nor have original targets been met. An exploration of the relationships between the different systems of oppression is needed in order to more fully explore the issues that girls experiencing disabilities may face.

In order to explore such relationships requires what has been described as 'relational analyses', which moves beyond more traditional methods of analyses associated with 'categorical' and 'distributive' approaches. Categorical research, for example, is useful in highlighting the differences that exist *between* categories, for example, participation rates in football for boys and girls, disabled and non-disabled people. Moreover, distributive research can be useful in identifying inequalities that exist between categories in terms of resources, access and opportunities. Within a football context this could include evaluating pitch times, coaching opportunities and sponsorship between categories. However, neither approach provides an explanation of why these differences occur nor explores the differences *within* groups. It has been suggested that relational analyses are more effective in providing these types of explanations by focusing on the social relations between different groups; exploring the hierarchies that are created by practices and discourses across different social spaces; and by looking at the macro-micro interface, the relationship between individual identities and the wider structural powers (Flintoff *et al.* 2008).

Despite research focusing on gender and sport there is a dearth of research that explores the experiences of girls experiencing learning disabilities and their involvement in football. The research reviewed in this chapter aims to contribute to discussions in this area and was undertaken within a special school and mainstream (regular) context. The following section introduces the schools, participants and data generation strategies adopted.

Research context

A case study approach was undertaken at Bryant Park Special School. Bryant Park Special School is situated in a suburb of a northern city of England and has approximately 100 students attending between the ages of 4 and 19. The students at the school experience a range of physical and learning disabilities. Bryant Park School was selected for the research as staff at the school were actively seeking to forge partnerships with other schools and community sport organizations within the area. In part this was as a result of the British government's Physical Education and School Sport Club Links strategy.[5] The research reported in this chapter focuses on a football intervention involving collaborative work with a local mainstream school, Liberty High, designated as a Specialist Sports College.[6] Six girls from Bryant Park Special School were supported to participate in an existing after-school football club based at Liberty High. In total, ten football sessions were facilitated to include the Bryant Park girls.

Semi-structured interviews were conducted with key stakeholders, including the head teacher of Bryant Park School, the football coach, School Sports Co-ordinator (SSCo) and five students experiencing learning disabilities from Bryant Park School. Where possible, repeat interviews were conducted. It was felt that approaching the research in this way would enable issues to be probed and more detail to be recalled and captured, relating to specific football experiences, during the six-month period of data generation. An important dimension of the research included gaining the insights of the girls experiencing learning disabilities participating in the football intervention. As Pitchford *et al.* (2004: 43) argue, a lack of consultation with young people can lead to 'problematic assumptions of many adult stakeholders'. In this study, I placed the students experiencing learning disabilities at the centre of my research and supplemented their insights with the perspectives of other stakeholders.

Findings – We want to play football

The challenges of change

In relation to 'the challenges of change' it became apparent that three challenges impacted upon the football intervention. Implementing change in schools, such as this football intervention, requires the commitment and enthusiasm of staff to lead and drive forward change. It was evident from the interviews that at times a number of challenges were encountered prior to, and during, the football intervention. A number of these challenges related specifically to the organization and planning of the intervention. For example, according to the head teacher, a key challenge encountered during the development of this football intervention was the lack of transport to support students to participate in the after-school club. Although some funding had been secured, this was insufficient to support all the girls at Bryant Park School who wanted to attend the club. The limited funding available was used to pay for one taxi to take the girls to the after-school club and afterwards take them home. This comment reiterates the head teacher's concern about suitable transport:

> Our biggest challenge encountered was transport. There were huge problems getting a female taxi driver on a Friday night. One driver was available with a taxi that could hold three girls. I had three more who were keen but given the geographical spread, it was not viable for them to go.

Although more girls had clearly expressed through their agency a desire to be involved in this football intervention, material constraints prevented this from happening for some girls. This challenge, relating to transport, has also been found elsewhere (Institute of Youth Sport 2000; Sleap and Wormald 2001) and seems to constrain participation for some young people in after-school clubs. The large geographical spread from which students are drawn is an issue often specific to special schools. In this intervention this prevented the possibility of car-pooling and consequently restricted the number of girls taking part in the football sessions.

Secondly, and beyond the intervention itself, the head teacher and SSCo frequently expressed concerns about the impending restructuring within the Local Education Authority (LEA) and seemed to be particularly preoccupied with the wider implications this may have on similar interventions in the future. In this environment of change, the head teacher was sceptical about the restructuring and the quality of future activity opportunities for the Bryant Park girls:

> Long-term, girls will not be coming through Bryant Park as the mainstream schools are supposed to look after their own [students experiencing learning disabilities]. The challenge for mainstream schools is how to encourage disaffected, behaviourally challenged, learning disabled individuals. If they try and provide 'special sessions' girls just won't go and that won't be good enough.

The SSCo also supported this view suggesting:

> A PE teacher will set up a segregated club, I'm not saying that's wrong but they'll do it without thinking and it may not be the best solution. You need to look at the kids first.

The implicit concern of the SSCo and head teacher seemed to be about the way in which they anticipated 'inclusion' would be operationalized in the new LEA structure. These stakeholders believed this would lead to dedicated provision (segregated clubs) that would not be well thought out. In their research, Flintoff and Scraton (2001) highlight the importance of the local context, including the culture of the school and PE department, and quality of student-teacher relations. They suggest teachers who listen to their students and recognize differences in aspirations and motivations, whilst in safe and supportive environments are more likely to be successful. This emphasizes the point that any future developments must include consultation with the young people. Indeed, the head teacher indicated that the strength of this intervention was the consultation with the girls who had been enabled to articulate their strong desire and willingness to play football: 'They were adamant they wanted to play football and they wanted to play with other girls.' This perhaps confirms MacDonald's (2002) concern for a praxis orientation. In this case the Bryant Park girls had been, to some degree, heard regarding their interests and desires.

The third key challenge emerging from the football intervention related to the sustainability of the intervention beyond the ten-week period. It was clear from the interviews with the girls from Bryant Park that there was an enthusiasm and desire to continue to participate in football:

> I wish we could still go to those [the coaching sessions]. I still play, at break times and at dinner times, but it's not the same as when we had the coach. (Edie)

> I miss the sessions and coach. I still go out with my friends, but we don't learn skills or anything. We just play a game. (Bree)

For all the Bryant Park girls football seemed to be an activity that they wanted to continue to play. However, beyond the intervention of the head teacher, the SSCo and coach seemed to have not considered or been aware of the possible player pathways that could have been accessed in order to extend activities beyond the ten-week intervention. Indeed, during the follow-up interviews with the head teacher, SSCo and the coach it was evident that there was a lack of awareness about dedicated (disability sport) player pathways. Only the SSCo mentioned a vague awareness of disability sport pathways: 'I think there are learning disability teams, but I don't know where.' Similarly, the head teacher pointed out the issues attached to encouraging the girls to go to local mainstream community football clubs:

> I'm not sure how well they would fair in that sort of environment, only because they need a lot of support, getting to the sessions and when they are there. I'm not really sure what other options would be open to them.

Apart from the possibility of further football sessions at Liberty High it seemed that the girls were not going to be supported to progress into other formal football settings such as those promoted in the Football Association's Development Strategies (2001, 2004).

Contexts of participation

Although the girls at Bryant Park school were involved in the football intervention at Liberty High school they also played football regularly, during break times, lunch times and sometimes in PE. It was apparent from the interviews with the girls that these experiences were seen as contrasting and *different*. At one level, the girls recognized the location, staff and other young participants as contributing to these differences. As Bree explained:

> At first we [the two schools] didn't mix well. They [Liberty High girls] seemed a bit funny . . . but the coach mixed us up and we got on. After the first session we knew all the names. It's not like break [time], we got some proper coaching.

What this account illustrates is that despite sharing the common identity marker of gender, there were other differences at play *within* the group such as class and disability. There may also be other dimensions to consider, for example, school affiliation and maturity levels. These differences contributed initially to the two groups remaining distinct and not fully integrating. However, over time, and with some intervention by the coach, these differences were less evident in the girls' discussions.

All the girls highlighted that the football intervention provided an opportunity to socialize with a new group of people:

> . . . I liked having a mix from two schools. (Edie)
>
> . . . enjoyed meeting new people our age. (Gaby)
>
> . . . had a right laugh with them. (Suzanne)

However, initially, according to Bree, there seemed to be some tension between the two sets of girls:

> At the start Gaby was getting picked on [by a Liberty High student] but the coach put a stop to it . . . it didn't happen again.

All too often the attitudes disabled people encounter can be as much of a barrier as can practical access issues (Tregaskis 2003). The comment from Bree does pose a question regarding Gaby's difference and why she was singled out from the other girls. Perhaps Gaby's production of her identity and the way that this was expressed within the initial football session contributed to this situation. It may be that the other girls' identities were more closely aligned to the hegemonic culture of the group and space within which they were operating.

In this intervention, apart from this initial incident, the attitude of the Liberty High students and the coach seemed to contribute to the positive experiences of the Bryant Park girls. Echoing the findings of Garrett (2004), the Bryant Park girls relished the opportunity to nurture new friendships during the intervention. Although these friendships were temporary, and constrained to within the football intervention, they were seen as a welcome change to those found at Bryant Park School:

> Not many of our [Bryant Park] girls play football, so it was good to find [Liberty High] girls who play. (Lynne)

A related issue to the girls' concern to socialize and make friends was a recognition that the Liberty High football sessions were single-sex sessions. According to the girls, this seemed to promote differing social dynamics to the Bryant Park break and lunch time football sessions. Indeed, at Bryant Park, during the informal break time sessions, boys outnumbered, and sometimes dominated, the girls. When reflecting upon these experiences girls referred to the boys as less than supportive, with negative attitudes towards both the girls' involvement in games and their playing abilities. The comment made by Lynne is similar to those made by other Bryant Park girls:

> They laugh if you don't do things right, you know, like miss a goal.

Similar to the work of McCallister *et al.* (2003), the boys are being seen to patrol the girls, through their actions and comments, as the girls move into the boys' sphere. Even when the girls were 'performing' in a way that was comparable with the boys this also seemed to be unacceptable:

> When we play with the boys they get all embarrassed when we tackle them. Some of them give me a hard time and I don't like it, feel funny, don't want to do it. (Edie)

When questioned about their interactions with boys in mixed sporting contexts, the girls suggested that the boys were often concerned that girls may be better than them. The girls believed this led to fear amongst the boys, resulting in them excluding the girls, or significantly reducing their involvement. It would appear from these comments that the informal football at Bryant Park Special School reinforced a hegemonic masculine culture. In this context, the dominant identity marker appeared to be gender. Following the Institute of Youth Sport (2000) research it appeared that the girls at Bryant Park preferred playing with other female students, in this case those at Liberty High. In this girl only environment they did not have to concern themselves with the way they were interacting and playing:

> Yeah, I have a really good laugh ... I don't have to watch what I do, the [Liberty High] girls just get on with it, no hassles. (Edie)

Within this social context the coach felt the Bryant Park girls learnt to adjust a number of aspects of their behaviour:

> It set boundaries. Early on there was some immature behaviour, which really stood out. Nothing major, some swearing, sulking, that sort of stuff. I didn't need to say anything though, it was just obvious from the responses they got that it wasn't acceptable. They changed their behaviour to fit in. Definitely, I think the [Bryant Park] girls learnt some boundaries, like socially acceptable behaviour.

In this instance, the coach recognized a positive social outcome for the Bryant Park girls.

Reflecting on the benefits

When both schools embarked on this football intervention each anticipated a range of outcomes and benefits. During the interviews all stakeholders were keen to discuss specific benefits of the intervention, including those associated with 'inclusive' provision; physical and skill development; and enhanced confidence.

The head teacher at Bryant Park believed that the intervention provided an 'unusual opportunity' for a number of reasons and felt that: 'The school is small and insular and opportunities like this help to overcome many shortcomings.' In relation to 'inclusive' provision it was felt that the intervention would provide an opportunity for the girls experiencing learning disabilities to be included in mainstream provision. The head teacher pointed out that there were limited opportunities for Bryant Park students to engage in sport with other non-disabled students. However, it also became apparent that benefits arose for both sets of girls. The head teacher indicated the intervention had opened up new possibilities for non-disabled and disabled students to participate in sport in a supportive environment:

> For the Liberty High girls the whole experience [of working with our students] probably opened their eyes a little by changing their perceptions of who goes to a special school.

The coach also believed this intervention benefited the Liberty High girls as it challenged negative stereotypical understandings of disability and students attending special schools. The coach emphasizes how this kind of experience would benefit all involved:

> I think it helped them [Liberty High students] appreciate difference ... and will be a massive influence on who they become.

From this perspective, it seems that difference, as it is expressed through inclusion, is being presented as positive rather than seen as negative or limiting. Despite the optimism of the coach we perhaps should be cautious about the longer term benefits that may come from this kind of short-term intervention.

For the coach, the 'automatic icebreaker' nature of sport helped create a positive and supportive environment. He believed the delivery strategies adopted enabled the pupils to mix well:

> Both sets of girls were shy at first, but I mixed teams, this forced them to communicate and interact. The Liberty High girls took their time though and were a bit uncertain . . . once they started playing it was OK. I think they [Liberty High] were probably intimidated at first, the Bryant Park girls were loud and a couple were swearing.

Another key benefit highlighted during the interviews concerned the development of new football skills. The head teacher at Bryant Park suggested: 'physical and skill improvements in the girls could be taken as read.' The SSCo also reported the development of some specific skills:

> They learnt tactics, and it was obvious just from the few times I watched that they had picked up skills they couldn't do before.

Research conducted by Pitchford *et al.* (2004) identified intrinsic, rather than extrinsic motivations, as being emphasized by the players. All the Bryant Park girls referred to intrinsic motivators including fitness and skill development. Here Edie talks about a number of skills:

> I think I got better at tackling and running with the ball . . . oh, and we did some goalkeeping work. I'd never done that before.

Interestingly, although all the girls recognized these kind of developments, as Lynne suggests, there was also an acknowledgement that these skills still required further development:

> I learnt about passing to teammates, like when to pass and how to swerve the ball, but I still need to work on it.

In addition to skill development the head teacher highlighted that this intervention provided an opportunity to support female only provision. He believed that as a consequence of the football intervention more football was being played at lunch and breaktimes:

> Now, more of our girls are more likely to come out at breaks and play with the boys, more than before the coaching. I'd say this is a good thing when you look at what most adolescent girls do.

The head teacher felt this was a positive trend given that many adolescent girls drop out of sport. In terms of confidence the head teacher felt some improvements had been made, although as this extract illustrates, this varied among the girls:

> It worked in different ways. For Gaby and Suzanne who are less mature their learning curve was greater and experiences were magnified. For Lynne and Bree, who had come from a mainstream school, the experience was less daunting, less new, if you like, changes were less likely.

It would appear from the data generated that two inter-related factors, the environment and skill development, contributed to enhancing confidence. The girls only environment had created a 'safe space' for them to engage, learn and develop their football experiences. In the presence of boys, the girls at Bryant Park had their behaviour and ability challenged by the boys, in an attempt to maintain a gender order. However, this was not the case in the girls only environment, which seemed to positively promote the development of new skills.

Conclusion

The research presented in this chapter focused on five young people's experiences of football. It would appear, from the data generated, that there is still work to be done to enhance the experiences of girls experiencing learning disabilities who want to play football. On the one hand, it would appear that although the key stakeholders of this intervention had good intentions they lacked an awareness of what football opportunities could be accessed beyond this ten-week intervention. This seemed to limit the extent to which the girls could progress beyond the after-school sessions. Indeed, when questioned about their engagement with football following the intervention, all girls reported that they had only continued to play in PE, at break and lunch times and at home with family and friends. Although the Football Association identifies clear player pathways the questions to be asked now would be: are these pathways being translated effectively into practice and are networks of support being communicated widely to football coaches and schools? Just like the women in Scraton *et al.*'s (2005) study negotiating by the girls at Bryant Park Special School led to increased opportunities (in this case football), albeit temporarily. Beyond these structural issues what this study illustrates is the understandings and insights that can be captured from young people, in this case, girls experiencing learning disabilities. They express a clear desire to engage in football and it seems to be an important part of their life. Like Scraton *et al.* (2005) I acknowledge the limitations of using interviews as a tool to generate data. Although useful on one level, they do not adequately capture the complex social identities or the lives of these young girls experiencing learning disabilities. We should be doing more to explore these kinds of insights.

Notes

1 PESSCL – The Government's national strategy for Physical Education, School Sport and Club Links, which has the aim of enhancing the take-up of sporting opportunities by 5–16-year-olds (DfES/DCMS, 2003).
2 It is recognized that the game of 'football' is also referred to as 'soccer' in other countries but for the purposes of this chapter it will be referred to as football.
3 For more information regarding the Inclusive Fitness Initiative see www. inclusivefitness.org
4 The Ability Counts scheme has a commitment to ensure opportunities are made available in all aspects of football regardless of a person's race, culture, religion, gender, ability, sexual orientation, ethnicity and social class (FA, 2004).
5 The PESSCL strategy has key strands, one of which is School Sport Partnerships (SSPs). SSPs are groups of schools that work together to develop partnerships and sporting opportunities for young people (DfES, 2003, 2004b).
6 Specialist Sports Colleges – These are at the hub of the PESSCL strategy. They place PE and sport at the centre of the curriculum as a vehicle to develop and improve learning opportunities for all (DfES, 2003, 2004b).

References

Anthias, F. and Yuval-Davis, N. (1982) *Racialized Boundaries*, London: Routledge.
Azzarito, L. and Solomon, M.A. (2005) 'A Reconceptualisation of Physical Education: The Intersection of Gender/Race/Social Class', *Sport, Education and Society*, 10 (1): 25–47.
Department for Education and Skills (2003) *Learning through PE and Sport*, Nottinghamshire: Department for Education and Skills Publications.
Department for Education and Skills (2004a) *Every Child Matters: Change for Children*, London: HMSO.
Department for Education and Skills (2004b) *Learning through PE and Sport: An Update on the National PE, School Sport and Club Links Strategy*, Nottinghamshire: Department for Education and Skills Publications.
Department for Education and Skills/Department for Culture, Media and Sport (2003) *Learning through PE and Sport: A Guide to the Physical Education, School Sport and Club Links Strategy*, Nottinghamshire: Department for Education and Skills Publications.
Ennis, C. (1999) 'Creating a Culturally Relevant Curriculum for Disengaged Girls', *Sport, Education and Society*, 4 (1): 31–49.
Fitzgerald, H. (2005) 'Still Feeling Like a Spare Piece of Luggage? Embodied Experiences of (Dis)Ability in Physical Education and School Sport', *Physical Education and Sport Pedagogy*, 10 (1): 41–59.
Flintoff, A. and Scraton, S. (2001) 'Stepping into Active Leisure? Young Women's Perceptions of Active Lifestyles and Their Experiences of School Physical Education', *Sport, Education and Society*, 6 (1): 5–21.
Flintoff, A. and Scraton, S. (2006) 'Girls and Physical Education', in D. Kirk, D. Macdonald and M. O'Sullivan (eds), *The Handbook of Physical Education*, London: Sage Publications, pp. 767–83.
Flintoff, A., Fitzgerald, H. and Scraton, S. (2008) 'Theorising and Researching Difference in PE: The Challenge of Intersectionality', *International Journal in the Society of Education*, 18 (2): 73–85.

Football Association (2001) *The Football Development Strategy 2001–2006*, London: The Football Association.

Football Association (2002) *Football For All*, London: The Football Association.

Football Association (2003) *Ethics and Sports Equity Strategy*, London: The Football Association.

Football Association (2004) *The Football Association's Football Development Programme Disability Football Strategy 2004–2006*, London: The Football Association.

Football Association (2005) *The Football Association Annual Review 2004–2005*, London: The Football Association.

Football Association (2006) *Football for Disabled People Strategy Update*, London: The Football Association.

Garrett, R. (2004) 'Negotiating a Physical Identity: Girls, Bodies and Physical Education', *Sport, Education and Society*, 9 (2): 223–37.

Goodwin, D.L. and Watkinson, E.J. (2000) 'Inclusive Physical Education from the Perspective of Students with Physical Disabilities', *Adapted Physical Activity Quarterly*, 17 (2): 144–60.

Hall, M.A. (2003) 'The Game of Choice: Girls' and Women's Soccer in Canada', *Soccer and Society*, 4 (2/3): 30–46.

Holroyd, R.A. and Armour, K.M. (2003), 'Re-engaging Disaffected Youth Through Physical Activity Programs', British Educational Research Association Annual Conference, Edinburgh, September.

Institute of Youth Sport (IYS) (D. Kirk, H. Fitzgerald, J. Wang and S. Biddle) (2000) *Towards Girl-Friendly Physical Education: The Nike/Youth Sport Trust 'Girls in Sport' Partnership Project, Final Report*, Loughborough: IYS.

Jinxia, D. and Mangan, J.A. (2002) 'Ascending then Descending? Women's Soccer in Modern China', *Soccer and Society*, 3 (2): 1–18.

McCallister, S.G., Blinde, E.M. and Phillips, J.M. (2003) 'Prospects for Change in a New Millenium: Gender Beliefs of Young Girls in Sport and Physical Activity', *Women in Sport and Physical Activity Journal*, 12 (2): 83–109.

MacDonald, D. (2002) 'Extending Agendas: Physical Culture Research for theTwenty-First Century', in D. Penney (ed.), *Gender and Physical Education: Contemporary Issues and Future Directions*, London: Routledge, pp. 208–22.

Oliver, K.L., Hamzeh, M., McCaughtry, N. and Chacon, E. (2007) 'Girly Girls can Play Games: 5th Grade Girls Negotiate Self-Identified Barriers to Physical Activity', paper presented at the American Educational Research Association Conference, Chicago, April.

Pitchford, A., Brackenbridge, C., Bringer, J.D., Cockburn, C., Nutt, G., Pawlaczek, Z. and Russell, K. (2004) 'Children in Football: Seen But Not Heard', *Soccer and Society*, 5 (1): 43–60.

Scraton, S., Caudwell, J. and Holland, S. (2005) ' "Bend It Like Patel": Centring "Race", Ethnicity and Gender in Feminist Analysis of Women's Football in England', *International Review for the Sociology of Sport*, 40 (1): 71–88.

Sleap, M. and Wormald, H. (2001) 'Perceptions of Physical Activity Among Young Women Aged 16 and 17 Years', *European Journal of Physical Education*, 6 (1): 26–37.

Sport England (2000) *Making English Sport Inclusive: Equity Guidelines for Governing Bodies*, London: Sport England.

Sport England (2001a) *Sports Equity Index*, London: Sport England.

Sport England (2001b) *Disability Survey 2000 – Young People with a Disability and Sport*, London: Sport England.

Stationery Office (2001) *Special Educational Needs and Disability Act (2001)*, London: Stationery Office.

Stationery Office (2005) *Disability Discrimination Act (2001)*, London: Stationery Office.

Tregaskis, C. (2003) 'Towards Inclusive Practice: An Insider Perspective on Leisure Provision for Disabled People', *Managing Leisure*, 8 (1): 28–40.

Valentine, G. (2007) 'Theorizing and Researching Intersectionality: A Challenge for Feminist Geography', *The Professional Geographer*, 59 (1): 10–21.

West, C. and Fenstermaker, S. (1995) 'Doing Difference', *Gender and Society*, 9 (1): 8–37.

Williams, J. (2003) 'The Fastest Growing Sport? Women's Football in England', *Soccer and Society*, 4 (2/3): 112–27.

Women's Sport and Fitness Association (2007) *It's Time. Future Forecast for Women's Participation in Sport and Exercise*, London: Women's Sport and Fitness Association.

Woolley, H., Armitage, M., Bishop, J. and Curtis, M. (2006) *Inclusion of Disabled Children in Primary School Playgrounds, Findings*, York: Joseph Rowntree Foundation.

7 Physical education as a normalizing practice

Is there a space for disability sport?

Hayley Fitzgerald and David Kirk

Introduction: viewing through lenses of inability

> We are seen as 'abnormal' because we are different; we are problem people, lacking the equipment for social integration. But the truth is, like everybody else, we have a range of things we *can* and *cannot* do, a range of abilities both mental and physical that are unique to us as individuals. The only difference between us and other people is that we are viewed through spectacles that only focus on our inabilities.
>
> (Brisenden 1986, cited in Shakespeare 1998: 22–3)

The inclusion of young disabled people within mainstream (physical) education has been at the forefront of international policy and programming for a number of years (Smith and Thomas 2005). However, in these new times some would suggest such developments have not changed practices in school subjects such as physical education, which continue to disadvantage many young people, including young disabled people (see Kirk 2005). Others have argued to the contrary that inclusion is morally unfair and disadvantages many young people (Barrow 2001). Both these positions expose a rather uncomfortable truth about physical education as it is currently practiced, which is that neither position, inclusion nor segregation, greatly assists young disabled people. Along with Bourdieu, we suggest that 'what is problematic is the fact that the established order is *not* problematic' (Bourdieu 1998: 56).

In this chapter, we seek to *make* problematic the established order by asking: should disability sports have a place within mainstream physical education? In seeking to answer this question we draw on data generated in an interview-based study with young disabled people and consider the way(s) in which disability sport is currently configured within physical education in relation to its position, place and value. Moreover, we utilize Bourdieu's (1990) concept of capital to understand young disabled people's experiences of physical education and disability sport. Like a number of writers within disability studies we believe Bourdieu's concept of capital bridges the structure/agency gap that limits the extent to which social and medical models can assist us to understand disability (Edwards and Imrie 2003).[1] Within physical education and youth sport research, a number of scholars have effectively employed Bourdieu's concepts and explored, among other issues, social spaces within physical education (Hunter 2004); young people, identity and physical culture (Holroyd 2003); cultural capital, masculinity and rugby union (Light and Kirk 2001); the social construction of gender (Gorely *et al.* 2003); and conceptions of 'ability' (Evans 2004). In this chapter, we seek to develop dialogue in this area and build on other recent work by focusing on issues relating to disability sport within physical education (Fitzgerald 2005).

We first of all focus on the different ways in which the identities of young disabled people are constructed within (physical) education and highlight how drawing on Bourdieu's notion of 'capital' helps us to understand the social positioning of disabled students within physical education. After this, we explore the main themes emerging from the data including: (1) 'it's just us'; (2) 'it's not a proper sport'; (3) 'people don't rate it'; (4) 'rule breakers'; and (5) 'I'd say it was a good success'. We then consider the possible consequences of these understandings for the ways in which disability sport is incorporated into physical education. In concluding we also discuss the implications these understandings may have on physical education more broadly.

Capital that counts in physical education and disability sport

> The children were constantly reminded that they were essentially different from their non-disabled peers, but they were also compelled to conform to specified ways of speaking, ways of walking, table manners and so on.
>
> (Davis and Watson 2001: 674)

As Davis and Watson indicate school is a significant site in which young disabled people begin to understand themselves and others. In this setting, the people, curriculum and organization all have a role to play in embedding and reproducing cultural norms and practices (Kirk and Colquhoun 1989). According to Priestley (1999), identities of young disabled people at school are constructed in a number of ways including 'becoming known' through institutionally embodied disciplines and discourses such as statementing, differentiation, adult support mechanisms and separate units. Informal discursive practices relating to how peers and teachers 'talk' about disabled students also contribute to identity formation. Furthermore, Priestley argues that identity is shaped by the way in which young disabled people 'make themselves known' through self-knowledge and speaking out. Identity selection is maintained through the creation of narratives about the self (Giddens 1990). Speaking out can sometimes lead to resistance of adult-formulated educational discourses and can come in many forms including silence, body language, aggression, humour and disassociation with other young disabled people (Corker 1999; Priestley 1999; Davis and Watson 2001). The way young disabled people experience physical education – the activities undertaken, the groups they are 'put in' and the way classmates and teachers perceive them – will all contribute to their understanding of self.

Within schools and mindful of the resources they provide for the construction of young people's identities, recent policy and programming developments focusing on inclusion are largely accepted as a 'good thing' and undoubtedly seen as a means of reducing the possibility of negative physical education experiences and disrupting inappropriate constructions of disability. The task remains though to generate the evidence that these new policies and practices are having the effects we would like to see. With this uncertainty in mind we focus our attentions on disability sport as this has been presented as one remedy for improving the physical education and youth sport experiences of young disabled people.

Some disability sports are adaptations of what could be considered 'mainstream sports' played by non-disabled people (for example wheelchair basketball, wheelchair tennis, seated volleyball and table cricket). Other disability sports such as goalball and boccia have been developed with specific impairment groups in mind. The *need* for adaptation or the creation of new sports would seem to signal a tension between sport, on the one hand, and disability on the other. To clarify this point, sport is about developing and refining techniques, adhering to rules and engaging in competition. For boys and men, these practices associated with sport are defining features of what Connell calls hegemonic masculinity (Connell 1995). Feminist scholars have debated the significance of this association between sport and masculinity for femininities and girls' and women's engagements with sport (Theberge 1984; Vertinsky 1992). Measured against the powerful construct of hegemonic masculinity in which physicality is so important, disability often signifies deficiency and impaired bodies are frequently viewed in negative ways. Male disabled bodies may not only be viewed as less masculine than non-disabled bodies, they also may be perceived as 'spoilt' (Goffman 1968) and 'flawed' (Hevey 1992). A tension then arises when disabled bodies engage with sport (Barton 1993). From this perspective, disability sport could be viewed as an accommodation of the symbolic importance of sport for hegemonic masculinity since these sports have been designed with disabled people in mind. 'Disabled sport' must by definition be a lesser form of sport if disability is a lesser form of being than to be non-disabled. While disability sport may be considered as 'fit for purpose' in the sense that it is 'fit for disabled people', tensions will inevitably surface around the social value attributed to ability over disability when disability sport is positioned within mainstream physical education.

Within physical education it is widely recognized that activities undertaken carry with them value and status. This can be manifested in a variety of forms including excelling or achieving performative success, participating in a high status sport, being a member of an exclusive sports club or having a certain kind of physical stature. In combination, these different forms of 'capital' contribute to the social positioning of those engaging in sport (Bourdieu 1991). According to Bourdieu capital can be considered in various forms including economic, social and cultural. Bourdieu also refers to physical capital and suggests this is the embodied state of cultural capital. Physical capital is associated with physical attributes and abilities and recognizes that the body is 'a possessor of power, status and distinctive symbolic forms, which is integral to the accumulation of various resources' (Shilling 2003: 111). It has been suggested that physical capital can be acquired and converted into other forms of capital and in this way can be used like an asset with 'exchange value' (Shilling 2003).

However, capital is neither easily acquired nor converted and individuals are limited to the levels of investment in the particular form of capital available to them. In this context, individuals are reliant on others within the 'field'[2] to recognize their capital as holding value (Shilling 2003). For example, within a sporting context, the most obvious form of conversion of physical capital is to be paid money to play sport. Another example of conversion is a person who excels in a team sport using this capital as a means of lobbying fellow teammates to support an attempt to become the next team captain. Beyond a sporting context, the same person may seek membership of an exclusive nightclub and use as leverage their sporting achievements to negotiate membership. Within physical education we need to learn more about the composition and nature of the capital held by young disabled people and the ways in which this is valued in different spheres of life.

While incorporating disability sports into physical education might make ethical sense there remain important questions unanswered about how disability sports are used within physical education, how they are valued by young disabled people and others around them, and what this all means for the ways in which disability more generally is understood.

In seeking to explore these issues we draw on data generated from two small-scale research projects that together represent fifteen focus group discussions with young disabled people attending six mainstream secondary schools in the Midlands of England. The young people participating in the research experienced a range of physical, sensory and learning disabilities. Each of the focus group discussions was recorded on an audiotape and then transcribed. The transcriptions were coded into categories, key themes developed and sorted (Glaser and Strauss 1967). Following the constant comparison method of analyzing data (Lincoln and Guba 1985) we continually reviewed and reworked these categories and themes. Analysis was conducted immediately following each focus group session. In addition to providing an ongoing and evolving insight into the data this also enabled preliminary results to be considered. Five key themes emerged from the data and provide an insight into the ways in which disability sport is configured within physical education.

The configuration of disability sport within physical education

'It's just us'

One of the distinctive features of disability sport emphasized by many of the focus group participants concerned a view that these sports were specifically for disabled students. We will see later that not all young disabled people recognized disability sports as legitimate sporting activities but rather perceived them as 'made-up sports' that other non-disabled people did not undertake. However, in either case, there was a sense that these sports were distinctively associated with young disabled people instead of all students engaging in physical education. A number of students discussed the characteristics of specific disability sports and the ways in which these features enabled participation. In this extract, we see how boccia is considered a 'good' sport for Sarah:

> Karen: [boccia] It's good for Sarah she can grip the balls and give 'em a good throw. There's no running, or that, so she's ok at boccia. It's a good disability sport for you and you can play with all us.
>
> Sarah: Karen, it's not my favourite. I like boccia games, I can be part of a team. In some sports I cannot get into them but with boccia I have a go, my throws count.

What is interesting in this comment is the understanding Karen has of Sarah's abilities and the way in which the skills related to boccia enable Sarah to participate in this sport. Indeed, Sarah also responds positively to playing boccia and is keen to highlight how she believes she is making a contribution to the game in the same way as other participants. Not all students though were complementary of disability sports and in relation to boccia Robin expressed frustration at the game's lack of dynamic movement suggesting 'the most action you get is when you collect the balls'. It would seem then, that the qualities of boccia considered as enabling for Sarah were precisely those that Robin identified as limiting. In this case, and others, it is clear that disability sports do not provide the all-encompassing solution for every disabled student. Like any physical education lesson if activities are not planned with reference to the students they are unlikely to promote skill development and be unfulfilling experiences.

Disability sports (or 'made-up' sport) were often understood by the students as activities that were undertaken as a group (of disabled students) and separate from the main physical education class. This student emphasizes a relationship between boccia and separate provision:

> Mike: It's just us doing boccia. The others don't, they do other sports.
>
> HF: What do you think about that, it just being you guys?

Mike: Yeah, well we're not with them, so it's just us. We are like away from the class. Boccia is for us so we have to be away from it.

A similar view was expressed by Kevin who suggested:

we are separate because we do different stuff. We can't do some sports so we do our own thing. I'd say we have good PE but I'd like to be with my friends.

Separation seemed to be rationalized by students on the grounds that they were engaging in different activities from the main physical education class. As Steve put it: 'We do different things, I'd say that's why we're not in the big class.' Opinion regarding the merits of this kind of separation were mixed with some students expressing relief that their classmates did not get to see them 'being really really bad at it [PE]' (Adam). In contrast, other students were concerned that they were missing important opportunities for interaction with friends. Tom was concerned a friendship with Jack would be affected because other students would use his absence from the main physical education class as an opportunity to 'take over' this friendship. The key issue at stake for students centred on maintaining their position, and associated capital, within and beyond physical education (Robbins 2000). In an era where inclusion is so vigorously promoted we wonder how this separation, both in terms of physical exclusion from the main physical education class and activity exclusion, can be justified. Indeed, promoting separate and different kinds of provision may be reinforcing negative differences between disabled and non-disabled students. From this position, this practice could be complicit in supporting other institutionally embodied disciplines and discursive practices in which young disabled students continue to 'become known' through negative and inferior representations (Priestley 1999).

'It's not a proper sport'

It is widely recognized that activities undertaken in physical education and sport carry with them value and status. Indeed, according to Bourdieu (1991), participation contributes to the social positioning of those engaging in such activities. A number of activities undertaken in physical education by the focus group students were not perceived in the same, or equal, manner as activities undertaken by other non-disabled students. One of the contexts in which students most frequently highlighted a sense of inferior status concerned their participation in disability sports during physical education. For example, at one school, the focus group students sometimes participated separately in table cricket instead of playing cricket in the main physical education class. As Anne put it: 'We get to do table cricket not grass cricket.' In this case, the students were not given the choice to participate in 'grass cricket' or table cricket; rather they were told they would have to undertake table cricket separately. The students perceived table cricket as a consolation and as having less value than playing 'proper cricket' (Robin). On a more general level, a few students conceded that on some occasions they understood that teachers would give them alternative physical education activities to undertake. However, in the case of table cricket, the students were unhappy with the alternative and at a loss to understand why they could not play 'grass cricket'. In the following exchange, students identify a number of limitations to table cricket.

> Robin: Have you seen the bat? It's for my baby brother not me!
>
> Anne: Baby balls too.
>
> Tom: Well, there is some skill needed. The bat makes, it makes things tricky . . . I just don't think we should do it in PE. Like I would say for me it's more of a fun thing, not proper exercise.

The reference to 'baby' illustrates that students considered table cricket to be inappropriate for their age and ability and subsequently holding little capital worth accumulating. The comment made by Tom during this exchange also suggests a feeling that this activity did not enable students to exhaust themselves in ways that they perceived they should within physical education. In addition to not valuing table cricket, the focus group students made similar observations about other tabletop games, boccia, parachute games and seated sports. In these contexts, comparisons were often made with other sports that were considered as holding more capital, as Keith put it: 'I want to do proper PE sports like everyone does in PE.' While on other occasions, students made comparisons with sports they had been exposed to through the popular media.

> I want to do sports from TV, like football, rugby, not boccia and gym fitness. I want to do sports like that. Some of the stuff we do is a waste of time, no one else does it so what's the point. I want to do the same, like everyone.
>
> (Michael)

In this case, it would seem there is capital to be gained by engaging in sports that are presented through the media or that are undertaken by friends. However, the students often positioned disability sports as holding limited capital. It was not only the focus group students that questioned the value of disability sport and the next theme illustrates their awareness that classmates and teachers viewed disability sport unfavourably.

'People don't rate it'

Within a school setting, social relations with teachers (Lavay 1987) and peers (Adler and Adler 1998; Ungar 2000) represent important contexts in which students are exposed to the 'talk' of others. These engagements, in part, provide the time and space in which identity is constituted and constructed (Priestley 1999; Jenkins 2002). Indeed, we have already seen the self-awareness that students have in relation to participating in disability sport. Students were also acutely aware of the ways in which others, including school staff, did not value disability sport. Their accounts include reflections of less favourable allocation of resources and limited recognition of sporting achievements. For example, at one focus group school students played boccia and occasionally attended after-school boccia sessions. Unlike other school sports teams, the boccia team did not train every week. Logistical problems relating to travelling home after clubs seemed to be a key issue. In addition, students were aware of the unavailability of a regular space to practise and play boccia, as James explained:

> Mr Jones has been trying for ages to get the gym, problem is it's used Monday, Tuesday, Wednesday, Thursday. Monday netball, Tuesday basketball, Wednesday badminton, Thursday fitness. We should have got it this term but didn't . . . we need a proper space.
>
> (James)

Although James was pleased with the occasional after-school boccia opportunities, he was far from happy with the space used to practise: 'The [dining] hall is for lunch, not sport.' In this context, it may be that the lack of regular after-school boccia and playing in the dinner hall served to reinforce the inferior value and marginality that other staff and students afforded to boccia. Therefore, attending the club, or indeed playing for the school boccia team, did not 'appropriate social energy' (Bourdieu 1986: 241).

Students who participated in community disability sport also recognized their achievements received minimal attention from school staff. In this extract, Tom discusses his participation in disability football:

> Tom: No one at school knows I play football in a team. People know I like watching but not playing. No one's interested.
>
> HF: Why do you think people are like that?
>
> Tom: When you're at school it's all to do with school. School sport is all to do with school teams, so we've got a football team and I play football but it's not for the school so it's down there. Like for me I guess people see me in PE and wouldn't believe I'm in a football team.

It would appear from Tom's reaction that more attention is given to school sports and, even though football is given high status at his school, it is specifically the school football team that is afforded the most attention. Within this school context, Tom is conforming, to some degree, by expressing an interest in a sport that is deemed to be 'popular'. However, it also seems that an interest in football needs to be articulated in a particular way in order to accumulate recognized capital. Contrary to the conclusions drawn by other writers (Walker and Kushner 1999), it would seem that the social capital often associated with the sporting participation of males was not evident in Tom's experiences of football.

At another school, James was particularly proud of the coverage he received in the school newsletter relating to his community disability football success.

> Our team won the finals of [the regional] football and school asked me for a photo and it got put in the newsletter and there was something written about the day. I got four copies gave one to me mum, nan, uncle and got one for the club. I've never been in the newsletter before and I was surprised they put it in. Erm, all my friends were coming up to me and saying you're in the newsletter, I was like 'yeah I know' and they couldn't believe I'd got in.
>
> (James)

On further discussions it was evident that the feature was in the 'Other News' rather than the 'Sports News' section. At one level, it is encouraging that the school recognized the achievements of James and publicized them. This illustrates that the school, to some degree, is recognizing the physical capital James has accumulated through his football interests and this is rewarded with exposure in the school newsletter. However, the position within the 'Other News' category perhaps demonstrates the work that still needs to be done to ensure more school staff recognize these 'sporting' achievements as comparable to those of other students.

'Rule breakers'

It was not only disabled students who participated in disability sports; in some instances these activities were imposed on non-disabled students. This practice seemed to reinforce the view that disability sports were unvalued activities. Focus group students recalled how on occasions non-disabled students who had forgotten their physical education kit or were naughty had been '*sent*' to work with them. Robin, a member of the table cricket group mentioned earlier, recalls when Jeremy was sent from the main physical education class.

> Well, there was that time when Jeremy came in. For starters he'd be late. He said he'd been sent 'cause he'd got no kit. He messed 'round and just, well messed 'round for the whole time of it and then said he'd not be forgetting his kit again, for next week.
>
> (Robin)

The rationale for this imposed membership was far from positive and instead granted on the grounds that other students failed to adhere to the rules, or expectations, of the main physical education class. According to Robin, Jeremy dismissed table cricket as a game for 'Blue Peter badge winners' and 'his gran'. Although the focus group students seemed to be annoyed by Jeremy's conduct in the lesson, they found it difficult to defend in any way the status of table cricket. Moreover, Robin was acutely aware of the broader implications their lack of defence may have on the attitudes of other students: 'Well it'll get round we play [cricket] with baby bats.' In this context, Robin was conscious of the ways in which Priestley's *et al.* (1999) 'peer talk' would impact on how the students playing table cricket were understood. 'They'll think we're babies' (Robin).

In other instances, within mainstream physical education, students recalled occasions where they had others imposed on them. During a basketball lesson two students described how they paired up together because they both use wheelchairs.

> We both use chairs so get put together in basketball. It's good 'cause we can practise passing, moving, defending. We're sitting at the same level and can work things out.
>
> (Jess)

These students were unhappy with the circumstances in which they were required to work with others, which included when other students had forgotten their kit or who were 'sitting out' because of illness or injury. Michelle describes how these students were sometimes encouraged to work with Jess and her.

> If you're sitting out you're sitting out and don't need me and Jess. I don't know what it is but Mrs Wood gets them to join us. If they're sitting out I don't want them. It's not fair on us.
>
> (Michelle)

In this situation, the physical education teacher may have been attempting to get the students who have forgotten their kit, or were ill, to engage in some activity. However, this kind of practice may reinforce a position that locates the focus group students and their physical education activities as less valued than that of other members of the class.

'I'd say it was a good success'

For many of the focus group students there was a feeling that they, and the disability sports they engaged in, were considered unfavourably and held less capital than other school sports. Indeed, we have already seen how table cricket and boccia were sometimes perceived as inferior. There were a few circumstances where specific activities were reported as holding some value. For example, Jane explained how the main physical education class had experienced three lessons of goalball.[3] The focus group students believed this sport was particularly popular with other non-disabled students.

> We have played a blind sport, have you heard of it, goalball? Everyone played and I'd say it was a good success. It got called 'Don't Dodge', I don't know why. May be 'cause you have to stop the ball. I really liked it. My sight, with me having poor sight I'm like used to the way I see. Now everyone else found it a bit scary. Once you get going, then you, well I'd say everyone got into it.
>
> (Jane)

In this instance, all students were given the opportunity in physical education to participate in goalball. Similar experiences were recalled in relation to wheelchair basketball:

> Mr Smith got some wheelchairs and we all played [wheelchair] basketball. I'd say it was the first time a lot of people had been in chairs and it was good 'cause they could see how hard it can be to control. Easy stuff and they couldn't do it like going fast backwards, turning fast, holding onto the ball and moving. I would say I was the best and a couple of them were asking for how to do things. Even Matt Jones said he'd liked it and wants to do it again.
>
> (Scott)

What these experiences illustrate are possibilities for more positive views to be constructed of disability sports. Through this limited exposure it is unlikely that these activities, or the students, will be able to gain or convert any valued capital. Although the teachers initiating the inclusion of disability sports into mainstream physical education may have had good intentions there are a series of critical questions that emerge from this practice: What is the purpose of these 'taster' lessons? Who benefits? Why don't the students experience concentrated periods of time focused on specific disability sports? Like any curriculum development, teachers need to have at least thought through these questions before they incorporate particular activities into their practice. Our concern is that this kind of piecemeal exposure reinforces the marginal position of disability sports. In other words, it is a brief experience, not leading to other activity possibilities and some may perceive this consequently enables more time to be devoted to other more legitimate sports.

Is there a space for disability sport within physical education?

In this chapter we have attempted to question the established order around notions of (dis)ability and physical education by focusing on young disabled people's views on the place of disability sport for young people as components of mainstream physical education programmes. We argued in the introduction that the current polarized positions around inclusion and segregation do not best serve the interests of young disabled people in terms of their physical education. Using disability sport as a lens, we have sought to scrutinize the extent to which physical education, as it is currently practiced in some schools in England, is fit for purpose for all young people.

Internationally, a number of programmes have been initiated which promote disability sports within physical education. At one level, the principles underpinning these programmes may seem to make ethical sense as they are supporting sports specifically designed for disabled people. However, we would suggest the inclusion of such activities within physical education raises a number of more complex issues that have not yet been explored by physical education and youth sport researchers. In particular, are disability sports serving to reinforce the inequalities that currently prevail within physical education? Should non-disabled students take part in disability sport and what may the implications of this be on disabled students and the broader physical education experience? Do disability sports, in fact, provide a different kind of vantage point to view disabled students? And if this is the case what other conditions need to be in place in order that (disability) sport is configured as a catalyst for greater equity within physical education for all young people?

The data and arguments presented in this chapter offer some initial insights into these issues. It would seem that if disability sports are included within physical education that careful consideration needs to be given to how teachers go about embedding these sports within the curriculum. For example, should disability sport be presented to all students as 'sports for all' rather than restricted to disabled students? Would adopting this strategy serve to lessen the distinction between disability and 'mainstream' sport? Or might this kind of strategy create an even wider gap between understandings of sporting ability? In this respect, the inclusion of disability sports may reinforce, rather than disrupt, normative paradigms that currently place greater value and status on 'mainstream' sport within physical education (Barton 1993; Fitzgerald 2005). At the very least, we believe young people should have the opportunity to critically assess the relationships between sport, hegemonic masculinity, (dis)ability, normativity and otherness in tandem with their practical engagement in disability sport, perhaps modelled on the 'cultural studies' approach developed by Kinchin and O'Sullivan (2003).

Another argument that could be presented is that there is no place for disability sports within physical education. This is not to suggest that those schools that presently do not offer such opportunities are 'doing it right'. Rather the absence of disability sport, along with rethinking the position of other sports, should be seen as a more radical attempt to develop a physical education curriculum that works towards rearticulating notions of ability (Evans 2004) in order that the normalized physical education habitus can be disrupted (Gorely *et al.* 2003). Indeed, the work of Kirk and Tinning (1994) and Oliver and Lalik (2001) perhaps provides some guidance in relation to this issue and signals a move towards teaching through a critical analysis of the body and supporting young people to become critical consumers of corporal information. By working in this way, articulations of ability can be recast and understood in ways that extend beyond narrowly defined measures of performance and normative conceptions of what it is to have a sporting body.

Notes

1 Debates about understandings of disability are not merely limited to critiques between medical and social model supporters. In particular, some social models advocates continue to deliberate the extent to which 'individual experiences' of impairment can be incorporated into understandings of disability (Patterson and Hughes 2000).
2 Bourdieu has been reluctant to encourage a specific definition of fields. However, he has offered this overview: 'A field may be defined as a network, or a configuration, of objective relations between positions. These positions are objectively defined, in their existence and in the determinations they impose upon their occupants, agents or institutions, by their present and potential situation (*situs*) in the structure of the distribution of species of power (or capital) whose possession commands access to specific profits that are at stake in the field, as well as by their objective relation to otherpositions (domination, subordination, homology, etc.)' (Bourdieu and Wacquant 2002: 97).
3 Goalball is a Paralympic team sport played with three visually impaired players on each team. All players wear blindfolds and the aim of the game is to roll the bell ball past the opposition defence and into the opponent's goal.

References

Adler, P.A. and Adler, P. (1998) *Peer Power: Preadolescent Culture and Identity*, New Brunswick, NJ: Rutgers University Press.

Barrow, R. (2001) 'Inclusion vs Fairness', *Journal of Moral Education*, 30 (3): 235–42.

Barton, L. (1993) 'Disability, Empowerment and Physical Education', in J. Evans (ed.), *Equality, Education and Physical Education*, London: Falmer Press, pp. 43–54.

Bourdieu, P. (1986) 'The Forms of Capital', in J. Richardson (ed.), *Handbook of Theory and Research for the Sociology of Education*, New York: Greenwood Press, pp. 241–58.

Bourdieu, P. (1990) *The Logic of Practice*, Cambridge: Polity.

Bourdieu, P. (1991) 'Sport and Social Class', in C. Mukerji and M. Schudson (eds), *Rethinking Popular Culture: Contemporary Perspectives in Cultural Studies*, Berkeley, CA: University of California Press.

Bourdieu, P. (1993) *Sociology in Question*, London: Sage Publications.

Bourdieu, P. (1998) *Practical Reason: On the Theory of Action*, Cambridge: Polity Press.

Bourdieu, P. and Wacquant, L.J.D. (2002) *An Invitation to Reflexive Sociology*, Cambridge: Polity Press.

Connell, R.W. (1995) *Masculinities*, Sydney: Allen & Unwin.

Corker, M. (1999) 'Differences, Conflations and Foundations: The Limits to "Accurate" Theoretical Representation of Disabled People's Experiences?', *Disability and Society*, 14 (5): 627–42.

Davis, J.M. and Watson, N. (2001) 'Where Are the Children's Experiences? Analysing Social and Cultural Exclusion in "Special" and "Mainstream" Schools', *Disability and Society*, 16 (5): 671–87.

Edwards, C. and Imrie, R. (2003) 'Disability and Bodies as Bearers of Value', *Sociology*, 37 (2): 239–56.

Evans, J. (2004) 'Making a Difference? Education and "Ability" in Physical Education', *European Physical Education Review*, 10 (1): 95–108.

Fitzgerald, H. (2005) 'Still Feeling Like a Spare Piece of Luggage? Embodied Experiences of (Dis)Ability in Physical Education and School Sport', *Physical Education and Sport Pedagogy*, 10 (1): 41–59.

Giddens, A. (1990) *The Consequences of Modernity*, Cambridge: Polity/Blackwell.

Glaser, B.G. and Strauss, A.L. (1967) *The Discovery of Grounded Theory: Strategies for Qualitative Research*, Chicago, IL: Aldane.

Goffman, E. (1968) *Stigma*, Harmondsworth: Pelican.

Gorely, T., Holroyd, R. and Kirk, D. (2003) 'Muscularity, the Habitus and the Social Construction of Gender: Towards a Gender Relevant Physical Education', *British Journal of Sociology of Education*, 24 (4): 429–48.

Hevey, D. (1992) *The Creatures Time Forgot: Photography and Disability Imagery*, London: Routledge.

Holroyd, R. (2003) 'Fields of Experience: Young People, Identity and Physical Culture', unpublished Ph.D. thesis, Loughborough University, Loughborough.

Hunter, L. (2004) 'Bourdieu and the Social Space of the PE Class: Reproduction of Doxa Through Practice', *Sport, Education and Society*, 9 (2): 175–92.

Jenkins, R. (2002) *Pierre Bourdieu*, revised edition, London: Routledge.

Kinchin, G.D. and O'Sullivan, M. (2003) 'Incidences of Student Support for and Resistance to a Curricular Innovation in High School Physical Education', *Journal of Teaching in Physical Education*, 22 (3): 245–60.

Kirk, D. (2005) 'Physical Education, Youth Sport and Lifelong Participation: The Importance of Early Learning Experiences', *European Physical Education Review*, 11 (3): 239–55.

Kirk, D. and Colquhoun, D. (1989) 'Healthism and Physical Education', *British Journal of Sociology of Education*, 10 (4): 417–34.

Kirk, D. and Tinning, R. (1994) 'Embodied Self Identity, Healthy Lifestyles and School Physical Education', *Sociology of Health and Illness*, 16 (5): 600–25.

Lavay, B. (1987) 'Is Mainstreaming in Physical Education, Recreation and Dance Working?', *Journal of Physical Education, Recreation and Dance*, November/December: 14.

Light, R. and Kirk, D. (2001) 'Australian Cultural Capital – Rugby's Social Meaning: Physical Assets, Social Advantage and Independent Schools', *Culture, Sport, Society*, 4 (3): 81–98.

Lincoln, Y.S. and Guba, E.G. (1985) *Naturalistic Inquiry*, Beverly Hills, CA: Sage Publications.

Oliver, K.L. and Lalik, R. (2001) 'The Body as Curriculum: Learning with Adolescent Girls', *Journal of Curriculum Studies*, 33 (3): 303–33.

Patterson, K. and Hughes, B. (2000) 'Disabled Bodies', in P. Hancock, B. Hughes, E. Jagger, K. Patterson, R. Russell, E. Tulle-Winton and M. Tyler (eds), *The Body, Culture and Society*, Buckingham: Open University Press, pp. 29–44.

Priestley, M. (1999) 'Discourse and Identity: Disabled Children in Mainstream High Schools', in M. Corker and S. French (eds), *Disability Discourse*, Buckingham: Open University Press, pp. 92–102.

Priestley, M., Corker, M. and Watson, N. (1999) 'Unfinished Business: Disabled Children and Disability Identities', *Disability Studies Quarterly*, 19 (2): 90–8.

Robbins, D. (2000) *Bourdieu and Culture*, London: Sage Publications.

Shakespeare, T. (ed.) (1998) *The Disability Reader Social Science Perspectives*, London: Cassell.

Shilling, C. (2003) *The Body and Social Theory*, London: Sage Publications.

Smith, A. and Thomas, N. (2005) 'Inclusion, Special Educational Needs, Disability and Physical Education', in K. Green and K. Hardman (eds), *Physical Education: Essential Issues*, London: Sage Publications, pp. 220–37.

Theberge, N. (1984) 'Towards a Feminist Alternative to Sport as a Male Preserve', *Quest*, 37, 193–202.

Ungar, M.T. (2000) 'The Myth of Peer Pressure', *Adolescence*, 25 (137): 167–80.

Vertinsky, P. (1992) 'Reclaiming Space, Revisioning the Body: The Quest for Gender-Sensitive Physical Education', *Quest*, 44: 373–96.

Walker, B.M. and Kushner, S. (1999) 'The Building Site: An Educational Approach to Masculine Identity', *Journal of Youth Studies*, 2 (1): 45–58.

8 Picture this!

Student co-researchers

Aspley Wood School

Our school

Aspley Wood School is a city, co-educational day school situated in the Midlands of England for children between the ages of 3 and 16 who have special educational needs associated with physical impairments and complex learning difficulties. Usually, there are 40 to 45 pupils on roll, some of whom also attend a mainstream school part-time. At Aspley Wood School we aim to:

- demonstrate respect for each person's unique qualities regardless of race, creed, gender or ability;
- maximize independence, whilst acknowledging the need for continuing support as pupils progress towards adult life;
- help pupils plan and prepare for the future;
- show respect for pupils' dignity at all times, establishing a climate of trust;
- present a stimulating curriculum designed to maximize individual potential;
- provide an education which is holistic, attending to the intellectual, social, physical, emotional and spiritual needs of pupils;
- recognize and give credit for effort and achievement;
- offer a network of support and information to facilitate the effective inclusion of disabled pupils in mainstream schools and the wider community;
- be sensitive to the need for adaptation in a changing climate, maintaining a commitment to continuous development;
- maintain a close and supportive relationship with parents;
- ensure that the school experience is enjoyable and motivating.

An important part of the school's ethos is recognizing and respecting the views of pupils. For example, the School Council provides a regular means through which pupils can exercise their autonomy and contribute to various issues impacting on their school experience. My staff and I are always exploring the possibilities of other ways to promote pupil engagement that enables their views to be heard. The 'pictured report' presented in this chapter represents an example of a successful collaboration between our pupils and a researcher. Six pupils were supported to develop their skills as co-researchers and it was these pupils who decided that a pictured report would enable more people to understand and access the research findings. There is nothing remarkable about these findings but perhaps the important message from this research project is that our pupils were recognized as having views that should be listened to and valued. Equally, the research was undertaken in a manner that centrally positioned our pupils as key contributors to the research process. I believe that more research needs to capture the views of young people in this way.

(Barbara Mole, Head Teacher)

Who did the research?

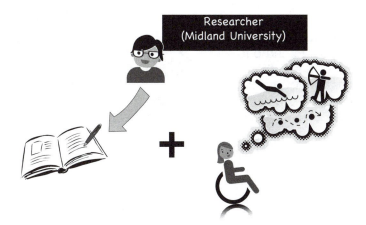

Not much research has been done about young disabled people, PE and sport. I wanted to find out more and tell other people.

I asked a school if I could work with some students and support them to be co-researchers.

Class 6 agreed to work with me.

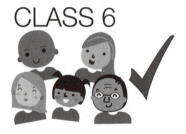

CLASS 6

What type of information did we collect?

We worked together to think of ways to find out about Class 6 and the other classes at the school. The ideas we used came from Class 6.

We did a number of things to find out about PE and sport.

The class took photographs. These were taken at school and during free-time away from school.

We went into other classes and Class 6 asked some questions.
Class 6 thought of the questions.

So we could remember what people said we recorded this. Tracey,
a Support Assistant, did the videoing.

Class 6 noticed that some people didn't say much. The class
decided we should send a survey home so parents and pupils
could answer questions together.

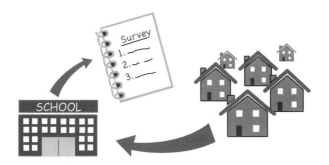

We also did another
survey which was
about school PE.

Everyone in Year 6
did this survey.

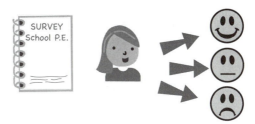

We had some discussions about why people do sport and why they don't.

During this research Class 6 had Keith (the teacher) and two Support Assistants (Tracey and Michelle) helping them. Sometimes they said things and gave their ideas.

What did we find out?

We found out a lot from Class 6 and the other classes about PE and sport. Here are some of the things we found out:

• Many benefits of PE and sport were recognized.

- Some pupils enjoy PE and sport and some dislike it.

- Table cricket and bowling were rated the best PE activities.

- Parachute games and 'thinking' games were rated the worst PE activities.

- Doing PE and sport helps to show other people that we can do a lot of things.

- When people say we 'can't' or 'shouldn't' do PE and sport – it's them with the problem!

- Many pupils spend a lot of free-time with their family.

- Many pupils spend a lot of free-time at home do these activities.

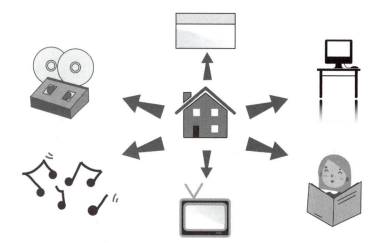

- A few pupils go sports clubs.

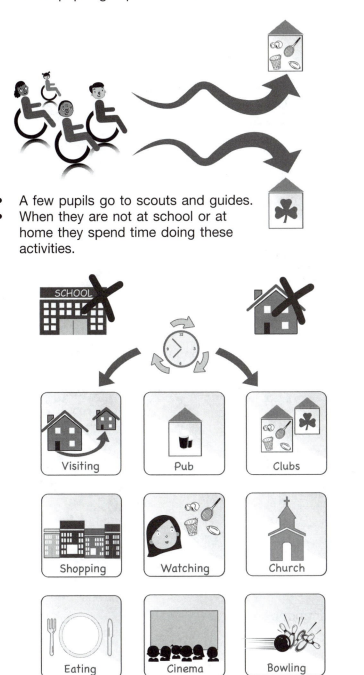

- A few pupils go to scouts and guides.
- When they are not at school or at home they spend time doing these activities.

- Everyone goes shopping and visits friends and family.

Providing better opportunities for young disabled people.

Many pupils want to do more activities including sport.

BUT...

They have to depend on family and carers.

Some people are not nice.

More sports should be provided in summer holidays.

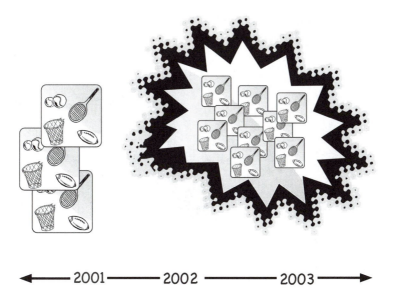

More accessible information would be helpful.

What will the researcher do next?

I would like to interview the Head Teacher and some other teachers at Aspley Wood School.

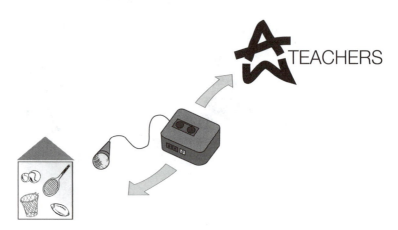

I would like to interview people working in sports development and others who are responsible for providing sport for disabled people.

I would like to send this report to different people. By doing this I hope more people will learn about your PE and sporting experiences. Maybe they will come and speak to you all.

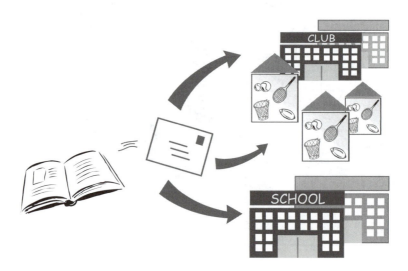

Part III

Inclusion in practice

9 The pedagogy of inclusive youth sport

Working towards real solutions

Pam Stevenson

I'm not playing 'games' – we need real solutions

As a practitioner I do not often read academic texts and it is not because I do not want to stretch myself. When I do bring myself to read I often get frustrated with the lack of immediacy and relevance presented. In my mind, if a paper is about 'inclusion', 'teaching styles' or 'skill development' it should have an underlying point that can be applied to a practical teaching or coaching situation. If the paper requires translation – and by this I mean having to grapple with theories and concepts to eventually come to some conclusion that you would have arrived at without actually reading the paper – then these papers can become rather pointless. My work is grounded in practice and I need to say this from the outset in order that you understand where I am coming from. I want to read papers that are creative, engaging and above all can make a real difference to youth sport practices. My chapter specifically focuses on practice and the realities of attempting to work with young disabled people and practitioners who work in youth sport. There is an absence of explicit theorizing, instead I present, what I consider to be an important story about a number of practitioners who strive to support others in order that they can navigate through the daily challenges and opportunities that inclusion in youth sport poses.

Attitudes towards the inclusion of young disabled people in youth sport have shifted dramatically in the past 10 years. From my experience, the majority of practitioners that now participate in training or professional development no longer question why young disabled people are included and they seem to have embraced the 'right' of young disabled people to take a full and meaningful part in youth sport. At the same time, I am aware that some practitioners are still unsure about how they can work towards enhancing the inclusive youth sport experiences of young disabled people. I believe that training and professional development has an important role to play in helping practitioners to develop their professional practice. During the training and development work that I have facilitated I have been fortunate to have teachers, support staff, coaches and development officers who have been keen and wanted to learn. I do worry about those practitioners that do not engage in any kind of professional development and I always want those that have done some work to view this as an on-going process. As practitioners working with young disabled people we can always learn and we should strive to nurture a professional culture that promotes thoughtful and reflective youth sport practitioners.

In this chapter, I want to offer an insight into the realities of professional development delivery in relation to including young disabled people in physical education and sport. As I do this, I am mindful of the criticism and debate that surrounds training and professional development (Armour and Yelling 2004 and 2007). I also acknowledge the broader debates about ablest practices within sport (Barton 1993) and calls by some scholars for radical reform (Kirk 1998). Although these discussions are important, I would argue that we also need to remember that our teachers, support staff and coaches need something, some help and direction and the opportunity to share good practice and discuss the reality of teaching in a diverse environment. So while the academic debate goes on and on about what the purpose of physical education is or should be, what inclusion is or should be and what 'high quality' provision really means, we still have young people in schools and community sport contexts who need coaching and practitioners who need support to work with these young people. I cannot wait or rely on the academics to provide answers or ask even more questions. The reality of youth sport is that practitioners want someone to give them guidance and something that they can use as a reference in their work or acknowledge and give credence to their positive exploration of practical inclusion methods.

In this chapter, I offer a practical view of what *is* being done to help these youth sport practitioners. I ask just one question: How can we present inclusion to practitioners in a way that will be useful to their work with young disabled people? In this chapter, I pose this question specifically in relation to 'games' activities within physical education and youth sport. I focus on this activity area as research continues to indicate that this is an activity area that young disabled people are more likely to be excluded from and have less favourable experiences (Smith 2004; Penney 2002). Whether we like it or not games activities are set to stay with us within physical education. They are also a staple diet for many people when they have left school and engage in community sport. The challenge for professional developers is to find ways to support practitioners to work inclusively as they attempt to deliver these activities.

Dreaded games!

Competitive, traditional games can be difficult to play successfully with a mixed group of young people unless the pedagogy is flexible. Typically, in traditional games activities the stronger players are advantaged and often tend to get more of the playing time. In contrast, weaker players are often excluded from the game in any meaningful way. The account given by this young person illustrates this point:

Most of the boys are bigger than me and I'm not going to get that tall and they're getting bigger and in basketball I haven't got a chance. What it's like, well, like I can't get the ball and they don't pass to me and they're bigger and faster and I'll run and try, I'm trying but, that's it, it's hard they're bigger than me.

(Young person, cited in Fitzgerald 2005: 50)

Similarly, the following teacher highlights what he perceives to be the limitations of games activities.

I think the difficult ones to include pupils with disabilities and special needs are team games. It's all right in situations when you are developing skills and fitness but when it comes to the actual game there is not a lot you can actually do.

(Teacher, cited in Smith 2004: 47)

Some practitioners may argue that within a competitive sports context player domination and marginalization can be justified. In this way, teams may use their stronger players in an attempt to win the game. I would suggest that within a physical education context this kind of experience is unacceptable and would seem to go against a broader philosophy of inclusion, which is 'about the participation of all children and young people and the removal of all forms of exclusionary practice' (Barton 1998: 85). Similar parallels could also be drawn in community sport settings, where I would encourage practitioners to not always have an overriding aim of tournament or league success. Instead, work to develop other qualities such as cooperation, leadership and teamwork could be emphasized (Siedentop 1994). In both these contexts of participation I would suggest that it is the environment that needs to be modified in order to make experiences more equitable for all young people. For example, this may be in the form of opening up the environment or additionally challenging the stronger players. Unless the environment is flexible, ever changing and not based solely on traditional activities we will always be trying to squash some young disabled people into an inappropriate environment where they will be disadvantaged and possibly alienated from engaging in sport.

During training and professional development I advocate an inclusive set of games sessions where: (1) Games must be reflective of all young people, (2) Levels of participation should be equal for all young people, and (3) Young people should be inspired and motivated to participate in games outside school. Balancing all the different needs of individual young people in a games context is very challenging. If a practitioner delivers games in only one way there will be a group of young people that benefit, enjoy and progress. There is also likely to be a group of young people that do not experience any form of success and may end up being excluded. MacDonald (2002) suggests a much broader concern for sports-related activities and also indicates that a range of young people may not be served well.

Professionals in exercise, physical education and sport may have served well the talented, able-bodied, skilled, physically fit, educated, middle classes. But what about the majority of our population?

(Macdonald 2002: 184)

Is this the kind of youth sport we want young people to continue to experience? By working with a games-based physical education curriculum I would argue that games activities have possibilities that can enable many young people to experience success and then want to go on to participate in youth sport. However, achieving this will require practitioners to think differently and challenge themselves beyond what they may currently know and understand about youth sport and games.

I have collaborated with a number of colleagues in what could be considered to be a community of practice (Lesser *et al.* 2000) and developed a practical working model of inclusion – the 'inclusion spectrum'. Later I illustrate how this model can be used to support practitioners to think inclusively when planning and delivering games-based activities. Meanwhile, in the following section I want to spend some time mapping out how the inclusion spectrum was developed. My intention in doing this is to highlight how different practitioners can come together and over time develop and refine a model for inclusion that, in a very practical sense, can make a difference to the way youth sport practitioners understand and work towards inclusion. By offering this model, myself and other collaborators recognize that further refinements will be made as we learn more from each other and other practitioners attempting to use this model. We are also aware that the inclusion spectrum may be criticized by some who may argue that it does not promote inclusive practice as it merely adapts or works with traditional sporting activities. To these commentators I would reinforce the view that the inclusion spectrum provides many practical working examples that move beyond the unhelpful theoretical abstraction that sometimes governs academic discussions and debates about inclusion.

The inclusion spectrum[1]

In 1987, Joseph Winnick published an 'Integration Continuum for Sport Participation' (Winnick 1987). The continuum presented in this paper focuses on five strategies for including disabled young people in physical activity, ranging from 'fully inclusive' activities to those where children participate in a 'segregated' environment. The fully included strategy was described as engagement in regular sport and in this context 'a particular sport should not be supplemented or supplanted by more restrictive participation in the same sport' (Winnick 1987: 159). In contrast, and at the other end of the continuum 'athletes participate in adapted sport in a totally segregated setting' (Winnick 1987: 160). The Integration Continuum is illustrated in Figure 9.1 and the strategies associated with it were presented as 'a framework for a

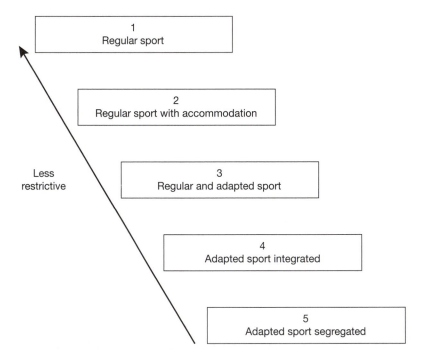

Figure 9.1 Integration continuum
Source: Winnick 1987: 158.

sport continuum to help enhance integration to the maximum extent possible, help guide decisions on sport participation, and help stimulate the provision of innovative opportunities along the continuum' (Winnick 1987: 158).

Drawing on the principles of Winnick's continuum, in 1996 Ken Black, then Inclusive Sport Officer at the Youth Sport Trust (YST), refined this model for inclusion in the TOP Play/BT TOP Sport supporting handbook – 'Including Young Disabled People'. The main alteration was to arrange the format of the continuum in a manner that gave each strategy equal importance. In essence, this changed Winnick's hierarchical structure that presented 'regular sport' activities as the ultimate aim and, in Winnick's terms, 'less restrictive'. This revised continuum was further refined following collaborative work between Ken and David Tillotson (at the time an advisory teacher of PE working for Birmingham Education). David and Ken produced the inclusion spectrum, which re-arranged the continuum in a circular format and provided more detailed explanation and examples of each approach. This arrangement is illustrated in Figure 9.2 and detailed examples were also presented in order to reinforce the idea that different strategies for participation could be adopted but that no one strategy is superior to another.

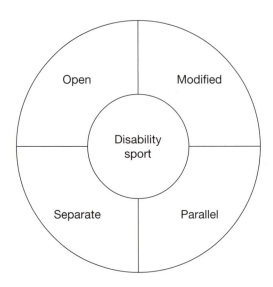

Figure 9.2 Inclusion spectrum

In a parallel development, my work at Liverpool Community College led me to start to use the inclusion spectrum in my practical work with students and teachers in the North West of England. I subsequently began to develop a practical course for teachers and other physical activity deliverers that emphasized the approaches advocated through the inclusion spectrum. In 1998, Ken and I were then brought together by the English Federation of Disability Sport (EFDS) to jointly develop a definitive course focusing on inclusion, young disabled people and physical education. The resulting 'Including Disabled Pupils in Physical Education' (IDP) workshop was piloted as part of the Sports Coach UK, Coaching Weeks in 1999 and subsequently adopted by the EFDS as the national curriculum practitioners inclusion course. During a curriculum review of physical education in England curriculum reviewers received information about the inclusion spectrum and some of the language used relating to the inclusion spectrum was embedded within the subsequently developed physical education curriculum (DfEE/QCA 1999). The inclusion spectrum has been used by a large number of international organizations, including the Australian Sports Commission (in their Disability Education Programme) and the Finnish Sports Association of Disabled People in their 'Ota Minut Mukaan' programme. In 2007, a further refinement to the inclusion spectrum was made by placing the Disability Sport strand (reverse integration) at the centre of the inclusion spectrum. As we learn more from teachers and coaches that use the inclusion spectrum I am sure this model will continue to evolve further. In this way, it is perhaps like the various theories that some of the contributors to this text may draw on, debate, challenge and then rearticulate. However, I believe what makes the inclusion spectrum different from this kind of theoretical development is the way in which it can, and does, continue to inform practice in a very real sense. It has been embraced by a range of individuals and organizations and continues to evolve in ways that enhance our work with young disabled people.

The inclusion spectrum and games activities

Having reviewed the development of the inclusion spectrum I will now move on by focusing on how this can be used to support inclusive work with games activities. Before I do this I want to stress that it is unrealistic to fully include and challenge all young people all of the time. However, we can strive to offer different types of games activities, in different ways, for different young people. The inclusion spectrum provides an activity-centred approach to the inclusion of pupils who have different abilities in physical activity. For example, in a games context inclusion can be achieved by changing the environment of the activity, or the way in which the activity is presented. The inclusion spectrum provides deliverers of PE and sport with options and different methods of delivery. I believe the inclusion spectrum is effective because it balances many different concepts that when added together can give more young people a positive environment for participation in sport. Each approach within the inclusion spectrum aims to empower, deliver and encourage activity involvement of disabled and non-disabled people. The five strategies, although different, overlap in principle and methodology.

Disability Sport

The disability sport circle within the inclusion spectrum encourages the teaching of games through adapted and disability sport-related games to compliment more traditional sports. The disability sport aspect of the spectrum promotes the notion of reverse integration (i.e. non-disabled people playing disability sport). For example, specific games designed for young disabled people like goalball (a game for visually impaired people) would be introduced to a group or class of predominately non-disabled people. Other disability sports that are an adaptation of mainstream sports, such as wheelchair basketball, could also be introduced. Here the emphasis need not be on having to access wheelchairs to play the game. Instead, changing the position of all players in a game or skill could effectively simulate an aspect of the game. For example, the group or class practising a basketball shot from a seated position would enable participants to reconsider the technique required to score a basket. By promoting reverse integration where disabled young people are participating with a predominantly non-disabled group it could be an important opportunity for these young people to feel confident, comfortable and even at an advantage. Opportunities to work with this dimension of the inclusion spectrum are diverse and could include 'one-off' inclusion of disability sport equipment or activities. Other opportunities associated with a disability sport focus week, festival or scheme of work could be initiated. Whichever of these developments is adopted care should always be taken to ensure there is a broader purpose underpinning the inclusion of such activities. Otherwise, as highlighted in Chapter 7 and other research (Medland and Ellis-Hill 2008) disability sport could be perceived as insignificant when compared to other sporting activities. If disability sports and adapted activities are threaded throughout the curriculum they can be accepted as the norm and not an 'add-on'.

The other four sections of the inclusion spectrum are a mechanism for delivering traditional and non-traditional games-based activities. Varying the method of delivery as well as the type of activity gives teachers and coaches a broader base to choose more equitable activity opportunities for all young people.

Delivering games in an open way

Open games work from a 'can do' premise and are an excellent way to ensure fair participation. In this way, components of the game that prevent a young person taking part are replaced with components that are open to all. For example, this could be a simple change of equipment; if a young person feels intimidated when anyone comes too close to them in a tag type game, a soft ball could be introduced and thrown to tag the person. In some cases, it is not the physical environment but the social interaction that prevents young people from being included. If a young person finds it too challenging to have other young people invade their space an interactive invasion game can be changed to one that confines participants in their own space. For example, a game of bench hockey, where young people are seated and play with shorter sticks would facilitate a less invasive activity environment. Similarly, for a young person experiencing a learning disability the complexity of a game may need to be changed. This is illustrated in a game of rounders where the whole team may move around the bases, instead of individually. This adaptation would give the young person repeated experiences to learn the pattern of movement he/she is expected to perform. Delivering games in an 'open way' enables all young people to take a positive and meaningful part in an activity. An open game focuses on what a group of participants can do and bases the game on those attributes. It is not concerned with sophisticated methods of modification. Indeed, any activity, sport or game can be delivered in an open way but key to delivery is to make the game open for each group.

Adopting the principle of delivering part of every lesson or coaching session in an open way has many other advantages. Where teachers have a bank of open style games they can be more confident to provide a session where everyone is included positively. Open games, because most are simple, allow the teacher or coach to observe, assess and reflect on the needs of the group. In addition, open games introduced as warm-up games set the tone for an inclusive session (traffic lights) or provide an opportunity for very high participation (snowball, where two teams try to send their non-threatening equipment over a line into their opponents' half). Open games provide a positive experience with the failure component taken out in a cooperative or non-competitive environment or provide an opportunity for people to play games with continually changing partners or groups or they can be used to teach isolated components of a game before becoming sports specific.

Delivering games in a modified way

Whereas open games do not try to stretch the more able young people, modified activities build on the principles of open games but move towards a differentiated environment. Young people are still playing games together regardless of their level of skill but the skill, task or game is changed to suit each person's needs. In a games session the skills, or the actual game, can be delivered in a modified way. This allows young people to access the activity in a way that best suits their needs.

A young person may find volleyball more accessible if a balloon is used in order to access volleyball-related skills while at the same time somebody else may use a volleyball. Similarly, a young person who needs space in an invasion game may play from their own zone while the rest of the game is unchanged. During a game of rounders young people may use different bats to strike the ball or score by completing laps round differently spaced cones, thus extending the challenge for the more able while still including everyone. In another context, a young person may need more time to control the ball and a rule could be created to give them a specific amount of unchallenged time (the disability sport of floor lacrosse has this rule).

In an environment where continual changing of the rules becomes the norm the whole group needs to understand the basis of inclusive delivery and be made part of this process. In this context we should always be mindful that how young people feel is as important as the quality of differentiation and inclusion. Indeed, some young people may be comfortable to have a rule or piece of equipment solely for them whereas others need to feel the modification is for the whole class. It is important to note that there is no method of modification that suits everyone but introducing the whole class to specialist equipment tends to normalize the activity and potentially prevents the modifications from being viewed as different.

A modified game is a game played by a group of young people where the aim is to treat young people differently to include everyone appropriately, challenging them differently dependent on their involvement in the game. Modifications can be a small part of the game to include one young person or the basis of the game. Zone hockey is an excellent example of a modified game as the layout of the game enables players to be matched with like ability or even be unmarked on the pitch. If a group of young people with very mixed abilities is going to practise and play games in a modified way it is essential that the teacher/coach flexibly adapts and modifies all aspects of the environment. Where there are a lot of young people with different impairments and different needs it is particularly useful to work with the whole class so they understand and are involved in the process of modification and adaptation. In this context, the whole class can explore and experiment with the impact of adaptation, make up their own games and set different challenges that encourage the inclusion of everyone. By working in this way with young people they are encouraged to plan and implement changes for themselves. I believe that all 'good' teachers practise differentiation through these kinds of modification and where young disabled people are involved it may just mean an extension of already existing good practice. In a games session when practising skills, each young person needs to be at a point, or level, that is right for them if they are going participate, enjoy and progress.

Delivering games in a parallel way

Usually, open and modified games are delivered to mixed ability groupings. In contrast, when delivering parallel games the group all play the same game in different ability groupings. In this way, each game is similar, based around the same sport or activity but set at a different level that suits each set of participants. The same class may be playing bench hockey, zone hockey and traditional hockey.

In any of these activities parallel games allow each group to participate at an appropriate level. Where young people are divided into sub groups for smaller sided games, in a parallel context they are divided according to their ability to play the game and then the game is set at the group's level. In essence parallel games are an extension of mini games but offer appropriate challenges for different groups of young people. In my view, parallel games involve some degree of streaming and in this they are a method of delivering inclusively when used alongside the other Inclusive Spectrum areas. For example, it may be appropriate to balance the use of parallel games with open games by first of all using open activities to promote social inclusion and introduce games that look different to the whole group. After this, parallel games can be used and this combined use of different segments of the inclusion spectrum may help to dispel any sense difference that the young participants feel. Of course participants may change groups in a set of youth sport sessions and it should not be assumed that it is the young disabled people who will need the simplest form of the game. A skilled wheelchair basketball player could play alongside her/his peers with a simple height rule introduced for the other players. Parallel games allow all young people to experience a full game at a level that suits them.

Delivering games in a separate way

A separate games option must be positive, planned and beneficial to the session taking place. It should not replace the search for innovative options to include all young people in games activities but instead should be seen as a way of supplementing existing good practice. Where practitioners and the young person are working cohesively together the separate option can positively contribute to youth sport experiences. In my view, where a young person has a substantially different need to the rest of the group or a real passion for a particular activity it makes sense to nurture these needs appropriately. When considering this separate option it is important to remember that there is no 'right' amount of separate provision for young disabled people. Indeed, consideration should be given to whether the young person wants to be included and if this is the case the amount of separate activity should be kept minimal. Conversely, if the young person resists or is distressed in group settings the amount of separate time may increase. Increasing numbers of young people on the autistic spectrum are attending mainstream schools and although changes need to be made to the core environment some of these young people do not, and will not, have a positive experience in a team game environment so the separate option may be more desirable. Some schools and community sport organizations that are working hard to provide inclusive youth sport experiences may need to be encouraged to see the separate option as a positive one that contributes to overall inclusion. This separate approach should not merely be seen as a way of excluding and assuming that young disabled people cannot be included in youth sport activities.

Conclusion

So, the inclusion spectrum that I have helped to develop does not have all the answers. Indeed, those who have attempted to work with the inclusion spectrum may reject it in the same way that I earlier rejected all the academic theorizing and procrastinating that goes on. Here I think the issue is about the reasoning behind the rejection. In relation to the inclusion spectrum, this may be rejected if practitioners are working in other ways to promote inclusion (Byra 2006). However, if practitioners are not concerned that their youth sport activities and programme should be inclusive then this would seem to be a more enduring issue that any kind of inclusion model cannot easily address. Attempting to reconcile this situation becomes a much wider issue that is about changing the mind set of practitioners so that 'The game is *not* the thing – the child is' (DES 1991: 16). Youth sport activities need to be flexible if all young people are going to be included positively and effectively. In many respects, I believe that non-disabled talented young people will take part in sport regardless of what we provide them with. However, ensuring that other young people, including young disabled people are inspired and enabled to engage in games-based activities is a bigger challenge for youth sport practitioners. To this end offering a range of games drawn from traditional, adapted and disability sport options will provide a breadth of options. Furthermore, if these activities are delivered in a variety of ways this is likely to increase the chance of hooking those young people into sport within and beyond a school context.

Note

1　I would like to acknowledge the support of Ken Black for contributing to the contents of this section.

References

Armour, K.M. and Yelling, M.R. (2004) 'Continuing Professional Development for Experienced Physical Education Teachers: Towards Effective Provision', *Sport, Education and Society,* 9 (1): 95–114.

Armour, K.M. and Yelling, M.R. (2007) 'Effective Professional Development for Physical Education Teachers: The Role of Informal, Collaborative Learning', *Journal of Teaching Physical Education*, 26 (2): 177–200.

Barton, L. (1993) 'Disability, Empowerment and Physical Education', in J. Evans (ed.), *Equality, Education and Physical Education*, London: Falmer Press, pp. 43–54.

Barton, L. (1998) *The Politics of Special Educational Needs*, Lewes: Falmer Press.

Byra, M. (2006) 'Teaching Styles and Inclusive Pedagogies', in D. Kirk, D. Macdonald and M. O'Sullivan (eds), *The Handbook of Physical Education*, London: Sage Publications, pp. 449–66.

Department of Education and Science (1991) *National Curriculum Physical Education Working Group. Interim Report*, London: Department of Education and Science.

Department for Education and Employment/Qualifications and Curriculum Authority (1999) *Physical Education. The National Curriculum for England*, London: HMSO.

Fitzgerald, H. (2005) 'Still Feeling Like a Spare Piece of Luggage? Embodied Experiences of (Dis)Ability in Physical Education and School Sport', *Physical Education and Sport Pedagogy*, 10 (1): 41–59.

Kirk, D. (1998) 'Educational Reform, Physical Culture and the Crisis of Legitimation in Physical Education', *Discourse: Studies in the Cultural Politics of Education*, 19 (1): 101–12.

Lesser, E., Fontaine, M. and Slusher, J. (eds) (2000) *Knowledge and Communities*, Oxford: Butterworth-Heinemann.

Macdonald, D. (2002) 'Critical Pedagogy: What Might It Look Like and Why Does it Matter?', in A. Laker (ed.), *The Sociology of Sport and Physical Education*, London: Routledge/Falmer, pp. 167–89.

Medland, J. and Ellis-Hill, C. (2008) 'Why Do Able-Bodied People Take Part in Wheelchair Sports?', *Disability and Society*, 23 (2): 107–16.

Penney, D. (2002) 'Equality, Equity and Inclusion in Physical Education and School Sport', in A. Laker (ed.), *The Sociology of Sport and Physical Education*, London: Routledge/Falmer, pp. 110–28.

Siedentop, D. (1994) 'The Sport Education Model', in D. Siedentop (ed.), *Sport Education: Quality PE Through Positive Sport Education*, Champaign, IL: Human Kinetics.

Siedentop, D. (2002) 'Junior Sport and the Evaluation of Sport Cultures', *Journal of Teaching in Physical Education*, 21 (4): 392–401.

Smith, A. (2004) 'The Inclusion of Pupils with Special Educational Needs in Secondary School Physical Education', *Physical Education and Sport Pedagogy*, 9 (1): 37–54.

Winnick, J.P. (1987) 'An Integration Continuum for Sports Participation', *Adapted Physical Activity Quarterly*, 4 (3): 157–61.

10 Deconstructing a narrative of physical culture

Catherine Morrison

Leo

An extract from the narrative 'Leo'.[1]

I reflect on the journey I made with Leo, my son, in the early years of his growing up. I had confidently assumed he would progress in certain ways throughout his schooling. Leo started school well equipped with number knowledge and the alphabet. As he was also able to recognize certain essential words, he seemed well prepared for this exciting schooling process. As a teacher, I was confident his handwriting would progressively develop. Initially, I was aware that some gross motor skills, such as riding a bike and climbing, were more difficult for Leo. I also battled with the fact he was unable to grip a pencil using the traditional tripod grip. What I found puzzling was that I knew he knew things, so why did he struggle physically to write them down? The confusion was that as Leo continued his junior schooling he proved to be an excellent reader for his age and of course, armed with running records[2] and with an aged Burt Test (Gilmore *et al.* 1981)[3] taken from my years of teaching I could prove this.

Over time, it became increasingly apparent that Leo had continuing difficulty with both fine and gross motor co-ordination skills. I observed the continuing reluctance he had trying to ride a tricycle and catching and throwing. In Year 3 at school, we began what was to be a year of frustration on both our parts as we struggled with the increasing challenge of homework. His difficulties with handwriting, involving the formation of letters, seemed to be taking a turn for the worse as the more complex skills to do with story writing, that required a number of planning skills as well, were introduced. As a teacher, I had some difficulty reconciling age-related expectations and what I believed Leo should be capable of doing. As the frustration built up he lost the motivation to complete anything much more than a sentence.

Leo was a member of not just a school culture but a family culture. He was brought up in a physically active and enriching environment. The sporting feats of his father, William, are celebrated in a scrapbook that only proud mothers could painstakingly spend time over and his cups and medals, although part of the toy box, are treasured. My family's ability to cut and paste seemed to have been overlooked but the team photos and years of involvement in provincial school-age athletics, netball and tennis are well documented in our oral history. As a family, we were confident about the values, lifelong skills and friendships Leo would gain from participation in sport.

At school, as his peers moved out of the sandpit and onto the sports field, I noticed that Leo played on the periphery of the playground boundaries in amongst the bushes. His interactions and engagement in play was often with girls. His difficulties with motor skills became more apparent with this shift from the playground to the sports dominated courts and fields. What was confusing for us was Leo's persistence in playing weekend rugby when at times the interactions with his team-mates were negative. As the competition became more focused on the winning, the environment began to highlight his co-ordination challenges and he was increasingly placed on the sideline. These difficulties have become more noticeable as he gets older, as is typical, particularly in boys, for children with co-ordination difficulties. We have come to realize that Leo will always struggle with the team-based sports setting and it is other sports we have encouraged him to participate in. Nevertheless, when visiting friends ask all the boys what sports they play, I observe an uncomfortable shift in Leo's body language as he waits quietly for the list of sports on offer to include taekwondo.

We eventually sought further explanation for the confusion of abilities that Leo displayed. He was finally diagnosed as having Developmental Coordination Disorder (DCD) or dyspraxia, by both a Pediatrician and Occupational Therapist. Dyspraxia is a medical label attached to children with a particular impairment as defined by the medical fraternity. According to the Diagnostic Statistical Manual of the American Psychiatric Association, children with DCD are children indicating poor motor coordination with no evident neurological defects (Hall 1988). This diagnosis not only provided us with an explanation but, I believed at the time, it also gave us understanding and insight into what Leo was experiencing.

Introduction

When I initially wrote the above reflection I assumed I was writing a personal narrative that described a journey with my son. The issues were initially what I had thought were questions in and around him and his (dis)abilities. But I am now well aware, through reflecting via post-structuralist lenses, that the issues I described were in fact more issues relating to the writer Catherine, as mother, and as someone who has been constructed as female, teacher, educator and athlete. Through employing post-structural resources, I have reflected on how a young person with motor coordination difficulties is positioned 'differently' and as our worlds merged, how Leo's lived experiences and the kinds of opportunities to live his life, are in fact largely contoured by the discourses that are available to him.

The purpose of this chapter is to identify and deconstruct the dominant discourses that are embedded throughout my earlier narrative. This involves explaining how positioning, agency, power, knowledge and resistance, operated within a particular discursive realm. This discourse analysis seeks to challenge 'taken for granted knowledge' of what is seen, written and spoken, as being the 'truth' (Foucault 1977). Firstly, I will examine the discourse of child development and how this positions Leo alongside what is traditionally regarded as 'normal' development. Secondly, I discuss the dominant medical discourse and, in this particular case, how this contours our understanding of disability. Thirdly, I explore how Leo's opportunities are situated within an educational context that can be influenced by political motivations, school curriculum and pedagogy. Here I argue that an intensification of governmental and professional interest and concern in children, young people and their bodies has ramifications for how boys with impairments, like DCD, live their lives. Finally, I will briefly examine discourses of masculinity within the New Zealand context and how these work to contour Leo's capacity to be understood and regarded by himself and others as a 'normal kiwi bloke'.

Child development discourse

Orthodox discourses of child development, together with the privileged place that medical discourses hold within western culture, position Leo as defective and as not normal because of his coordination difficulties. He does not meet the expected milestones that are part of the dominant child development discourses of our time and is, therefore, positioned as a young person in 'need' (Billington 1996: 45). If we examine the social practices historically surrounding child development discourses, as Foucault (1977) would have us do, we become aware of how the notion of a 'normal child' has been constructed and the role specific scientific models of child development have had, and continue to have, in our lives from birth. The predominance of notions of linear sequential stages of development is reflected in physical education texts (Gabbard 1992) where, for instance, crawling, standing and walking are signalled as being inevitable steps in the passage of childhood. Of course, as is the case with any 'normalized' set of expectations about development, there are those that do not 'fit', those who do not 'develop' in the expected ways and those who fail to meet the expected 'milestones' as articulated in these developmental psychological texts. The very presence of a 'norm' implies that those who fall either side of it need fixing or remediation.

Erica Burman (1997) points to the numerous ways in which everyday practices highlight and consolidate the 'naturalness' of developmental knowledge. This is the case with Plunket books where pages featuring normative weight and height for age tables are displayed. Expected milestones (truths) and questions relating to each age group throughout their growing years reinforce the notion that medical experts and developmental scientists know more about how a child should develop and, indeed, are more attuned to what a child may need at various stages of its life than their parent(s).

Burman points out that: 'we all have notions – reinforced by the media and by our own hazy memories of childhood – of how children are "supposed" to develop.' She further states that there is a 'failure to notice that behaviour norms are ethnocentric, androcentric, and patriarchal' and that they serve 'the interests of dominant groups' (Burman 1997: 134). We therefore need to ask the question of who is normal and who is not? Contemporary 'reality' television programmes, such as New Zealand's *Demons to Darlings* and Britain's *Supernanny* reinforce the belief that there is in fact a 'normal' way to raise children and a 'normal' way they should behave. Programmes like these show families with behavioural challenges that can be 'fixed' by experts. *Supernanny* and the psychologists from *Demons to Darlings* enter the family home as experts capable of making so called bad or 'developmentally delayed' behaviours acceptable. In these contexts, however, behaviour is regarded as solely a parental problem, at the exclusion of all the other social influences which, in reality, families may face. The families selected for parading on such shows are inevitably rendered suitable for family television viewing and typically exhibit no signs of violence, drug abuse or similar problems, which, in reality, many may face.

Medical discourse

Contemporary understandings of disability, usually founded on either medical or social model perspectives, can be viewed in several ways. Within the medical discourse disability has historically been defined as a defect or sickness that must be cured through medical intervention (Barnes, Mercer and Shakespeare 1999; Oliver 1996). Despite the best efforts of sociologists and those working in the field of critical disability studies, the medical 'view' of disability still predominates. The New Zealand Ministry of Education Report on Curriculum Policy and Special Education Support (2004: 15), for example, states: '[the] most pervasive and influential of these [discourses], is the medical [or expert] discourse of disability, with its professional and clinical focus on the body.' Within this discourse I, as a mother, am positioned as being without knowledge. Burr concurs that I, as both a teacher and a parent, am 'addressed as non–medic, and positioned with lesser rights to make decisions, make diagnoses and use medical terminology' (Burr 1995: 143). Within the expert or medical discourse, Leo's needs are seen as beyond the understanding of the lay person and improving his outcomes depends on specialized, scientifically based, interventions. The Ministry of Education Report (2004: 15) further states that: 'discourse analysis of special education language reveals expert and medical discourse at work in the highly specialized "treatments" and "interventions" developed for students who have particular labels or diagnoses.' If the role of intervention and the goals of the professional are to cure, this assumes that the individual wants to be fixed – an interesting reflection on the powerful positioning of medical discourses in our culture.

In this context, parental knowledge can, potentially, conflict with medical practice. For example, at one stage Leo was being treated by an Occupational Therapist (OT). At one meeting, conversation between the OT and myself became uneasy as I tried to explain my view that the deficit model of improving handwriting had limited relevance outside the classroom and that, for Leo, writing was now more about expressing his ideas and not just the formation of letters. Evidently regarding herself as the one with the 'knowledge', the OT questioned my hesitation to improve Leo's handwriting skills, despite my clear articulation of why I would rather he spent his evenings doing things other than practising drawing circles. I wanted to ensure that his precious time was spent on extending his ability to communicate by utilizing new technologies, such as a laptop, that enabled him to engage in learning opportunities, share his knowledge and move on from the sole focus on letter formation. I was initially positioned as without knowledge. By taking up agency and subverting her planned intervention, I resisted and challenged the OT's position of power within the medical discourse.

Foucault's notion of agency can be seen here as the subject (Catherine), although constituted by discourse, was able to 'recognize that constitution and to resist, subvert and change the discourses ... through which one is being constituted' (Davies 2000: 67). In order to achieve this, I re-positioned myself as someone with knowledge, resisted the medical discourse and drew on teacher discourse to do so. As Foucault suggests, we can 'exercise power by drawing upon discourses which allow our opposing actions to be represented in an acceptable light' (Burr 1995: 64). For Foucault, 'there are no relations of power without resistances; the latter are all the more real and effective because they are formed right at the point where relations of power are exercised' (Foucault 1977: 142). Interestingly, we could ask whether or not I would have felt able to do this, if I had not had a teacher discourse to draw upon. From this perspective, the power implicit in one discourse, in this case the medical discourse, only became apparent through the resistance of another.

Educational discourse

In the educational setting, we can see a number of issues arising for Leo. For example, the fact that funding is linked to a diagnosis, not by parents or teachers, but predominantly by medical experts, clearly shows the influence of the medical discourse within the educational sector. As the Ministry of Education regards such diagnoses as necessary for allocating resources, Leo must fail the 'normal test' devised by those who, more often that not, are located within a scientific field in order to receive funding.

In a school interview, Leo's teacher questioned whether or not Leo would cope in the secondary school system. Within this discussion I re-positioned myself as teacher, as opposed to parent, and explained that, within the model of learning I ascribe to, the child – task – environment are conceived relationally. The problem was not how Leo would cope, but how the teacher would adapt the task or environment to ensure Leo would continue to learn.

What was interesting as I re-positioned myself from 'mother' to 'teacher' was the silence emanating from his teacher. In terms of discourse analysis as methodology, Burr (1995) refers to indicators of silence and absences as being just as significant as what *is* actually said. Perhaps this teacher was resisting my views as those of a mother or maybe felt challenged by my re–positioning of myself as a teacher?

An increasingly dominant theme in Ministry of Education literature of the late 1990s is the notion of students meeting their 'full potential' (1993). Morss (1996) suggests that this rhetoric of the child as an 'individual' with a set of potential abilities needing to be fulfilled is, in fact, an example of how educational practices regulate how children, their parents and their teachers will be treated. Both the *Health and Physical Education Curriculum* (1999) and the *New Zealand Curriculum* (2007) place emphasis on the self and the individual taking responsibility for decisions made and practices undertaken. As in the example outlined above, where the teacher refers to Leo as the one that should be 'doing the coping', the discourse of self-development has the potential to become victim blaming. If individuals fail to reach their expected potential, or do not take personal responsibility for their own learning, does it follow that this is the child's fault? Interestingly, new initiatives from the Ministry of Education, such as *Let's Talk About: Personalised Learning* (2007) again accent the need for children and young people to take 'control of their own learning'. In this case, however, they also place emphasis on teachers having 'high expectations of every student', by knowing how they learn, where they come from and adjusting their teaching to meet the diverse range of students' learning needs. The supporting booklet suggests that New Zealand and overseas research is a backdrop to these 'shifts that are happening in our education system' (Hon. Steve Maharey, Minister of Education). Is it now that the teachers are the ones who are expected to reach their full potential through this 'talk of personalized learning'?

By drawing on a social model of disability, rather than a medial model, we can re-frame the 'problems' alluded to above. That is, under a social model, the impairment of DCD cannot be considered in a vacuum, as a physical ailment similarly affecting all to whom that label is applied. Each of the young boys or men who find themselves labelled DCD are situated within particular familial and cultural contexts and with varying kinds of educational, financial and therapeutic resources within their grasp. More broadly, from this perspective boys labelled DCD exist within a wider educational, social and political context – one that is currently replete with admonishments and initiatives pertaining to the 'body' and its 'performance' both within and outside of school contexts (Evans and Davies, 2004b).

Masculinity, sport and the Kiwi 'male'

The last decade has seen a push toward physical fitness and physical activity in schools as a way to address the avowed obesity epidemic. Within a New Zealand context, Sport and Recreation New Zealand (SPARC),[4] the government organization responsible for delivering sports-related benefits to the nation, currently has numerous initiatives in place to address issues such as physical activity and nutrition. These include programmes, such as 'Mission On', 'The Physical Activity Initiative', 'Active Families', 'Active Movement', Sportfit' and 'Active Schools', which place particular focus on children and have gained strong footholds in the early childhood sector and primary schools. The changing fabric of what we see in schools with an emphasis on fitness alongside these programmes is increasingly apparent. Evans and Davies (2004a) suggest that these kinds of initiatives and practices work to produce classroom codes and contexts that shape a pedagogical conscience in and around 'the body'. As the programmes introduced by SPARC bring a renewed emphasis on physical activity, schools are under pressure to produce fit, active citizens. Burrows and Gillespie (2006) propose that, as a result, a scientific and prescriptive view of the body may be returning to schools in New Zealand.

In recent years, policy makers in the UK have presented physical education and physical activity initiatives as a public health, rather than education, agenda (O'Sullivan 2006). As Rawlins (2007) claims, the implicit theme of messages in UK secondary schools is one that emphasizes becoming a 'good' citizen which, in turn, means making the 'right' choices when it comes to lifestyle decisions, such as eating and physical activity practices. Research is suggesting that new 'orthodoxies' relating to the body, health and self, within health and physical education programmes in schools, are emerging as a result of a move toward making young people fit and thin (Davies and Evans 2004; Rich, Holroyd, and Evans 2004; Gard 2004). How often do we consider the extent to which government policies drive teacher and learning programmes and how this can leave a student feeling excluded and, therefore, contribute to their apparent lack of personal development in and around, for example, specific bodily performances as opposed to enjoyment? The Beep Test,[5] for example, has been a twice yearly regime for Leo since the age of ten years. This test has students running a series of shuttle runs and as they progressively drop out they are thereby ranked according to a very visual and hierarchical order which inevitably creates an 'ideal' level of ability. We can anticipate a number of issues arising for young people in such a climate and here specifically within a visual landscape that encourages such measures of performance. We can, in fact, view this 'landscape', as Clandinin would suggest, as 'narratively constructed: as having a history with moral, emotional, and aesthetic dimensions' (Clandinin 1998: 3).

Sporting prowess and knowledge is widely valued in New Zealand society, particularly if you are male (McConnell and Edwards 2000; Phillips 1996; Pringle 2005). Studies of the historical discursive practices that have shaped sporting discourse reveal that certain males have been excluded and marginalized because they have failed to live up to a normalized notion of what constitutes the kiwi 'male' (Ferguson 2004; Phillips 1996). Volkerling (2000) further states that in colonial countries, in particular Australia and New Zealand, sporting values have been integral to, and have informed the practices of, elite secondary schools for boys. Moreover, the cultural power of these discourses of control is seen to be magnified in these two countries in particular. This is evident today with single sex boys' schools known to dominate traditional sporting codes and boys choosing to attend certain schools because of the culture and value they place on sport.

In its *High Performance Strategy 2006–2012*, SPARC stated that their mission was to have: 'New Zealand athletes and teams winning in events that matter to New Zealand' (SPARC 2006: 3). As a measure of success, with regard to the 'results of New Zealand athletes and teams in events that matter to New Zealand', the Strategy declares that, by '2012 the system will have contributed to: New Zealand being World Champions in cricket, netball and rugby' (SPARC 2006: 5). From this perspective, it is not surprising that physical competence in 'particular' sports in New Zealand is very important to children and adolescents. It is also one of the major criteria contributing to children's social acceptance by their peers (McPherson, Curtis, and Loy 1989; Weinberg and Gould 1995).

Hickey and Fitzclarence propose that 'competitive male team sports . . . continue to dominate the sporting landscape in most Western societies' (Hickey and Fitzclarence 2004: 7). Leo's continued desire to play rugby, despite his earlier experiences, becomes understandable when one recognizes the 'value and status' (Fitzgerald 2005: 47) widely attached to sport. How does a person like Leo, a young person labelled with dyspraxia, negotiate school and the physical cultures therein if he is unable to compete in such contexts? Leo, as a male, whom I earlier positioned as having coordination difficulties compared to those of his age, is seen as being somewhat less of a 'boy' alongside contemporary truths about what constitutes masculinity. Taekwondo, as his sport of engagement, is not one of the multiple choice answers on offer to him by well-meaning adults. This conveys a message to Leo about what is 'valued' and what is not.

Normalizing discourses that produce particular truths are entangled in our lives in ways that are often difficult to recognize: these truths are not a set of by-laws in a constitution; instead, they are part of everyday life.

(Hardin 2001: 15)

During the 1990s I was a secondary school Physical Education teacher. Historically sport-based programmes have dominated physical education, as has been well documented in Australian and British schools (Kirk 2002). Accordingly, I believed that all students would gain from involvement in movement, including competitive sport. My urge for Leo to be involved in sport stemmed from my experiences in my own culturally constructed world, which I had believed would be rich and rewarding for all. Wellard proposes that listening to adult sporting recollections draws our attention to the contrasting experiences of young people and points to the fact that those who suggest 'all children benefit from sport fail to recognize the differing experiences faced by boys and girls, particularly in organized sport and school physical education' (Wellard 2006: 116–17).

Concluding thoughts

Wright suggests that 'research drawing on a post–structuralist perspective offers a powerful means to make visible the relationship between the ways individuals construct their sense of self/their identity and the sets of social meaning and values circulating in society' (Wright 2004: 29–30). Knowledge has been traditionally viewed as something people either do or do not have. That is, those at the 'top' of a society are regarded as having the appropriate knowledge and, therefore, the power. We can, however, view knowledge as something that is acquired through the social interactions between people and through language exchanges that are ever changing. In this respect, our sense of who we are is structured around the particular knowledge valued by our culture at any one time and is intimately bound up with relations of power.

If we understand that people inevitably experience the world, and make meaning from it, in ways circumscribed by the discourses available to them, then having opportunities to interrogate discourses that dominate, or indeed that are the most predominantly available to individuals, is imperative. However, this is not simply to state how things are, rather by revealing the manner in which lives are constantly being made and remade in relation to different discursive possibilities, we can uncover some of those which have more 'power' to infuse our lives than others, at different moments in time. 'Understanding the relationship between knowledge and power is contingent upon the notion that "truth" is always contextual, construed, and established by communities of individuals' (Hardin 2001: 17).

Through the narrative 'Leo', I reflected on my son's earlier years. After engaging with post-structural theoretical tools and reflecting on this narrative, it became apparent to me that each and every one of our practices needs to be scrutinized for their intent and for what assumptions they are premised on, with a view to considering the 'effects' of our practices on those to whom they are applied.

Leo forced me to re-examine the educational framework I had trained in and now work within. How often do we consider dominant discourses like developmentalism and the medical model that positions 'Leo' and constrains his opportunities to learn? How do current political initiatives influence the school curriculum and pedagogy, and how can the curriculum, in turn, possibly leave a student feeling excluded and therefore contributing to a lack of personal development and self-esteem? It is a challenge for Leo to live his life in and around the gendered discourses of what it means to be male in New Zealand culture. That is, how to function, live and be regarded as a 'male', despite his (limited) capacities to engage in the sports that are privileged in New Zealand society.

Catherine

> But what I also know now through this writing of the narrative 'Leo' is that I can also exercise choices that will support Leo, build his self-esteem, foster resilience and all the while celebrate the uniqueness of him as an individual. While he may not have to experience the compulsory cross-country, he will still be able to achieve excellence on that day. In fact, we will have gone to the beach at Moeraki, dug sandcastles, sat on the boulders and looked out to sea while eating our ice creams together.
>
> In doing this 'talk' throughout this chapter, I have shared Leo, but in fact I shared much more of Catherine.

Acknowledgement

I am grateful to Lisette Burrows (University of Otago, New Zealand) for the support and very helpful comments she gave me during the drafting of this chapter.

Notes

1 The following passage is an extract from a narrative entitled 'Leo' that I earlier wrote for a course 'Reflecting on Learning and Teaching through Narrative'.
2 Teachers use running records to get reliable information about their students' reading skills and fluency. A student reads aloud while the teacher records exactly what the student reads or does. After completing the record the teacher scores it. Through observation, scoring and interpretation, the teacher gains an insight into a student's reading behaviour.
3 This widely used test has been revised and standardized for use in New Zealand. It is an individually administered test, which provides a measure of an aspect of a child's word reading skills, i.e. word recognition. The Test Card consists of 110 words printed in decreasing size of type and graded in approximate order of difficulty. Used in conjunction with other information, the Burt Word Reading Test should allow teachers to form a broad estimate of a child's reading achievement to aid decisions about appropriate teaching and reading materials, instructional groupings, etc. In addition, the Burt Word Reading Test should prove useful as an indicator of possible wider reading problems.
4 More information can be found about SPARC at: www.sparc.org.nz/.
5 This multi-stage fitness test is a commonly used maximal running aerobic fitness test. It is also known as the 20 metre shuttle run test, beep or bleep test among

others. The test involves running continuously between two points that are 20 m apart. These runs are synchronized with a pre-recorded audio tape or CD, which plays beeps at set intervals. As the test proceeds, the interval between each successive beep reduces, forcing the athlete to increase velocity over the course of the test, until it is impossible to keep in sync with the recording. The recording is typically structured into 23 'levels', each of which lasts around 63 seconds (the shortest level is level 1, lasting 59.29 seconds, the longest is level 8, lasting 66 seconds). Usually, the interval of beeps is calculated as requiring a speed at the start of 8.5 km/h, increasing by 0.5 km/h with each level. The progression from one level to the next is signalled by 3 rapid beeps. The highest level attained before failing to keep up is recorded as the score for that test.

References

Barnes, C., Mercer, G. and Shakespeare, T. (1999) *Exploring Disability: A Sociological Introduction*. Cambridge: Polity Press.

Billington, T. (1996) 'Pathologizing Children: Psychology in Education and Acts of Government', in E. Burman, G. Aitken, P. Aldred, R. Allwood, T. Billington, B. Goldberg, A. Gordo Lopez, C. Heenan, D. Marks and W. Warner (eds), *Psychology Discourse Practice: From Regulation to Resistance*, London: Taylor & Francis, pp. 36–54.

Burman, E. (1997) 'Developmental Psychology and Its Discontents', in D. Fox and I. Prilleltensky (eds), *Critical Psychology: An Introduction*, London: Sage Publications.

Burr, V. (1995) *An Introduction to Social Construction*, London: Routledge, pp. 134–49.

Clandinin, J. (1998) 'Stories to Live By on the Professional Knowledge Landscape', paper presented at the New Zealand Teacher Education Conference.

Davies, B. (2000) *A Body of Writing. 1990–1999*, Walnut Creek, CA: AltaMira.

Evans, J. and Davies, B. (2004a) 'Pedagogy, Control, Identity and Health', in B. Davies, J. Evans and J. Wright (eds), *Body Knowledge and Control: Studies in the Sociology of Physical Education and Health*, London: Routledge, pp. 3–18.

Evans, J. and Davies, B. (2004b) 'Endnote: The Embodiment of Consciousness', in J. Evans, B. Davies and J. Wright (eds), *Body Knowledge and Control: Studies in the Sociology of Physical Education and Health*, London: Routledge, pp. 207–17.

Ferguson, G. (2004) *You'll be a Man if you Play Rugby. Sport and the Constitution of Gender*, Palmerston North: Dunmore Press.

Fitzgerald, H. (2005) 'Still Feeling Like a Spare Piece of Luggage? Embodied Experiences of (Dis)Ability in Physical Education and School Sport', *Physical Education and Sport Pedagogy*, 10 (1): 41–59.

Foucault, M. (1977) *Power/Knowledge. Selected Interviews and Other Writings 1972–1977*, New York: Pantheon Books.

Foucault, M. (1994) *The Order of Things*, New York: Vintage Books.

Gabbard, C. (1992) *Lifelong Motor Development*, Dubuque, IA: Wm C. Brown Publishers.

Gard, M. (2004) 'An Elephant in the Room and a Bridge Too Far, or Physical Education and the "Obesity Epidemic"', in J. Evans, B. Davies and J. Wright (eds), *Body Knowledge and Control: Studies in the Sociology of Physical Education and Health*, London: Routledge, pp. 68–82.

Gillespie, L. and Burrows, L. (2006) *Submission to the Health Select Committee on the Inquiry into Obesity and Type 2 Diabetes in New Zealand*, Wellington: Physical Education New Zealand/Te Ao Kori Aotearoa.

Gilmore, A., Croft, C. and Reid, N. (1981). *Burt Word Reading Test*, Wellington: New Zealand Council for Educational Research.

Hall, D. (1988) 'The Children with DCD', *British Medical Journal*, 296: 375–6.

Hardin, P. (2001) 'Theory and Language: Locating Agency between Free Will and Discursive Marionettes', *Nursing Inquiry*, 8 (1): 11–18.

Hickey, C. and Fitzclarence, L. (2004) '"I Like Football When It Doesn't Hurt": Factors Influencing Participation in Auskick', *Australian Council for Health, Physical Education and Recreation*, 51 (4): 7–11.

Kirk, D. (2002) 'The Social Construction of the Body in Physical Education and Sport', in A. Laker (ed.), *The Sociology of Sport and Physical Education*, New York: Routledge, pp. 79–91.

McConnell, R. and Edwards, M. (2000) 'Sport and Identity in New Zealand', in C. Collins (ed.), *Sport in New Zealand Society*, Palmerston North: Dunmore Press, pp. 115–29.

McMenamin, T., Millar, R., Morton, M., Mutch, C., Nuttall, T. and Tyler-Merrick, G. (2004) *Report to the Ministry of Education on Curriculum Policy and Special Education Support*, Christchurch: Christchurch College of Education, New Zealand.

McPherson, B., Curtis, J. and Loy, J. (1989) *The Social Significance of Sport*, Champaign, IL: Human Kinetics.

Ministry of Education (1993) *The New Zealand Curriculum Framework*, Wellington: Learning Media.

Ministry of Education (1999) *Health and Physical Education in the New Zealand Curriculum*, Wellington: Learning Media.

Ministry of Education (2004) *Teachers' Experiences in Curriculum Implementation: General Curriculum, the Arts, and Health and Physical Education*, Wellington: Learning Media.

Ministry of Education (2007) *Let's Talk About: Personalised Learning*, Wellington: Learning Media.

Ministry of Education (2007) *The New Zealand Curriculum*, Wellington: Learning Media.

Morss, J. (1996) *Growing Critical: Alternatives to Developmental Psychology*, London: Routledge.

O'Sullivan, M. (2006) 'Supporting Professional Learning Communities for Physical Education, Sport and Recreation Professionals', paper presented at the International Council for Health, Physical Education, Recreation, Sport and Dance, Oceania Congress.

Oliver, M. (1996) *Understanding Disability: From Theory to Practice*, Basingstoke: Macmillan.

Phillips, J. (1996) *A Man's Country? The Image of the Pakeha Male – A History*, Auckland: Penguin.

Pringle, R. (2005) 'No Pain is Sane After All: A Foucauldian Analysis of Masculinities and Men's Experiences in Rugby', *Sociology of Sport Journal*, 22, 472–97.

Rawlins, E. (2007) 'Citizenship, Health Education and the UK Obesity Crisis', paper presented at the University of Otago, New Zealand.

Rich, E., Holroyd, R. and Evans, J. (2004) '"Hungry to be noticed": Young Women, Anorexia and Schooling', in J. Evans, B. Davies and J. Wright (eds), *Body*

Knowledge and Control: Studies in the Sociology of Physical Education and Health, London: Routledge, pp. 173–90.

SPARC (2006) *High Performance Strategy 2006–2012*, Wellington: Sport and Recreation New Zealand.

Volkerling, M. (2000) 'Sport as Culture: Passion and Possibility', in C. Collins (ed.), *Sport in New Zealand Society*, Palmerston North: Dunmore Press, pp. 65–82.

Weinberg, R. and Gould, D. (1995) *Foundations of Sport and Exercise Psychology*, Champaign, IL: Human Kinetics.

Wellard, I. (2006) 'Able Bodies and Sport Participation: Social Construction of Physical Ability for Gendered and Sexually Identified Bodies', *Sport, Education and Society*, 11 (2): 105–19.

Wright, J. (2004) 'Post-Structural Methodologies: The Body, Schooling and Health', in J. Evans, B. Davies and J. Wright (eds), *Body Knowledge and Control: Studies in the Sociology of Physical Education and Health*, London: Routledge, pp. 19–32.

11 Are you a 'parasite' researcher?

Researching disability and youth sport

Hayley Fitzgerald

Introduction

We have already seen in a number of chapters in this edited collection that engaging in research provides an important means of exploring and understanding the insights and experiences of young disabled people in youth sport. In this chapter I consider the ways in which (young) disabled people have traditionally been positioned within research. I highlight how research focusing on disabled people has often involved others and in this way marginalized their direct contributions. After this, I focus on the nature of research found in youth sport and map out a similar trajectory to that evident in research more broadly. The chapter then considers a number of strategies that have been adopted in order to generate insights about experiences of young disabled people and youth sport. These examples illustrate the possibilities and ways in which youth sport research can enable many young people to take a meaningful part in the research process. A central concern of this chapter is to critically question many of the taken-for-granted assumptions that we have as researchers and to begin to rearticulate these in ways that enable research to be more inclusive.

Researching disability

Historically, research focusing on disabled people has been underpinned by a medical model understanding of disability. In this context, disabled people have been treated as passive recipients to be researched on rather than with. The medical profession, and other associated experts, were seen as the primary source from which to generate research information (Mercer 2002). Within this environment it is not surprising that many disabled people became hostile and suspicious of researchers. Hunt (1981) described researchers as 'parasite people' and drawing on his encounters with (non-disabled) researchers concluded that they are 'definitely not on our side' (Hunt 1981: 39). What was it then that researchers were doing so wrong? According to Hunt (1981) we were on the side of the oppressors, interested in our own research careers and consequently exploiting disabled people.

It would seem then that over thirty years ago we, and here I am referring to earlier contributors to research, were failing the people we were researching with, or should I say researching on. This then raises a question about contemporary research and youth sport – how we are doing today? Are we perpetuating the research orthodoxies of our predecessors and remain 'parasite researchers', essentially engaging in disablist research? Or have we taken heed from the concerns expressed by Hunt (1981) and others (Barnes and Mercer 1997; Mercer 2002), and re-orientated our thinking and approaches to research? Just over ten years ago Oliver (1992) argued that we had actually done little to improve this situation.

> It also became apparent that there was increasing anger, hostility and suspicion amongst organisations of disabled people that much that passed for 'disability research' was nothing more than 'rip-off'.
>
> (Oliver 1997: 15)

In response to the dissatisfaction with research, disabled activists and academics established a new paradigm driven by an emancipatory philosophy (Oliver 1992 and 1997; Barnes 2003). As Oliver (1992) argues emancipatory disability research is underpinned by a desire to confront social oppression.

> The development of such a paradigm stems from the gradual rejection of the positivist view of social research as the pursuit of absolute knowledge through the scientific method and the gradual disillusionment with the interpretive view of such research as the generation of socially useful knowledge within particular historical and social contexts. The emancipatory paradigm, as the name implies, is about the facilitating of a politics of the possible by confronting social oppression at whatever levels it occurs.
>
> (Oliver 1992: 110)

This socially critical research presented 'a radical alternative to mainstream research theory and methods' (Barnes and Mercer 1997: 5). It has been suggested that emancipatory disability research is underpinned by praxis-orientated research that exposes social oppression and supports political action in order to transform society (Humphries 1997). A number of central tenets feature in emancipatory disability research including a rejection of the medical model of disability, support of partisan research, reversal of researcher/ researched relations and the promotion of diverse choice in methodologies (Zarb 1992; Mercer 2002; Oliver 1992). According to Stone and Priestley (1996) the aspirations of emancipatory disability research have still to be achieved by many researchers. Within youth sport research there seems to be an increasing trend to *talk* of *doing* emancipatory disability research. However, on closer inspection, the majority of these works have yet to fully understand the epistemological and ontological thinking supporting this paradigm.

For many advocates of emancipatory disability research a key issue of concern relates to who is doing the research and if it is a non-disabled researcher then this is deemed inappropriate. For example, Branfield (1998) and Oliver (1992) argue that non-disabled researchers have not experienced discrimination and prejudice like many disabled people and therefore cannot possibly understand these experiences. ' "Non-disabled" people are not where we are and can never be. This is the political impossibility of their relation to the disability movement' (Branfield 1998: 143). In this context, it is argued that research perpetuates social inequalities and serves to reinforce the disempowerment of disabled people (Barnes and Mercer 1997). As a non-disabled researcher I recognize that I have not experienced oppression in the same way as many disabled people and cannot begin to understand the impact that this has on experiences of life. However, I would also argue that to exclude non-disabled researchers is to preclude the possibilities of research endeavours that do contribute to understandings of the ways in which disabled people are oppressed within society (Kitchin 2000).

Researching disability and sport

A medicalized imperative similar to that found in broader disability research has dominated research concerned with youth sport (DePauw 1997 and 2000). Indeed, since the 1940s a professional body, known as Adapted Physical Activity, has engaged in research focusing on exercise physiology, biomechanics, motor learning and motor development (Hoover and Wade 1985; Pyfer 1986; Broadhead and Burton 1996). Much of this research is positioned within a positivist paradigm and adopts quantitative methods of data collection. Given that sport is often driven by the desire to develop, refine and perform athletic techniques and practices it is probably not surprising that sports science research has developed and has gone someway to extending understandings of disabled athletes' bodies. However, from this quantitative and medicalized perspective, disability and 'the disabled body' have extensively been treated as an object to be tested, modified and retested. A number of writers have acknowledged that such data only provides a partial understanding of the experiences of disability, with DePauw suggesting:

> To most in our field . . . The object of our study is the body or specific aspects of the performing body, but traditionally our study has not focused on the body as whole, the body in a social context, or the body in connection with self.
>
> (DePauw 1997: 419)

Within much sports related research disabled people have a subservient role, as research subjects, and the research findings seem not to challenge social oppression. As already indicated, some would argue we need to question why we are doing research if it is not to serve this fundamental purpose (Zarb 1992; Mercer 2002; Oliver 1992).

In the previous section I highlighted how disabled people have traditionally been marginalized in research and treated in an inferior manner. It is important to recognize that young people have also been positioned in this way. Indeed, it has been suggested that 'most research about children has been carried out on them rather than with them. Often they have been the objects of observation or experimentation' (Hill *et al.* 2004: 86). When consideration is given to young disabled people it is evident that much research mirrors the way in which young people and disabled people are perceived within society. Typically, researchers listen to the views of parents, carers and professionals and dismiss young disabled people as illegitimate sources of research information (Priestley 1999; Smith, 2007). Without insights from young disabled people it is difficult to see how practitioners or researchers can effectively and legitimately advance change within different spheres of life including youth sport. Currently, it could be argued that we cannot advocate for young disabled people in youth sport, as we actually know very little about their experiences. A change of mindset is required that recognizes young disabled people as 'expert knowers' (Barnes and Mercer 1997: 7): they know more about themselves and researchers need to find ways of capturing these expert insights.

The willingness and desire of young disabled people to engage in youth sport research is also apparent and was a striking feature in the research conducted by Murray who found:

> many disabled young people were frustrated by the gap they perceived between the rhetoric of the legislation and their experience of exclusion. Not surprisingly, therefore, they were eager to be involved in a project that sought to make their experiences visible.
>
> (Murray 2002: 3)

This view exemplifies a position in which young disabled people recognize inconsistencies between legislation and practice and want to ensure that their agency is mobilized through research in order that they can express their views about this situation.

More recently, the complexion of research relating to disability and youth sport has begun to change and move beyond a medicalized imperative. In part, this shift in thinking is a result of broader changes within society concerned with inclusion and the need to explore these developments. However, as I discuss in the next section traditional orthodoxies underpinning research continue to impinge on the position and value given to young disabled people.

Challenging orthodoxies in youth sport research

Research, it has been suggested, encompasses a number of key phases including identifying a focus, planning, data generation and dissemination

(Robson 2002). In each of these phases there is a range of traditions that govern the assumptions, actions and values afforded to research. For example, many researchers perceive they have achieved success in dissemination when their research paper is published in a 'renowned' journal. This though is only one approach to dissemination and we have already seen in Chapter 8 how equally valued dissemination strategies can be employed. In this instance, the pictured report provides relevance and meaning not only to academics and practitioners but also to the participants and recipients of research. The central issue of concern here would seem to lie with how researchers value different kinds of dissemination strategies and the purposes that their research is serving.

Similarly, researchers who want to seriously engage with young people need to think about the data generation strategies they adopt. Interviews and questionnaires may not always be the best means of capturing insights from potential research participants. However, these approaches seem to be the dominant strategies that most researchers assume will generate new insights. Ironically, this lack of reflexivity represents a significant contradiction. That is, youth sport researchers often advocate in research findings for more inclusive practice in sport and yet fail to embrace these very ideals in their research. A key question to consider then is: How can we ensure the experiences and views of young disabled people are captured within youth sport research in ways that reflect and recognize their social agency? I pose this question to you in relation to including, for example, young people experiencing profound and multiple disabilities, severe or moderate learning difficulties. In my experience, it is assumed by many youth sport researchers that these young people cannot be included, or in fact, that a 'smiley face' will solve the problem and enable inclusion in research.

There are some examples of research that illustrate the ways in which disabled people can be involved and valued in research. Indeed, much of this work draws on participatory approaches found within childhood studies (Christensen and James 2003) and disability studies (Barnes and Mercer 1997). This research utilises drawings and photography (Prosser and Loxley 2007), drama and role play (DIY Theatre Company and Goodley 1999; Goodley and Moore 2000), narrative (Roets and Goedgeluck 2007; Smith and Sparkes 2008) and other augmented forms of communication (Germain 2004). In different ways, each of these approaches disrupts the normative and traditional ideas associated with researching disability. In the following section I outline a number of examples of youth sport research that build on this kind of participatory research activity. I have intentionally selected a number of generation strategies that may be less familiar to youth sport researchers including working with drawings, using drama and collaborating with young disabled people as co-researchers. Rather than presenting the results from this research I instead outline the approach and explore a number of methodological issues arising from using a diversity of strategies to generate data from young disabled people about youth sport.

Drawings: connecting conversations in research

When research has explored the experiences of young disabled people and youth sport it is important to note that these research encounters have essentially been 'one way' conversations. To clarify this point, research has either sought the views and opinions of one group – for example teachers or coaches about youth sport (Smith 2004; Meegan and MacPhail 2006). Alternatively, research has engaged with a number of groups – for example teachers and young disabled people but viewed these engagements as discrete exchanges (Morley *et al.* 2005). Although this work is valuable, I would suggest that researchers have missed a vital opportunity to draw on the views of one group in order to stimulate the thinking of others. Given earlier discussions about the marginalization of young disabled people in research it is perhaps even more important that further consideration is given to how the views of these young people can be conveyed within research in order to generate responses from other research participants such as teachers, coachers, sport development staff and support workers.

Visual images such as drawings, photographs and other montages have already proved to be a valuable source of data in youth sport research (MacPhail and Kinchin 2004; Oliver 2001; Fitzgerald *et al.* 2003; Murray 2002). In seeking to create some connectivity in the conversations between young disabled people and adult stakeholders I have developed three task-sheets focusing on the drawings and interview commentary of young disabled people. Initially, the young disabled people participating in this research generated a drawing focusing on their physical education experiences. After this, they came with the drawings and contributed to a series of focus group interviews. By using these data generation strategies new insights were gained about their physical education experiences. Rather than limiting the use of this data to merely reporting the findings, I used some of this data as a catalyst to capture other data by creating the adult stakeholder task-sheets. In addition to the student drawings and interview commentary the task-sheets also include a number of questions for the responding adult stakeholders to consider. For example, one task-sheet incorporated Mary's drawing and commentary and reflects discussions focusing on working with a support worker and experiencing physical education in different settings. During an interview Mary described her drawing and explained that each week she has two physical education lessons, one with the main physical education class and the other was a 'one-to-one' experience with her support worker. Of these two experiences, Mary indicated that she preferred the 'one-to-one' experience. I used this drawing and commentary to 'tap' the views of adult stakeholders and asked two key questions. *Why do you think Mary has these distinct PE experiences? Why do you think Mary prefers to work separately with her support worker?*[1] By posing these questions adult stakeholders had to grapple with the ongoing theoretically and practical debates concerned with understandings of inclusion, success and affiliation in youth sport.

Stakeholder responses from the task-sheets then became an additional source of data generated. Importantly, this data was generated by making a direct connection between the experiences of the young disabled people and the stakeholders.

When reflecting upon using these task-sheets I considered, amongst other things, the benefits of adopting this data generation strategy. As I reflected, I was immediately struck by the impact of a combination of the young persons' drawing and commentary on the adult stakeholders. This was in terms of empathy expressed towards the experiences of the young disabled people and also the willingness of stakeholders to reply to my request for their response. Although this approach to data generation enabled connections to be made between young disabled people and adult stakeholders not all young people will find this approach to data generation accessible. Next, I discuss the use of drama in research as a potential strategy for generating a diversity of engagements.

Drama: capturing movement, gestures and words

Researchers that choose to use drama usually do so in two key dimensions of the research process. Some researchers use drama as a strategy for presenting data generated (Donmoyer and Yennie-Donmoyer 1995; DIY Theatre Company and Goodley 1999) and others use drama as an interactive form of data generation (Norris 2000; Barnardo's 2001). In relation to the latter approach, the data generated, becomes the engagements between the drama facilitators and research participants. I have collaborated in a number of research based drama projects with professional drama facilitators, young people experiencing severe learning disabilities,[2] support workers and physical education teachers. Unlike conventional research I used drama as I wanted to recognize, value and include a breadth of responses (Stalker 1998). By actively engaging in an interactive drama session the young disabled partici-pants were able to convey their views and preferences about physical education, communicate about the nature of their free-time experiences and provide an indication of activities they would like to undertake more regularly. I have outlined elsewhere a number of challenges and opportunities concerned with using drama for eliciting the insights from young disabled people including tensions between research and creative performance, the inclusive-ness of drama, the student and school experience and re-presenting the insights captured during the drama session through transcription (Fitzgerald 2007). In this section, I focus on one these issues concerned with the process of transcription and in particular the challenges of capturing voice and movement.

I attempted to capture voice and movement during the drama sessions by recording and reviewing video footage. Following Collier and Collier (1986) I transcribed the verbal and visual aspects of the video recording simulta-neously. Undertaking the transcription in this way was particularly important given that students communicated through a variety of means. I noted which student, facilitator or support assistant was engaging and what response was given (verbal response, signing through a support assistant or movement). I also recorded if this response stimulated responses of other students, support assistants or drama facilitators. In addition, where relevant, I recorded further observations relating to the manner of individual participants responses and actions. I also noted additional contextual information about specific aspects of the pilot session. Tables 11.1 illustrates a short segment of the transcript and the format in which data were transcribed.

Although this segment is only part of the response given by students it serves to illustrate the complex nature of the transcription process and the kinds of non-verbal insights that can be gained from transcribing the drama sessions in this way. This approach seemed to be particularly useful for capturing non-verbal responses from the students who did not verbally communicate. For example, Table 11.1 illustrates how Kate finds expression through movement by joining Richard and demonstrating 'running'. This exchange also shows how the students were able to make alliances and collaborate with each other in order to express themselves in a meaningful way. Indeed, throughout the transcript it was evident that student responses were key stimuli for other students to follow-up through movement, gestures or verbal responses. Clearly, the use of drama and the process of transcription are not without limitations and there was sometimes uncertainty and some imprecision when re-presenting the drama sessions through transcription. That said other traditional methods of data generation have done little to embrace the different ways people experiencing learning disabilities communicate (Atkinson 2004). This drama research perhaps then signals the research possibilities when attention is given to the diverse communication abilities of students rather than giving priority to research methods merely relying on verbal exchanges.

Co-researchers: Young disabled people as competent researchers

And now for what some people may consider being the unthinkable, young disabled people working as co-researchers. I have collaborated on a number of projects where I have taken the role of facilitator and in this way supported co-researchers through the research process. Elsewhere I have outlined a number of methodological issues and challenges arising from attempting to research in this way (Fitzgerald *et al.* 2003). Indeed, two issues of particular significance concern the researcher supporting rather than directing the focus of research and perceptions of co-researcher competencies. In order to illustrate how these two issues impacted on my thinking when working with co-researchers I will draw on some reflective field notes I compiled during one research project.

These field notes were taken while facilitating a project located in a mainstream school where 12 young disabled worked as co-researchers. The co-researchers working on this research project were divided into three

Table 11.1 Format of the transcription

Respondent	Response given	Nature of response	Response stimulated by others	Observations
John	'Football, I like football (R1)	Verbal response		John is the first to respond and does so immediately following the facilitators question
Jane	[the verbal response and gestures seen through the video were unclear] (R1)	Verbal and gestures	Support Assistant (3) (See R2)	The Support Assistant bends down closely to Jane (in her wheelchair) and Jane makes some purposeful hand movements
Support Assistant (3)	'Jane says she likes PE when we play with colourful balloons' (R2)	Verbal response		When verbalising her response SA (3) ensures she gets the attention of Facilitator (1) who nods to acknowledge the response
Richard	'Running' (R3)	Signed response	Support Assistant and James respond while Richard demonstrates (See R4 below)	Richard runs around two other students to demonstrate his running Kate also starts running with Richard. She does not say or sign any responses at this time
Support Assistant (1)	'Richard, yes he says he likes running in PE lessons'	Verbal response		
	'Good, running' (R4)	Signed and verbal response		Response directed towards Richard
James	'I like running' (R4)	Verbal response	Support Assistant 2 responds to James (See R6 below)	James points with his hand over to the playground
Drama Facilitator (1)	'Oh yes I can see you two like running' (R5)		Facilitator (1) responds to Richard and Kate running	Facilitator (1) moves his arms in a running action
Support Assistant (2)	'Yes James, you run over there don't you' (R6)	Verbal response		James nods his head and continues to point to the playground

Note: The number after the 'R' signifies the specific timing of the response and where numbers are repeated this indicates simultaneous responses.

groups and each group regularly met to plan and conduct their research activities. The initial project activity I facilitated focused on agreeing the content and nature of a 'Research road map' and the key components to this are illustrated in Figure 11.1.

This became a frame of reference for each group throughout the research project. For example, it provided the co-researchers with a reminder of the key themes that the research would focus upon, options for the kind of research activities that could be undertaken, sampling options and dissemination strategies. After joint group discussions and some negotiation each group identified itself with a name that related to the activity or task they were going to plan and work towards. The groups were the 'Interviewers', 'Design team' and 'Survey group'. These groups worked separately on their selected research activities and then came together periodically to update each other on their progress and coordinate aspects of the project work that overlapped.

From the outset these co-researchers made their own decisions about what they wanted to find out about PE and sport and from whom. Interestingly, the research that developed did not extensively focus on the co-researchers experiences of PE and sport but instead their non-disabled peers. In some ways this decision by the co-researchers provided the first tension that I had to reconcile as a researcher seeking to work collaboratively with co-researchers. My field notes reflect a concern that the research project would not yield the research data that I had originally anticipated.

> Today we talked about who the co-researchers are going to research and it's not going to be them. They want to open their project up to everyone

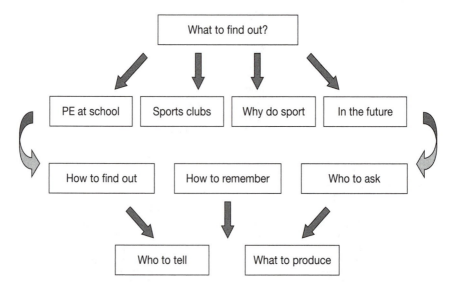

Figure 11.1 Research road map

at the school. I've gone into the school thinking that I'd find out about the co-researchers experiences of PE but this isn't going to happen. Should I, or can I redirect them in any way? I've already asked them to focus on PE and sport so by doing this I have dictated what I want. If I ask for the research to be based on them this is not enabling them to make any important decisions. I do need to go with what they want to do but this completely changes what I was hoping for. I think I needed to have had a more open mind at the beginning rather than focusing on my agenda and interests.

(Notes, 14 October 2001)

This reflection illustrates how the power dynamics of research were moving, to some degree, away from me as the researcher to my fellow co-researchers. However, as the field notes show this was a far from straightforward process and even though my intensions were to promote greater autonomy for the co-researchers the reality of supporting this had perhaps not been sufficiently thought out on my behalf.

As each group began to plan and work on their allocated activities my concerns often focused on the co-researchers abilities to undertake and complete the tasks adequately. This is evident in the following field notes where I was unconvinced that the 'Interviewers' were going to be adequately skilled to competently undertake the interviews.

The Interviewers, the liveliest group at the school, very chatty, sometimes I couldn't get a word in! At times, they became very competitive, 'I've said the most ideas'. It'll be interesting to see how the interviews go, I'm sure they'll be able to ask the questions but will they be able to then sit and listen?

(Notes, 16 November 2001)

At the start of the session all James seemed to talk about was 'when can we do the proper interviews'. He didn't seem to understand that he needed to practise . . . They are still not listening to the answers.

(Notes, 30 November 2001)

The interviews, like many other aspects of this research project, were completed in a more than competent manner. In relation to the 'Interviewers' my field notes recognize that they actively listened and demonstrated effective probing skills during the interviews. As I have discussed earlier in this chapter young disabled people are often perceived in negative ways and positioned at the margins of research. At times, in my research role, I too had many doubts about the co-researchers' abilities and throughout this particular research project had to reconcile the tensions between me as 'research expert' and the co-researchers position as non-researcher school children. It would seem though that throughout this research it was me learning as much as my co-researchers – they had no doubts about their abilities.

Concluding thoughts

Research with young disabled people, including that outlined in this chapter, may at times marginalize the role of the researcher, challenge assumptions about how to communicate and destabilize the very conventions on which traditional research methods are constructed. In part, this kind of repositioning has contributed to concerns about participatory research and the 'quality' of data generated (Lewis and Lindsay 1999). Such concerns are premised on a methodological discourse that requires research to be systematic and grounded within parameters that demonstrate, amongst other things, reliability and validity (Miles and Huberman 1994). On this issue, I support the thinking of Stalker (1998) who argues that viewing research in this way is disablist and fails to recognize the circumstances of researching issues relating to disability. Although there are some limitations to the generation strategies reviewed in this chapter I would argue that these are minimal and must be weighed against the insights and understandings that these kinds of participatory approaches bring.

I believe that as a research community it is imperative that more value is placed on the insights and experiences of young disabled people in youth sport. Indeed, is it not sufficient to merely listen to young people but rather we should seek to support an environment in which their voices are heard and celebrated. Within our society, when we consider young disabled people we all too often think of inadequacies, limitations and the need to 'help' these youngsters. However, this chapter illustrates that their contributions to youth sport research can provide an opportunity to rearticulate this marginalized position and instead situate these young people as active, thoughtful and valued contributors to the research process. This perspective is clearly encapsulated by Murray (2002) when reflecting upon the participants contributing to a research project.

> The meeting that took place was completely ordinary – what was extraordinary was the fact that neither of the young men had previously has such an opportunity. The occasion rendered undeniably visible the fact that the preoccupations of these two young men were similar to those of the majority of young people – friendships, music, education, exams, future prospects – in spite of their particular experience of exclusion. In many ways, their methods of communication added to the depth of the dialogue as each word spelled out took great effort and was therefore carefully considered.
>
> (Murray 2002: 6)

As 'responsible researchers' (Edwards, 2002) in youth sport we all should be working harder to ensure young disabled people are recognized rather than ignored in research.

Notes

1   Another task-sheet incorporated a drawing and commentary that focused on the competitive dimensions of youth sport and how this can sometimes demoralise students who are unable to achieve on these terms. The third task-sheet incorporated a drawing and commentary focusing on the nature of the activity undertaken which does not reflect progressive skill development.
2   These young people typically communicated using 'a limited verbal vocabulary' and responded in short sentences to the drama activities. Some young people also communicated using Makaton and other movement or gestures.

References

Atkinson, D. (2004) 'Research and Empowerment: Involving People with Learning Difficulties in Oral and Life History Research', *Disability and Society*, 19 (7): 691–702.

Barnardo's (2001) *Children's Disability Resource Centre: Barnardo's Consultation with Children and Young People*, London: Barnardo's.

Barnes, C. (2003) 'What a Difference a Decade Makes: Reflections on Doing "Emancipatory Disability Research"', *Disability and Society*, 18 (1): 3–17.

Barnes, C. and Mercer, G. (eds) (1997) *Doing Disability Research*, Leeds: The Disability Press.

Branfield, F. (1998) 'What Are You Doing Here? "Non-Disabled" People and the Disability Movement: A Response to Robert Drake', *Disability and Society*, 13 (1): 143–4.

Broadhead, G.D. and Burton, A.W. (1996) 'The Legacy of Early Adapted Physical Activity Research', *Adapted Physical Activity Quarterly*, 13 (2): 116–26.

Christensen, P. and James, A. (eds) (2003) *Research with Children: Perspectives and Practices*, London: Falmer Press.

Collier, J. and Collier, M. (1986) *Visual Anthropology: Photography as a Research Method*. Albuquerque, NM: University of New Mexico Press.

DePauw, K.P. (1997) 'The (In)Visibility of DisAbility: Cultural Contexts and "Sporting Bodies"', *Quest*, 49 (4): 416–30.

DePauw, K.P. (2000) 'Social-Cultural Context of Disability: Implications for Scientific Inquiry and Professional Preparation', *Quest*, 52 (4): 358–68.

DIY Theatre Company and Goodley, D. (1999) 'People with Learning Difficulties Share Views on Their Involvement in a Performing Arts Group', *Community, Work and Family*, 1 (3): 367–79.

Donmoyer, R. and Yennie-Donmoyer, J. (1995) 'Data as Drama: Reflections on the Use of Reader's Theatre as a Mode of Qualitative Data Display', *Qualitative Inquiry*, 1 (4): 402–28.

Edwards, A. (2002) 'Responsible Research: Ways of Being a Researcher', *British Educational Research Journal*, 28 (2): 157–68.

Fitzgerald, H. (2007) 'Dramatising Physical Education: Using Drama in Research', *British Journal of Learning Disabilities*, 35: 253–60.

Fitzgerald, H., Jobling, A. and Kirk, D. (2003) 'Valuing the Voices of Young Disabled People: Exploring Experiences of Physical Education and Sport', *European Journal of Physical Education*, 8 (2): 175–201.

Germain, R. (2004) 'An Exploratory Study Using Cameras and Talking Mats to Access the Views of Young People with Learning Disabilities on their Out-of-School Activities', *British Journal of Learning Disabilities*, 32: 157–204.

Goodley, D. and Moore, M. (2000) 'Doing Disability Research: Activist Lives and the Academy', *Disability and Society*, 15 (6): 861–82.

Hill, M., Davis, J., Prout, A. and Tisdall, K. (2004) 'Moving the Participation Agenda Forward', *Children and Society*, 18 (2): 77–96.

Hoover, J.H. and Wade, M.G. (1985) 'Motor Learning Theory and Mentally Retarded Individuals: A Historical Review', *Adapted Physical Activity Quarterly*, 2 (3): 228–52.

Humphries, B. (1997) 'From Critical Thought to Emancipatory Action: Contradictory Research Goals?', *Sociological Research* (Internet), 2 (1), available from: www.socresonline.org.uk/socresonline/2/1/3.htm (accessed 4 February 2005).

Hunt, P. (1981) 'Settling Accounts with the Parasite People: A Critique of "A Life Apart" by E.J. Miller and G.V. Gwynne', *Disability Challenge*, May: 37–50.

Kitchin, R. (2000) 'The Researched Opinions on Research: Disabled People and Disability Research', *Disability and Society*, 15 (1): 25–47.

Lewis, A. and Lindsay, G. (eds) (1999) *Researching Children's Perspective*, Buckingham: Open University Press.

MacPhail, A. and Kinchin, G. (2004) 'The Use of Drawings as an Evaluative Tool: Students' Experiences of Sport Education', *Physical Education and Sport Pedagogy*, 9 (1): 87–108.

Meegan, S. and MacPhail, A. (2006) 'Irish Physical Educators' Attitudes Towards Teaching Students with Special Educational Needs', *European Physical Education Review*, 12 (1): 75–97.

Mercer, G. (2002) 'Emancipatory Disability Research', in C. Barnes, M. Oliver and L. Barton (eds), *Disability Studies Today*, Cambridge: Polity Press, pp. 228–49.

Miles, M.B. and Huberman, M.A. (1994) *Qualitative Data Analysis: An Expanded Sourcebook*. Thousand Oaks, CA: Sage Publications.

Morley, D., Bailey, R., Tan, J. and Cooke, B. (2005) 'Inclusive Physical Education: Teachers' Views of Including Pupils with Special Educational Needs and/or Disabilities in Physical Education', *European Physical Education Review*, 11 (1): 84–107.

Murray, P. (2002) *Disabled Teenagers' Experiences of Access to Inclusive Leisure*, York: Joseph Rowntree Foundation.

Norris, J. (2000) 'Drama as Research: Realizing the Potential of Drama in Education as a Research Methodology', *Youth Theatre Journal*, 14: 40–51.

Oliver, K. (2001) 'Images of the Body from Popular Culture: Engaging Adolescent Girls in Critical Inquiry', *Sport, Education and Society*, 6 (2): 143–64.

Oliver, M. (1992) 'Changing Social Relations of Research Production?', *Disability, Handicap and Society*, 7 (2): 101–14.

Oliver, M. (1997) 'Emancipatory Research: Realistic Goal or Impossible Dream?', in C. Barnes and G. Mercer (eds), *Doing Disability Research*, Leeds: The Disability Press, pp. 15–31.

Priestley, M. (1999) 'Discourse and Identity: Disabled Children in Mainstream High Schools', in M. Corker and S. French (eds), *Disability Discourse*, Buckingham: Open University Press, pp. 92–102.

Prosser, J. and Loxley, A. (2007) 'Enhancing the Contribution of Visual Methods to Inclusive Education', *Journal of Research in Special Educational Needs*, 7 (1): 55–68.

Pyfer, J. (1986) 'Early Research Concerns in Adapted Physical Education, 1930–1969', *Adapted Physical Activity Quarterly*, 3 (2): 95–103.

Robson, C. (2002) *Real world Research: A Resource for Social Scientists and Practitioner-Researchers*, Oxford: Blackwell.

Roets, G. and Goedgeluck, M. (2007) 'Daisies on the Road: Tracing the Political Potential of Our Postmodernist, Feminist Approach to Life Story Research', *Qualitative Inquiry*, 13 (1): 85–112.

Smith, A. (2004) 'The Inclusion of Pupils with Special Educational Needs in Secondary School Physical Education', *Physical Education and Sport Pedagogy*, 9 (1): 37–54.

Smith, A.B. (2007) 'Children as Social Actors: An Introduction', *The International Journal of Children's Rights*, 15 (1): 1–4.

Smith, B. and Sparkes, A. (2008) 'Narrative and Its Potential Contribution to Disability Studies', *Disability and Society*, 23 (1): 17–28.

Stalker, K. (1998) 'Some Ethical and Methodological Issues in Research with People with Learning Difficulties', *Disability and Society*, 13 (1): 5–19.

Stone, E. and Priestley, M. (1996) 'Parasites, Pawns and Partners: Disability Research and the Tole of Non-Disabled Researchers', *British Journal of Sociology*, 47 (4): 699–716.

Zarb, G. (1992) 'On the Road to Damascus: First Steps Towards Changing the Relations of Disability Research Production', *Disability and Society*, 7 (2): 125–38.

12 Future directions in disability and youth sport

Development, aspirations and research

Hayley Fitzgerald and Anne Jobling

Rhetoric, confusion and no real change?

Over the past fifty years the nature and meaning of sport for young people with disabilities has changed significantly and yet not at all. We would argue that this rather contradictory statement best reflects the current position facing young people with disabilities who (want to) participate in sport and those policymakers, educators and coaches responsible for facilitating such opportunities. So why do we consider there to be a contradiction? From one perspective, it would seem that many developments have been made that legitimize the position and place of people with disabilities within the community of sport. Indeed, Chapter 2 outlines a major shift in thinking that has extended the meaning of sport for people with disabilities beyond that merely associated with rehabilitation. In this way, there is increasing recognition that people with disabilities, like their non-disabled counterparts, may want to engage in sport for recreational or competitive purposes. The elite development goal that Siedentop (2002) believes is a central component of the constitution of youth sport can now be worked towards as athletes with disabilities compete on a world stage in the Paralympics and other international events. Similarly, Chapter 3 reviews British policy developments in relation to physical education and youth sport that seek to promote more inclusive practices. Internationally, these kinds of policies have also been coupled with legislation and other mandates that articulate a desire to promote more equitable (sporting) opportunities and rights for people with disabilities (Peters 2007). Moreover, Chapter 4 discusses the development and adoption of the social model of disability within policy and legislation reflecting a radical shift in positioning that views material conditions and relations within society as key contributors to the marginalization and discrimination that people with disabilities encounter. Whilst these various developments within wider social life and youth sport may have heightened the recognition given to people with disabilities they are limited in so much as we cannot assume they have, or will, automatically lead to positive change. Evidence from research continually confirms that people with disabilities are disadvantaged in many spheres of life including sport (Priestley, 2003).

Legislation and policy imperatives can be used to challenge inequitable opportunities and within a range of youth sport contexts some individuals and groups are exercising their rights to challenge such inequalities. For example, in Britain, the Equality and Human Rights Commission (EHRC) recently challenged the eligibility rules of an event overseen by a prominent national youth sport organization. As the statement from the EHRC illustrates, the Youth Sport Trust narrowly averted legal action.

A ban on children with learning disabilities taking part in the UK School Games has been dropped after the threat of legal action by the Equality and Human Rights Commission. The Commission told the Youth Sport Trust, which runs the games, that excluding children was discriminatory and unlawful. The Trust has now agreed that these young people can compete in bespoke athletics, swimming and table tennis events at future games.

(Equality and Human Rights Commission 2007)

Similarly, inadequate access to other sports programmes and facilities has also been challenged through the legislative frameworks put in place and disabled athletes continue to dispute a range of rules set out by governing bodies of sport (see Moorman and Masteralexis 2001; Swartz and Watermeyer 2008). Spectators and Internet viewers have also challenged the nature of provisions made in relation to accessibility (Worthington, 2001).

Although these developments may seem to be positive they also bring us to the contradictory position we alluded to earlier. From this perspective, we would contend that enduring social inequalities have not yet been disrupted (Rioux 2002), and in fact, that sport in particular has not made much progress to redress the ongoing inequities experienced by people with disabilities. We observe this contradiction in Chapters 3 and 4 where both contributors, in different ways, point to the gap between policy rhetoric and practice in youth sport. Indeed, a commitment to the policy of inclusion seems not to have significantly changed practices, the content of activity opportunities or experiences of young people with disabilities. This latter issue is vividly illustrated at the beginning of Chapter 1 where we hear the commentary of two people with disabilities. In many respects there is nothing significant about the recollections given by Margaret and Luke about physical education. However, what we find striking is the forty-year gap between these accounts and the compelling way in which each reflection echoes the other. Although these are two isolated accounts they remind us so much of the other voices of young people with disabilities we continue to hear in research who also express similar views (Fitzgerald 2005). We are also reminded in Chapter 4 of the work of Hahn (1984) and his concerns that as a 'gatekeeper' sport seeks to promote inequalities rather than erase them. The durability of sport to be measured through non-disabled normative ideals becomes apparent in Chapter 7 where, for example, tensions surface around the social values attributed to disability sport. It would seem that sport has to be practised in a particular way in order to be valued and remains largely the preserve of the non-disabled majority. Like others (Barton 1993; DePauw 1997 and 2000) we believe that while people with disabilities and disability sport attempt to assimilate into the world of sport that the gauge will always be pointing towards the marker indicating inferiority. For us, this issue remains a central and unresolved problem in sport.

Having mapped out what would seem to be a rather contradictory and inconsistent journey that people with disabilities have been, and continue to be, exposed to in relation to engaging in youth sport, we will move on by exploring a number of associated concerns that are reflected, to differing degrees, throughout the chapters in this edited collection.

Inclusion – a pedagogy or a place?

The philosophy of inclusion involves the belief that all individuals are entitled to equity of opportunity. Chapters 4 and 5 highlight how inclusion is not only associated with the environments in which life activities take place but also with the social contexts and personal feelings individuals gain when interacting with others. Inclusion is about both belonging and being. In order to implement this philosophy, many commentators argue that inclusion needs to be considered as a process, not just a place (Barton 1998; Cheminas 2000). This process involves the development of collaborative teamwork both across and within the various aspects of an individual's life that comprise the interaction between the individual, activity and environment. These interactions take place at many differing levels and are interwoven and complex. They require the conceptualization of shared goals based on a common and shared framework of beliefs, values and assumptions between the individual, professionals involved and the environmental context. All stakeholders need to own the inclusion process – administrators, managers, students, teachers, players and coaches. Although in principle many acknowledge the benefits of inclusion there also remains some scepticism and a view that inclusion is an ideal that is perhaps unreachable (Barrow 2001). A critical question to consider here is: How can we embrace inclusion in a meaningful way if in reality there is evidence suggesting that there appears to be little change to the constitution of youth sport or its practices?

In part, the challenge for PE teachers and coaches is how to meet the individual needs of young people with disabilities more effectively while at the same time meeting broader curriculum content and programme requirements. As we have seen in Chapter 3, where changes are made to accommodate different needs they are frequently minor or 'add-ons' to the learning rather than being substantially incorporated into the class or activity. In this edited collection, various contributors have discussed how youth sport can be inclusive of those with disabilities. For example, in Chapter 9 it is argued that there is a need to do something that provides *real solutions* for youth sport practitioners and the inclusion spectrum is presented as one viable option to adopt. Similarly, activities that move away from traditional competitive sports have also been advocated as a means of supporting more inclusive youth sport experiences. In particular, it has been argued that dance has the potential to create a new or more prominent subject position for physical education (Gard 2004; Jobling *et al.* 2006). Competitive sport, practised through Sport Education, has also been presented as a means of moving beyond decontextualized skill development and instead replicating game-like situations (Siedentop 1994; Kinchin 2006). Furthermore, from a scientific perspective, numerous programmes have been developed in response to, or based on, motor behaviour data and are designed to facilitate individual aspects of motor performance – in other words, 'up skill' a young person with a disability (see Kodish *et al.* 2006). There are also many critics to these kinds of activity, curriculum or programme innovations (Wright and Forrest 2007; Jobling 2007). Indeed, there are those that are more radical in thinking and call for reform and recontextualization (Kirk 1998 and 2004; Ennis 1999; Evans 2004; Gorely *et al.* 2003). Such developments in physical education would require a shift in emphasis away from specific forms of physical practice (e.g. direct instruction of motor skills) towards practices engaging young people in physical activities that are related to popular culture and developing more reflective and self-directed learners (Wright 2004). In many ways, this shift seems to be critical to lifelong physical activity as learners would be encouraged to become reflective about 'what they learn' and 'how they learn' as well as how to transfer their learning to new situations in which they find themselves. In this context, young people examine the impact of their actions on themselves, others and the environment. We would suggest that it is these kinds of reflective engagements that should be pivotal and embedded within PE and youth sport rather than those that are limited to measuring performative success.

A journey of professional development

In youth sport contexts it has been shown that teaching/coaching skills are critical to effectively include young people with disabilities. That said, research repeatedly confirms that youth sport practitioners feel unprepared and uncertain about their abilities to effectively support these young people (Morley *et al.* 2005; Smith 2004; Meegan and MacPhail 2006). In part, we would suggest that professional development has an important role to play in bridging the gap between policy and practice in youth sport settings. In this way professional development can enhance the practices of youth sport practitioners. However, many professional development opportunities are 'stand alone' courses or training and have no follow-up support for participants. Programmes in Australia, Britain and New Zealand have been particularly good at providing one-off training and rewarding participants with resource cards or equipment. Our concern is that there are unlikely to be any significant pedagogical changes from these kinds of development activities, and the knowledge gained is also unlikely to be incorporated into the values, structures or day-to-day activities of schools or sports clubs. In this context, if inclusion is a place where equipment is used and activities are participated in rather than the development of a pedagogy incorporating the use of these resources, the inclusion process is likely to have only partial success.

In a similar way to inclusion, Tomlinson (2004) has argued that differentiation of instruction is a journey, not an end point, and that expertise develops over time. Over a decade ago when considering the experience of teaching David, a student with a disability, Bailey offers the following reflective commentary:

> But what about everyday PE lessons? We cannot say it has been easy. There have been times when we have not done what we should. Sometimes the weather, the activity and group do make integration almost impossible. On occasions David himself has chosen what he will do. On occasions he has chosen to participate but perhaps in isolation. He has very rarely opted out.
>
> (Bailey 1997: 18)

Bailey's account provides a sense of the journey that a teacher and student have embarked on in order to enable physical education to be experienced within a mainstream setting. Written in an era prior to explicit policy and programming concerns to promote inclusion it is interesting to note that Bailey held a professional commitment to ensuring David positively experienced and made choices about his physical education. In this instance, we can only speculate about the kind of teacher Bailey became. However, we are sure that this particular journey, and those of other youth sport practitioners, would be enhanced if they were supported over an extended period of time with on-going professional development (Armour and Yelling 2007). Chapter 9 shows that practitioners do participate in and are willing to learn about inclusive practices through workshops and training. In the same way that Pam Stevenson collaborated with colleagues to create and refine the inclusion spectrum we believe there remains a need to develop purposeful, 'professional learning communities' that work towards achieving the best outcomes for all young people in youth sport (Stroll and Louis, 2007).

Conceptualizing disability and (youth) sport

Central to the notions of physical education and youth sport is physicality. Indeed, it is a certain kind of physicality that is promoted and practised in youth sport. For boys, this is often associated with aggression, prowess, competition and masculinity (Connell 1995; Light and Kirk 2000), while girls are concerned with issues focusing on femininity (Oliver and Lalik 2004) and conscious of presenting the self to the gaze of others (Henderson 1996). Importantly, the very nature of these understandings of self-contrast with the ways in which dominant notions of disability are recognized and understood. DePauw acknowledges the tensions between sport and disability, arguing that 'sport, as a place where physicality is admired, has presented a challenge for individuals with disabilities and their active participation in sport appears as somewhat of a contradiction' (DePauw 1997: 423). Moreover, Chapter 4 alerts us to this tension by outlining an incompatibility when 'disabled bodies' are expected to conform to the normalized practices that promote a type of physicality that may not be obtained by many people with disabilities. In addition, the importance of physicality and, in particular, differences in physicality were prominent in the research findings discussed in Chapter 7 where young people with disabilities compared themselves less favourably to their non-disabled peers. Having presented what would seem to be a binary between disability and sport we would caution against constructing such simplistic inferior/superior identity constructions.

Identities are complex and the school, family, peers, media and physical culture represent key sites in which young people socialize and engage in 'identity work'. It has been argued that within contemporary society the body has become a 'project', a malleable commodity to be refined, reshaped and reproduced in order that its keeper can (re)negotiate their place(s) in social life (Shilling 2003). For some people with disabilities their sporting experiences provide a context and possibility for their identities to be re-constituted (Fitzgerald 2007). For example, the South African athlete Oscar Pistorius (who runs using carbon fibre prostheses) challenges normative assumptions of what it means to be an elite track and field sprinter (Swartz and Watermeyer 2008). Similarly, the wheelchair basketball players in the film *Murderball* disrupt stereotypical assumptions often associated with wheelchair users and instead construct themselves through a 'jock-ish masculinity' (Gard and Fitzgerald 2008). In both these cases, though, it seems to be rather normative ideas that are strived for and this may marginalize those people with more severe impairments who may remain at the periphery of (disability) sport and continue to have an inferior identity imposed on them. Indeed, as Giddens (1999) cautions, the fluidity of identity is not limitless and a particular kind of 'disabled' identity remains deeply embedded within the social and cultural norms that permeate different spheres of life. It should perhaps also be acknowledged that disability is not the only way in which individuals may be recognized and understood. Indeed, Chapter 6 extends these kinds of discussions by moving beyond a single aspect of identity and explores the intersections of disability and gender. This chapter serves to remind us that young people with disabilities have complex identities that are constituted, in different ways and at different times, through gender, sexuality, ethnicity, class and age (Connor 2008).

Future directions in research

In Chapter 1 it was suggested that an initial immersion into disability studies helped Hayley begin to see research in a different light and ask critical questions about 'why' and 'how' we do research. We believe that the reason 'why' you should engage in research is to tell the stories about people, their lives, experiences and the ways in which youth sport touches them. 'How' we do research is also important, and in telling stories we need to ensure that young people are actively engaged with, rather than seen as an insignificant part of, the research process. In Chapter 11 it is suggested that within a youth sport context, the stories of young people with disabilities have often been ignored. Although this is largely the case it is also evident in Part 2 of this edited collection that inroads continue to be made that attempt to capture the views and experiences of young people with disabilities. Building on these developments we would suggest there are a number of possible directions future research could take in relation to disability and youth sport.

First, as briefly indicated in the previous section, there is a need to recognize and research 'difference' in youth sport and in this way move beyond one-dimensional understandings of individuals' identities. A small but growing body of work has begun to theorize and research difference in PE and sport (see Wright *et al.* 2003; Sparkes and Smith 2002; Oliver and Lalik 2004; Azzarito and Solomon 2006). However, much of this work has failed to recognize disability within these analyses of difference. We see a real need for researchers to acknowledge and explore disability in relation to other identity markers in order that disability does not continue to be perceived as somewhat separate to the core business of youth sport research (Flintoff *et al.* 2008). Second, as a research community we have undertaken limited longitudinal research and this has hindered our understandings of a range of issues. For example, although there have been short-term evaluations of the various programmes and interventions that have been initiated internationally to promote inclusive youth sport, we actually know very little about the sustained impact that these initiatives have had, and continue to have, on teachers, coaches, young people, schools and community sport. Similarly, we know very little about the kinds of professional journeys that teachers and coaches, like Bailey mentioned earlier, navigate as they attempt to work inclusively in youth sport. Our stories from young people with disabilities are also partial and we have limited insights of sporting experiences throughout schooling and into adulthood. Third, much of the research completed in the area of disability and youth sport tends to retain a focus on specific individuals and groups, for example, coaches or teachers, or young people. Such research is also usually context specific, for example, school or community sport or family. There is a need to undertake research in a manner that reflects lived experiences through multi-dimensional spaces.

These suggested developments in disability and youth sport research also bring with them associated theoretical challenges and developments that require attention. In particular, we would encourage those working within disability studies to recognize and contribute to theorizing and researching about youth sport. Having said this, we are conscious that many writers within this field do not want to engage with sport. In Chapter 4, Len Barton rehearses the need to develop some critical dialogue and contends:

> The importance of understanding disability as a significant means of social differentiation and the need to develop a critical analysis which challenges the barriers to inclusion within society and particularly in terms of PE and sport can be seen as an urgent and serious necessity.

We would suggest that it is this very conversation from within disability studies that could provide new theoretical and conceptual challenges to many of the taken-for-granted discourses dominating understandings of sport, ability and difference. We need to forge closer alliances with these scholars and those drawing on feminist and critical race theory in order that our thinking and theorizing can be collaboratively developed and challenged.

Afterword: (un)intentional silences

In preparing this concluding chapter we read through all the contributions and there were many excited emails sent between us about individual chapters and the combination of contributions making up this edited collection. We are mindful though that there are some silences within the text concerning, for example, specific academic disciplines (including psychology, motor development, motor learning and physiology). We are not concerned about these silences as they continue to be researched and explored in other publications such as *Adapted Physical Activity Quarterly* and the plethora of other 'adapted' textbooks that are continually published. Similarly, little has explicitly been said from a socially critical perspective about issues related to socialization into youth sport; elite youth sport; relations between school and community sport; and participation in youth sport by people with specific impairments (including those with profound and multiple disabilities). These absences need to be addressed in another volume and also within broader sports-related literature. On this issue, and reflecting back to the title of the introductory chapter 'Bringing disability into youth sport', we want to highlight the importance of developing in tandem a dedicated literature (such as this text) but also see a need for issues relating to disability to be embedded within the diverse range of books and journals that now contribute to socially critical sports-related scholarship. In our view, there should be less separation and concentrated efforts to re-position disability within, rather than apart from, broader scholarship in youth sport.

Beyond concerns about 'what is said' and 'where it is discussed' we must also acknowledge that within this edited collection, and indeed the majority of scholarly activity focusing on sport and disability, there is largely an absence of people with disabilities contributing as scholars to discussions and debates. Whilst we do not wish to suggest that non-disabled people have no place within this area of work, we would argue that our research community needs to be more reflexive about this silence. Why are there few researchers with disabilities interested in researching sport? In what ways have sport and sports researchers contributed to this position? And how can, or should, researchers in youth sport work to remedy this situation?

Although there are omissions in this edited collection, it has attempted to redress one particular silence that remains evident in much youth sport research – that is, re-presenting the views and experiences of young people with disabilities. Some may perceive that this bias imbalances this edited collection. We suggest that this emphasis merely reinforces the need for all researchers and practitioners to actively engage, and take seriously, the voices of young people on matters that affect their lives such as youth sport.

References

Armour, K.M. and Yelling, M.R. (2007) 'Effective Professional Development for Physical Education Teachers: The Role of Informal, Collaborative Learning', *Journal of Teaching Physical Education*, 26 (2): 177–200.

Azzarito, L. and Solomon, M.A. (2006) 'A Post-Structural Analysis of High School Students' Gender and Racialized Bodily Meanings', *Journal of Teaching in Physical Education*, 25 (1): 75–98.

Bailey, S. (1997) 'David: A Study in Integration', *British Journal of Physical Education*, Winter: 17–18.

Barrow, R. (2001) 'Inclusion vs Fairness', *Journal of Moral Education*, 30 (3): 235–42.

Barton, L. (1993) 'Disability, Empowerment and Physical Education', in J. Evans (ed.), *Equality, Education and Physical Education*, London: Falmer Press, pp. 43–54.

Barton, L. (1998) *The Politics of Special Educational Needs*, Lewes: Falmer Press.

Cheminas, R. (2000) *Special Education Needs for Newly Qualified and Student Teachers*, London: David Fulton Publishers.

Connell, R.W. (1995) *Masculinities*, Sydney: Allen & Unwin.

Connor, D. J. (2008) *Urban Narratives Portaits in Progress: Life at the Intersections of Learning Disability, Race and Social Class*, New York: Peter Lang.

DePauw, K.P. (1997) 'The (In)Visibility of DisAbility: Cultural Contexts and "Sporting Bodies"', *Quest*, 49 (4): 416–30.

DePauw, K.P. (2000) 'Social-Cultural Context of Disability: Implications for Scientific Inquiry and Professional Preparation', *Quest*, 52 (4): 358–68.

Ennis, C. (1999) 'Creating a Centrally Relevant Curriculum for Disengaged Girls', *Sport, Education and Society*, 4 (1): 31–49.

Equality and Human Rights Commission (2007) 'Children with Learning Disabilities to Compete in UK School Games After Ban Dropped', available from: www.equality humanrights.com/en/newsandcomment/Pages/SchoolGameBanDropped.aspx (accessed 15 May 2007).

Evans, J. (2004) 'Making a Difference? Education and "Ability" in Physical Education', *European Physical Education Review*, 10 (1): 95–108.

Fitzgerald, H. (2005) 'Still Feeling Like a Spare Piece of Luggage? Embodied Experiences of (Dis)Ability in Physical Education and School Sport', *Physical Education & Sport Pedagogy*, 10 (1): 41–59.

Fitzgerald, H. (2007) 'Still Feeling Like a Spare Piece of Luggage? Young Disabled People's Construction of Embodied Identities within Physical Education and Sport', unpublished Ph.D. thesis, Loughborough University, Loughborough.

Flintoff, A., Fitzgerald, H. and Scraton, S. (2008) 'Theorising and Researching Difference in PE: The Challenge of Intersectionality', *International Journal in the Sociology of Education*, 18 (2): 73–85.

Gard, M. (2004) 'Movement, Art and Culture: Problem Solving and Critical Thinking in Dance', in J. Wright, D. Macdonald and L. Burrows (eds), *Critical Inquiry and Problem Solving in Physical Education*, London: Routledge, pp. 171–82.

Gard, M. and Fitzgerald, H. (2008) 'Tackling *Murderball*: Masculinity, Disability and the Big Screen', *Sport, Ethics and Philosophy*, 2 (2): 126–41.

Giddens, A. (1999) *Modernity and Self-Identity*, Cambridge: Polity Press.

Gorely, T., Holroyd, R. and Kirk, D. (2003) 'Muscularity, the Habitus and the Social Construction of Gender: Towards a Gender Relevant Physical Education', *British Journal of Sociology of Education*, 24 (4): 429–48.

Hahn, H. (1984) 'Sports and the Political Movement of Disabled Persons: Examining Non-Disabled Social Values', *Arena Review*, 8 (1): 1–15.

Henderson, K.A. (1996) 'Just Recreation for Girls and Women', *Journal of Physical Education, Recreation and Dance*, 67 (2): 45–6.

Jobling, A. (2007) 'Motor Behaviour and Adapted Physical Activity: What Do We Know and Where Should We Go?', *Journal of the Brazilian Society of Adapted Motor Activity*, 12 (1): 31–41 (supplement).

Jobling, A., Virji-Babul, N. and Nichols, D. (2006) 'Children with Down Syndrome: Discovering the Joy of Movement', *Journal of Physical Education, Recreation and Dance*, 77 (6): 34–8.

Kinchin, G.D. (2006) 'Sport Education: A Review of the Research', in D. Kirk, M. O'Sullivan and D. Macdonald (eds), *Handbook of Research in Physical Education*, London: Sage Publications, pp. 596–609.

Kirk, D. (1998) 'Educational Reform, Physical Culture and the Crisis of Legitimation in Physical Education', *Discourse: Studies in the Cultural Politics of Education*, 19 (1): 101–12.

Kirk, D. (2004) 'Towards a Critical History of the Body, Identity and Health: Corporal Power and School Practice', in J. Evans, B. Davies and J. Wright (eds), *Body Knowledge and Social Control Studies in the Sociology of Physical Education and Health*, London: Routledge, pp. 52–67.

Kodish, S., Kulinna, P.H., Martin, J., Pangazi, R. and Darset, P. (2006) 'Determinants of Physical Activity in Inclusive Settings', *Adapted Physical Activity Quarterly*, 23 (4): 390–409.

Light, R. and Kirk, D. (2000) 'High School Rugby, the Body and the Reproduction of "Hegemonic" Masculinity', *Sport, Education and Society*, 5 (2): 163–76.

Meegan, S. and MacPhail, A. (2006) 'Irish Physical Educators' Attitudes Toward Teaching Students with Special Educational Needs', *European Physical Education Review*, 12 (1): 75–97.

Morley, D., Bailey, R., Tan, J. and Cooke, B. (2005) 'Inclusive Physical Education: Teachers' Views of Including Pupils with Special Educational Needs and/or Disabilities in Physical Education', *European Physical Education Review*, 11 (1): 84–107.

Moorman, A.M. and Masteralexis, L.P. (2001) 'Writing an Amicus Curiae Brief to the United States Supreme Court, PGA Tour, Inc. v. Martin: The Role of the Disability Sport Community in Interpreting the Americans with Disabilities Act', *Journal of Legal Aspects of Sport*, 11 (3): 285–315.

Oliver, K. and Lalik, R. (2004) '"The Beauty Walk": Interrogating Whiteness as the Norm for Beauty Within One School's Hidden Curriculum', in J. Evans, B. Davis and J. Wright (eds), *Body Knowledge and Control: Studies in the Sociology of Physical Education and Health*, London: Routledge, pp. 115–29.

Peters, S. (2007) '"Education for All"? A Historical Analysis of International Inclusive Education Policy and Individuals with Disabilities', *Journal of Disability Policy Studies*, 18 (2): 98–108.

Priestley, M. (2003) *Disability: A Life Course Approach*, Cambridge: Blackwell.

Rioux, M.H. (2002) 'Disability, Citizenship and Rights in a Changing World', in C. Barnes, M. Oliver and L. Barton (eds), *Disability Studies Today*, Cambridge: Polity Press, pp. 210–27.

Siedentop, D. (ed.) (1994) *Sport Education: Quality PE Through Positive Sport Education*, Champaign, IL: Human Kinetics.

Siedentop, D. (2002) 'Junior Sport and the Evaluation of Sport Cultures', *Journal of Teaching in Physical Education*, 21 (4): 392–401.

Shilling, C. (2003) *The Body and Social Theory*, London: Sage Publications.

Smith, A. (2004) 'The Inclusion of Pupils with Special Educational Needs in Secondary School Physical Education', *Physical Education and Sport Pedagogy*, 9 (1): 37–54.

Sparkes, A.C. and Smith, B. (2002) 'Sport, Spinal Cord Injury, Embodied Masculinities, and the Dilemmas of Narrative Identity', *Men and Masculinities*, 4 (3): 258–85.

Stroll, L. and Louis, K.S. (eds) (2007) *Professional Learning Communities: Divergence, Depth and Dilemmas*, Buckingham: Open University Press.

Swartz, L. and Watermeyer, B. (2008) 'Cyborg Anxiety: Oscar Pistorius and the Boundaries of What It Means to be Human', *Disability and Society*, 23 (2): 187–90.

Tomlinson, C.A. (2004) *How to Differentiate Instruction in Mixed Ability Classrooms*, London: Prentice Hall.

Worthington, T. (2001) 'Olympic Failure: A Case for Making the Web Accessible', paper presented at the INET 2001, Internet Society Conference, available from: www.tomw.net.au/2001/bat2001f.html (accessed 10 May 2007).

Wright, J. (2004) 'Critical Inquiry and Problem Solving in Physical Education', in J. Wright, D. Macdonald and L. Burrows (eds), *Critical Enquiry and Problem Solving in Physical Education*, London: Routledge, pp. 3–15.

Wright, J. and Forrest, G. (2007) 'A Social Semiotic Analysis of Knowledge Construction and Games Centred Approaches to Teaching', *Physical Education and Sports Pedagogy*, 12 (3): 273–87.

Wright, J., Macdonald, D. and Groom, L. (2003) 'Physical Activity and Young People: Beyond Participation', *Sport Education and Society*, 8 (1): 17–34.

Index

The Routledge Physical Education Reader

Richard Bailey, Birmingham University UK
and **David Kirk**, Leeds Metropolitan
University, UK

Physical Education teaching and research is fundamental to the physical and social health of our communities.
The Routledge Physical Education Reader presents an authoritative and representative selection of the very
best international scholarship in PE, drawn from across the full topical range of the discipline.
Containing a rich blend of contemporary, 'classic' and hard-to-find articles, this book helps students gain a
full understanding of the historical context in which current issues and debates within PE have emerged.
Leading international scholars Richard Bailey and David Kirk weave a thoughtful editorial commentary
throughout the book that illuminates each key theme, making insightful and important connections between
articles and approaches. The book is divided into eight thematic sections, each of which includes an extensive
guide to further reading:

- Nature and values of physical education
- Physical education and sport
- Physical education and health
- Learners and learning
- Teachers and teaching
- Curriculum and content
- Social construction of bodies
- Researching physical education

Addressing the most important topics in contemporary physical education, and representing a comprehensive
'one-stop' resource, The Routledge Physical Education Reader is essential reading for all serious students of
physical education, sport, coaching, exercise and health.

Contents
Introduction
Part One: The Nature and Values of Physical Education
Part Two: Physical Education and Sport
Part Three: Physical Education and Health
Part Four: Learners and Learning
Part Five: Teachers and teaching
Part Six: Curriculum and content
Part Seven: The social construction of bodies
Part Eight: Researching physical education
Conclusion

R Routledge
Taylor & Francis Group

September 2008
HB: 978-0-415-44600-6: **£95.00**
PB: 978-0-415-44601-3: **£29.99**

www.routledge.com/sport

Physical
Activity and Health
Second Edition
The Evidence
Explained

Adrianne Hardman, Loughborough University, UK
David Stensel, Loughborough University, UK

Now in a fully updated and revised edition, Physical Activity and Health explains clearly, systematically and in detail the relationships between physical activity, health and disease, and examines the benefits of exercise in the prevention and treatment of a wide range of important health conditions.

The book critically considers the evidence linking levels of physical activity with disease and mortality. It explores the causes of specific health conditions and syndromes prevalent in developed societies, such as cardiovascular disease, Type 2 diabtetes, obesity and cancer, and discusses the role of physical activity in their prevention or alleviation. Throughout, the book draws on cutting edge research literature and is designed help the student to evaluate the quality and significance of the scientific evidence. A concluding section explores broader themes in exercise and public health, including therapeutic uses of exericse; exercise and ageing; children's health and exercise, and physical activity and public health policy, and includes a critical appraisal of current recommendations for physical activity. Containing useful pedagogical features throughout, including chapter summaries, study activities, self evaluation tasks, guides to 'landmark' supplementary reading and definitions of key terms, and richly illustrated with supporting case-studies, tables, figures and plates, Physical Activity and Health is an essential course companion. It is vital reading for degree-level students of sport and exercise science, public health, physical therapy, medicine, nursing and nutrition.

R Routledge
Taylor & Francis Group

April 2009
PB: 978-0-415-42198-0: **£29.99**
HB: 978-0-415-45585-5: **£85.00**

www.routledge.com/sport